AGEING GIANT

For Peregrine

AGEING GIANT

CHINA'S LOOMING POPULATION COLLAPSE

TIMOTHY BEARDSON

Edited by Nick Fielding

Signal

Signal Books
Oxford

First published in 2021 by
Signal Books Limited
36 Minster Road
Oxford OX4 1LY
www.signalbooks.co.uk

A catalogue record for this book is available from the British Library

ISBN 978-1-909930-98-8 Cloth

Cover Design: Tora Kelly
Typesetting: Tora Kelly
Cover Images: (front) Alexander F, Yuan/Yuan Images, New York;
(back) Dmitry Chulov/Shutterstock
Printed & bound in Great Britain by TJ Books, Padstow, Cornwall

CONTENTS

Foreword by Sir Andrew Burns.. vii

Editor's Introduction ix

Acknowledgements xv

1. A Brief Population History of China...................................... 1

2. Ageing 15

3. Gender Disparity 37

4. Voluntary Population Collapse 75

5. Assessing the Key Forecasts.. 142

6. Labour Losses and Economic Prospects 162

7. The Military Effect 206

8. The International Context 215

9. Has Pronatalism Worked? 255

10. Potential Policy Solutions 275

Index 309

FOREWORD

Sir Andrew Burns
British Consul-General to Hong Kong and Macau, 1997-2000

By the time of his untimely death in October 2020, Tim Beardson had more or less completed this calmly dispassionate analysis of the demographic challenges facing China. He thus complements and further illuminates one of the major themes that emerged from the sobering assessment he made of the threats to China's future in his influential book *Stumbling Giant: The Threats to China's Future*, published in 2013.

Much has changed in the intervening years and China's future relationship with the rest of the world has become a topic of even more pressing concern. But demographic changes in China, and indeed the world over, have a glacial inexorability which needs to recognized and faced up to honestly and realistically by governments and critics alike.

Every student of China is warned that Chinese statistics are unreliable and to be treated with caution. But as Beardson shows, a diligent study of the figures that have emerged, and a careful comparison with what we know from the experience of other countries, can give us a pretty confident view of the demographic trends over the next 50 years. This leads to some seemingly realistic conclusions about the dramatic consequences for China and the decisions its leaders will need to take.

Growing numbers of older people retired from the workforce, living longer and dependent on their single children for support are one part of the picture. A shrinking workforce, declining fertility and birthrates and an increasing reluctance among the young, especially educated women, to marry or have children is another. China's population may be about to decline by over half before the end of the century, its workforce is declining while its pensioners grow in number, and 50 million of its young men face the prospect of not being able to find a wife.

Such a country will face major new challenges for which it does not seem well prepared. But neither does the rest of the world.

One great merit of Beardson's approach is that he requires the US, Europe and the UK to face up too to the inevitable implications of demographic change in our own countries as well as in China. The issues raised and the consequences for inter-generational fairness seem quite as dangerous and far-reaching as those of climate change.

From Mrs Clair Beardson

Tim loved China and had wonderful experiences there, one of which was his being an Honoured Guest lecturer at the Central Party School, which made this true capitalist chuckle. By writing this book he wanted to open up for debate his thoughts on the looming demographic problems he saw facing China. I feel the concepts in the book not only relate to China but to a future audience in many countries of the world. My husband was a master at looking at things from an upside viewpoint, which works well in a world that is currently resetting its paradigms of creating a more harmonious world.

The pandemic has shown us the importance of community life and the joy of being an individual of integrity, but part of a bigger whole. China is a big community and yet now is an integral part of our world. I hope you, readers of this book, will also open your mind to this.

Clair Beardson
Hong Kong, May 2021

EDITOR'S INTRODUCTION

The untimely death of Tim Beardson in October 2020 deprived his family and many friends and acquaintances of the insightfulness and intellectual rigour that stemmed from a lifetime of work and experience at the cutting edge of business in China and Hong Kong. Although no longer working full-time in banking and finance, he continued to hone his remarkable analytical skills and to apply them to the study of China, his enduring passion.

Tim's first book, *Stumbling Giant: The Threats to China's Future*,[1] published in 2013, argued with characteristic aplomb and contrary to the views of most commentators that China was unlikely ever to replace America as the next superpower. He pointed to social instability, a devastated environment, a low-tech economy where innovation was seldom in evidence, the lack of an effective welfare safety net and an official party structure that was ossified and incapable of dealing with the country's many problems.

More particularly, and long before most analysts, Tim also recognized the impending demographic catastrophe that was inexorably creeping up on China. Even a decade ago he spotted that a shrinking labour force, the relentless ageing of the population, massive gender disparity and a falling population were all likely to make their presence felt before long. None of this, he argued, was the result of the Chinese state's draconian birth control policies. Indeed, several countries in Eastern Asia had seen their populations fall more sharply than China, despite not implementing such policies.

The issue, he argued, was the massive and rapid switch from a largely rural to a largely urban society. City dwellers are less inclined to have large families when rents and the cost of living are so high. Even after the Chinese state relaxed some of the restrictions on family size in recent years, uptake was negligible. There is simply no desire by most young couples to have more than a single child. Average marriage age for both men and women in China has risen inexorably and the number of children being born each year is now at its lowest level for 70 years.

---

1   Timothy Beardson, *Stumbling Giant: The Threats to China's Future*, Yale, 2013.

These ideas were set out in a chapter in *Stumbling Giant*, but it soon became clear that the subject deserved a more detailed examination. In 2018 Tim began studying China's demographic outlook in earnest. This required an enormous effort simply to get a grip on the statistics. Official Chinese statistics are notoriously unreliable and often contradictory. Determined to get to the bottom of the issue, Tim read everything he could on the subject. Dozens of reports on birthrates and every aspect of demography were pored over, dissected and assessed. He spoke to many leading academics, expanding his knowledge and expertise and eventually obtaining the information that now informs this book. Despite the uncertainty over official statistics, he was able to develop a highly credible analytical framework, backed by the best available facts and figures.

By the autumn of 2020, when Tim passed away, much of the work for the book had been completed. The text had been through three major edits. The fast-approaching 2020 Chinese Census, carried out in November 2020, meant that some textual changes would have to be introduced, but these did not challenge the general thrust of this book. In the event, with China not releasing results of the Census until the late spring of 2021, we took the decision to add an initial assessment of the Census data at the beginning of the book to take the new information into account. Otherwise, the book is as Tim intended it to be. He always made it abundantly clear that whatever his criticisms of China, they were words of advice from one good friend to another.

China's 2020 National Census

On 11 May 2021, after an unprecedented four-week delay, Ning Jizhe, Commissioner of China's National Bureau of Statistics, finally announced the release of data from the country's Seventh National Census, conducted on 1 November the previous year.[2] More than seven million officials carried out the survey, which took place during the Covid-19 pandemic. For the first time, much of the data was collected electronically, with respondents allowed to fill in online forms and submit them to the authorities.

Of course, we cannot be sure of the accuracy of all the data or even if the data was correctly interpreted. Statistics from China

---

2   http://www.stats.gov.cn/english/PressRelease/202105/t20210510_1817185.html

have often been problematic in the past and these should come with a health warning, particularly considering the long delay in their publication. Nonetheless, the figures are important, not least because they will be the data used by Chinese officials to plan for the future. The full details of the report are not yet available and will be issued over the course of the next year.

Despite much speculation, the figures as published did not show an absolute decline in China's population over the last decade, but instead posted a small increase.[3] The total was given as 1.443 billion, up by 5.38 per cent from the figure given for the Sixth National Census conducted in 2010 - an annual growth rate of 0.53 per cent. However, several demographers have previously stated that China's population could already be as low as 1.2 billion and has been in decline for several years. Officially, only 12 million babies were born in 2020, the lowest number since 1961.

On the basis of the new Census China's population decline could begin as early as next year, almost a decade earlier than the previous official estimates. Already these figures show the slowest population growth since the 1960s. Family size has shrunk over the last decade from 3.1 persons to 2.62 and births are continuing to decline. The official figure for total fertility rate is given as 1.3 - well below the 2.1 figure needed to ensure that the population simply remains stable, without decreasing. This is one of the lowest fertility rates in the world, with only five countries having lower rates.

There are no figures on the size of the working population, which many experts say has been in absolute decline for a number of years. These are among the figures that analysts will hope to see as the results are gradually rolled out during the next year.

The Census also showed that 91 per cent of the population was Han Chinese. Two of China's 31 provinces now have a population of more than 100 million, nine have between 50-100 million, 17 have 10-50 million and three have less than 10 million. The top five provinces accounted for 35 per cent of the national population. In all,

---

3   See, for example, this article from the *Financial Times*, which said the Census was expected to report that China's population had fallen to less than 1.4 billion, after reaching this figure in 2020: https://www.ft.com/content/008ea78a-8bc1-4954-b283-700608d3dc6c?accessToken=zwAAAXkTj48wkc8AjqeKi8FJVNOyg3A GCNPcbA.MEQCIDcFji_BkdpQQ9qj8SC-4ooUEu7JyKB3c3fy6OnFO5Q-AiBmp7-ULuo_1PqSJZiGeel9DUFimOKIqzz9exDvFx47oA&sharetype=gift?to ken=2ed6d6fc-82e2-40ee-b59d-f9195e2b0eb1

25 provinces have seen a population increase over the last 10 years.

As expected, the Census confirmed that China's skewed sex ratio continued to be a problem, although we will have to wait for more details before we can see the exact number of surplus adult males. There are 723 million males (51.24 per cent of total population), and 688 million females, giving an official sex ratio of 105.07:1. Most demographers believe the real figure would show a higher percentage of males. Only two provinces had a sex ratio below 100.

In terms of ageing, 18.7 per cent (264 million) were aged over 60, of which 190 million were over 65. In 2010 the figure for over-60s was 13.26 per cent. Figures for the over-60s were up by 5.44 per cent and for over-65s by 4.63 per cent. These are likely to be the most worrying figures for Beijing, in that they indicate the population is ageing much faster than expected. Further breakdown of the figures will show the provinces which are ageing fastest.

In terms of educational attainment, 218 million Chinese were educated to university level, with another 213 million having had senior secondary school education. Those with university education have risen from 8,930 per 100,000 in 2010 to 15,467 per 100,000 in 2020. At 15 per cent of the adult population, this is still way below the figures for many developed countries, where around 40 per cent of people have gone through tertiary education. And unless China can create jobs for its new graduates, it is likely that fertility will fall even further, as lack of financial stability will discourage couples from starting families. Figures for the number of children in junior and primary education appear to be falling, indicative of an overall decline in the national birthrate. Illiteracy has decreased from 4.08 per cent of the national population, to around 2.67 per cent, a drop of around 17 million.

The move from the country to the cities - one of the principal reasons behind the fall in fertility - continues unabated in China, with the urban population increasing during the decade by 235 million (up 14 per cent) and the rural population falling by 164 million. Nonetheless, roughly a third of China's population still lives in rural areas.

Demonstrating the fact that many people have become internal migrants in China, we are told that 492 million people live in places other than their household registration areas. Around 125 million of these had moved to other provinces. The number who live in places other than their household registration area has increased by 88 per cent over the decade.

Just before the Census figures were published in May 2021, the People's Bank of China published a detailed working paper on population trends.[4] It noted that developed countries had underestimated the role of population and the severe consequences of ageing and declining birthrates. For China, the report stated, the situation was even worse, in that its population was ageing faster and the extent of sub-replacement fertility was more severe: 'China must recognise that the demographic situation has changed, the demographic dividend was used comfortably at the time and that it is a debt that needs to be repaid afterwards.' It also stressed that population inertia is 'a huge force across generations, and its reactionary force will lead to changes in the population in the opposite direction.' Education and technological progress cannot compensate for the decline in population, it argued. Instead, China should fully liberalize and encourage childbirth, removing difficulties faced by women during pregnancy, childbirth, kindergarden and school enrolment.

This theme was echoed in much of the coverage of the Census results. The official *Global Times*, for example, reported that over the next few years China will increase the retirement age.[5] It also quoted independent demographer He Yafu saying that there is 'no doubt' that China will fully lift the remaining birth restrictions and will more than likely remove its family planning policy as early as the autumn of 2021 during the sixth plenary session of the 19th Central Committee of the Communist Party of China. It added: 'Fully lifting birth restrictions will not be enough to avert a fall in China's total population, or prevent China from becoming another Japan, demographers said, noting that China should come up with more measures to encourage childbirth, such as subsidizing couples who choose to have more than one baby.'

Readers of this book will understand that there is no simple way of reversing demographic trends. They tend to be settled over decades, rather than years. And the reasons that are preventing

---

4   http://www.pbc.gov.cn/redianzhuanti/118742/4122386/4122692/4214189
     /4215394/2021032618473569432.pdf
5   https://www.globaltimes.cn/page/202105/1223120.shtml

Chinese women from having children, many of them economic, are unlikely to change even in the medium to long term.

The Census details that have emerged so far fully vindicate many of the main themes of this book, namely that China's population is on the cusp of a major, possibly catastrophic, decline in population. Its working population is already in decline. The number of elderly is climbing relentlessly as a percentage of the population and the sex ratio at birth is heavily skewed towards excess males.

Nick Fielding
May 2021

ACKNOWLEDGEMENTS

Tim would have wished to thank his many friends and acquaintances for their advice, comments and contributions during the years since his first visit to China in 1978 and especially while writing this book.

In particular he would have liked to thank Zhou Xiaochuan, Liu Hongru, former Vice President of the People's Bank of China, Wang Ruipu at the Communist Party Central School, Li Yining, the late Jing Shuping at CITIC and Ma Hong at the Development Bank Research Centre of the State Council, amongst many for their early perspectives. Later he benefited from Liu Mingkang's views. Thanks are also due to Robbie Lyle, who encouraged him to expand his views on China, and to Cheng Siwei, former Vice Chairman of the Standing Committee of the National People's Congress. He also spoke with Professors Kang Shaobang, Gon Li, Qin Zhilai of the Communist Party Central School, Zhang Weiying at Peking University, Wu Qidi, formerly Vice Minister of Education, Li Pelin and Wang Zhimou of the Chinese Academy of Social Sciences (CASS) and Larry Lau, the then-president of the Chinese University of Hong Kong. In particular, he would have thanked Dan Esty for encouraging him to embark on this project.

In Hong Kong he would have thanked Roger de Basto, Peter Churchouse, Lucy Isler, Peregrine Moncrieff, Simon Rigby, Dominic Horsfall and Raymond Tang for their advice on the text, Sir Andrew Burns, former Consul General in Hong Kong during the transition in 1997, for his preface and comments and Professor Stuart Gietel-Basten from the Hong Kong University of Science and Technology. He would have extended his particular thanks to the China Oxford Scholarship Fund students, all from one-child families, who at the summer lunches reminded him of how difficult it was to have four grandparents and two parents all focusing on their every move.

Doubtless there are others whom Tim would have thanked and whose names, through circumstance, have not made it into the book. Some held very different views to him and would not have shared all the conclusions he drew. Others have asked not to be acknowledged due to sensitivities. That does not lessen their contribution and his family remain grateful for their efforts. Most importantly, he would have wanted to thank his wife Clair and son Peregrine for their constant support, particularly during 2020. As Tim did not have sight of the final manuscript it means that his editors take full responsible for any errors and omissions that remain.

Tim always retained the original copy of Mao's little red book given to him by the Chinese Embassy in London in 1960, so it was a particularly poignant moment when he founded what was the only foreign institution invited onto the working party to set up the Shanghai stock exchange and which became the first foreign firm to be authorized by the People's Bank of China to open up in the country in 1989. Although the opinions expressed here are not always closely aligned to official views, Tim put them forward as an old friend who had spent over 30 years working with China and who wished it well.

He had no hesitation in dedicating this book to China which has had such a terrible nineteenth and twentieth centuries and which fully deserves a prosperous, successful and happy twenty-first century.

1

A BRIEF POPULATION HISTORY OF CHINA

This chapter examines China's history for forerunners of today's severe population threats and also uncovers the origins of China's invasive birth control policies, first introduced in the 1970s.

It can be argued that the modern history of China began as far back as the Qin Dynasty, which was founded by Qin Shi Huang, the first (and most notable) Emperor of *Qin* and which lasted only a few years, from 221-206 BCE, in an area that is now known as Gansu and Shaanxi. The Qin Emperor forcibly unified the warring kingdoms and created the early Chinese state. More importantly, his was one of the world's first attempts to build a totalitarian society. The state brooked no intermediary institutions between itself and the people. Officials replaced the role of the aristocracy. The state interfered expansively in the personal lives of its citizens.

Qin Shi Huang was noted for building an efficient and effective state, simplifying Chinese script and for major construction feats such as the 34-kilometre Lingqu Canal, which links the Yangtze River and Pearl River systems and hence north and south China, and the Great Wall. It is his (still unexcavated) mausoleum that is guarded by the Terracotta Army. Equally he was infamous for his ruthlessness and was known to execute not only his enemies, but also their relatives to the third degree (cousins, uncles, aunts).

The Qin state's philosophy of administration, known as legalism, was the only acceptable school of thought. Legalism emphasized order and the need for powerful and efficient government. It embraced the view that the state was unconstrained in its ability to invade private life. Qin Shi Huang instructed his officials to destroy - with certain exceptions - all books not centred on his reign. He also had 460 scholars buried alive and reportedly another 700 stoned to death. Sima Qian, the prominent historian

1

of early China, described Qin Shi Huang as 'a man of scant mercy who has the heart of a tiger or wolf'.[1]

While the system itself ostensibly terminated with the Dynasty in 206 BCE, elements of this thinking became deeply implanted within Chinese political culture, regularly resurfacing throughout imperial history. For example, Professor Timothy Brook has referred to the Ming Dynasty (1368-1644) as a 'Legalist gulag'. This kind of thinking returned again with the 1949 communist victory in the civil war.[2]

Qin China introduced the notorious *baojia* (or *pao chia* or *li chia*) system, in which communities were divided into groups of five or ten families which were made collectively responsible for any breach of laws and informing officials of the perpetrators. This weakened family and social bonds and strengthened the state. The system was publicly re-energized in 2016 as social control under the title of 'grid management'.[3] In such a society the cardinal virtue becomes obedience rather than volition. This leads to a stunting of personal moral development but in today's China that is regarded as an acceptable price for a peaceful, orderly and efficient state.

China's present leader, Xi Jinping, has cited approvingly the writings of Han Fei Tzu,[4] the most prominent of the legalist theoreticians. Mao Zedong is reported as saying he embodied 'Emperor Qin and Marx in one'. Many of the themes of Emperor Qin's reign, such as the primacy of the state, the relish for large-scale projects, the disdain for private space and the absence of moral nicety, anticipated today's communist China.

Through using data collected by Chinese officials for censuses and registration, researchers have been able to calculate population growth in China over the last two millennia.[5] The figures - which need

1   https://web.stanford.edu/dept/archaeology/journal/newdraft/miller/paper. pdf
2   See Timothy Brook, *The Troubled Empire: China in the Yuan and Ming Dynasties*, Harvard University Press, 2010, p. 8.
3   JK Fairbank and M Goldman, *China: A new history*, Belknap Press, 2006, p. 55.
4   See, for example, Jianying Zha's 2020 essay, 'China's Heart of Darkness: Prince Han Fei and Chairman Xi Jinping', accessed at http://chinaheritage. net/journal/chinas-heart-of-darkness-prince-han-fei-chairman-xi-jinping-prologue/
5   See, for example, Dudley L Poston Jnr and David Yaukey, *The Population History of China*, Plenum Publishing Co, 1992.

to be treated with caution, as do all Chinese population statistics[6] - show that for more than a millennium China's population was stable, at between 37 and 60 million. The first period of sustained population growth - at around 1.6 per cent a year - was recorded in the last half of the eleventh century under the Song Dynasty. It was, however, reversed by a combination of dynastic struggle, bubonic plague, civil war and Mongol invasion.

Beginning in the early years of the Ming Dynasty in the late fourteenth century China then experienced six consecutive centuries of population growth. It was checked only twice - once because of the fall of the Ming Dynasty in the early seventeenth century and once during the Taiping Rebellion towards the end of the Qing Dynasty in the late nineteenth century. From 1749-1851 China's population expanded rapidly, doubling during this period - an annual growth rate of 0.9 per cent. This in turn led to a huge growth in agricultural food production by increasing the land under cultivation, importing new varieties of high-yielding rice seeds and importing food crops from both North and South America.

Table I. China Population Estimates, CE 2-1953

Date (CE)	Dynasty	Persons Counted	Implied persons per Household	Adjusted to PRC boundaries
2	Han	59,594,978	4.9	
88	Han	43,356,367	5.8	
105	Han	53,256,229	5.8	
125	Han	49,690,789	5.2	
140	Han	49,150,220	5.1	
144	Han	49,730,550	5.0	
145	Han	49,524,183	5.0	
146	Han	47,566,772	5.1	
156	Han	56,486,856	5.3	
606	Sui	46,019,956	5.2	

---

6   Lee and Wang call China's population the largest but least understood in the world. See James Lee and Wang Feng, *One Quarter of Humanity: Malthusian Mythology and Chinese Realities, 1700–2000*, Harvard University Press, p. 29.

705	Tang	37,140,000	6.0	
726	Tang	41,419,712	5.9	
732	Tang	45,431,265	5.8	
734	Tang	46,285,161	5.8	
740	Tang	48.143.609	5.7	
742	Tang	48.909,800	5.7	
754	Tang	52,880,488	5.8	
755	Tang	52,919,309	5.9	
1290	Yuan (Mongol)	58,834,711	4.5	
1291	Yuan	59,848,964	4.5	
1381	Ming	59,873,305	5.6	
1393	Ming	60.545,813	5.7	
1749	Qing	177,495,000		176.5
1776	Qing	268,238,000		267.0
1791	Qing	304,354,000		303.0
1811	Qing	358.610.000		357.0
1821	Qing	355,540,000		353.7
1831	Qing	395,821,000		393.8
1841	Qing	413,457,000		411.3
1851	Qing	431,896,000		429.5
1953	PRC	582.603.417		582.6[7]

Population Fall

The lack of reliable data makes it hard to make firm statements about many aspects of dynastic China. Population data are particularly ambiguous. Despite frequent censuses throughout Chinese history, the numbers are contested. They often do not increase despite, say, ten-year intermissions. There are good reasons for this; as rising provincial populations attracted increasing central demands for tax contributions it is likely that bureaucrats discouraged the reporting

---

7   Judith Banister, *China's Changing Population*, Stanford University Press, 1987, p. 4.

of population growth. Other demographers stress the impact of frequent natural and man-made disasters. A third group defends historical data. Accordingly, what little data there are have to be interpreted, weighed and adjusted to provide credible estimates.

Another area of confusion is that different dynasties had different boundaries and thus during their reigns the empire both expanded and contracted. Hence determining China's population is complicated by the fact that its territory often changed from dynasty to dynasty and also within dynasties. It did not matter whether the emperor was Han Chinese or foreign. And few things through its history have been as fluctuating as China's borders. In fact, the only constant over the centuries seems to be that the territorial area of the state was larger when ruled by foreigners than when it was ruled by native Han Chinese.

Yet, when the Song Dynasty was broken in two and only operated in the southern half, there was a feeling that the lands in the north, conquered by non-Chinese, were somehow still China. One might also note that the foreign Qing Dynasty (1644-1911) grew to rule over twice the land area of the preceding native Ming Dynasty (1368-1644) at their respective apogees. Nonetheless - surprisingly - the accretion of lands did not itself always absorb substantial new populations. Huge new territories such as Tibet and Xinjiang were lightly populated relative to their enormous areas. However, during the Qing Dynasty there was genuine large-scale growth in births in the domestic heartlands.

China's An Lushan rebellion (755-763 AD) was - proportionately - one of the world's bloodiest events; some accounts suggest that during the rebellion the equivalent of 5 per cent of the entire world's population may have died in combat and through starvation. Accounts and academics differ but on a like-for-like basis up to 40-50 per cent of the Tang Dynasty's population may have died during this period. Figures suggesting a two-thirds fall in China's population seem extreme but could be explained by the fact that whole classes of people were removed from the census after the rebellion for taxation reasons and parts of the Tang Dynasty lands were no longer under the empire.

Where there are data, for example, the period between the fracturing of the Song empire and the final collapse of the Southern Song, from 1187 and 1292, the population of what had earlier been

Song Dynasty China fell by about a third as a result of war in the north, the Mongol invasion, sieges of cities and bubonic plague.

Plague also devastated the population during the Ming Dynasty in the 1580s. Cao Shuji, the Chinese demographic historian, traced this epidemic to the resumption of trade between the Mongols and Chinese farmers, a process that disturbed the Mongolian gerbil, a known vector for plague. He has suggested death rates in north China of 'between 40 and 50 per cent' although some critics suggest this figure is on the high side. (Rodents from Mongolia have also been blamed for the devastating Black Death in fourteenth-century Europe.[8])

Again, from about 1600 in the late Ming period until around 1680 in the early Manchu time, the population fell by a third to two-fifths as a combined result of natural disaster, civil war, invasion and disease. Ming census reports from the fifteenth century onwards have been described - controversially - as 'the least trustworthy in the whole of Chinese history' and so analysis is vital. This is an academic battlefield. Some of the Ming collapse was caused by China's all too frequent and savage climate change, in this particular case, global cooling.[9]

If we require reminding of the repetitive waves of climate cooling and warming, we need only recall Mark Elvin's remark that only 4,000 years ago the semi-arid area surrounding Beijing was once the habitat of a substantial elephant population. A thousand years later the temperature had cooled and the elephants had moved on.[10]

Wars in particular had an enormous impact on China's population. The Manchu invasion that created the Qing Dynasty is estimated to have caused the direct deaths of 20 per cent of the population. China is also particularly prone to natural disasters. WH Mallory published a list of 1,828 such disasters between 211 BC and 1911 AD.[11] The year 1811, for example, was particularly deadly, the country ravaged by drought, flood, earthquake and

8   Brook, *op. cit.*, p. 67.
9   Jacques Gernet, *A History of Chinese Civilization*, Cambridge University Press, 1972, p. 392,
10   Mark Elvin, *The Retreat of the Elephants: an environmental history of China*, Yale University Press, 2006.
11   See Walter H Mallory, *China: Land of Famine*, American Geographical Society, New York, 1926.

plague, causing an estimated 20 million deaths - about 5 per cent of the population. To measure the impact of these events, much depends not only on the estimates of casualties but also on the varying estimates of the then population.

However, during most of the Qing Dynasty, the country underwent what has been described as 'an extraordinary demographic expansion'. While accepting the frailty of the data, it seems reasonable to estimate that China's population at the founding of the Qing in 1644 may have been under 100 million. By 1850 it was possibly over 400 million. To quadruple the population in 200 years is a brisk annual growth rate of 0.7 per cent.

But for the latter part of the Qing Dynasty, well into the twentieth century, from 1851-1949, the growth of the previous century slowed down dramatically, due to social breakdown, the weakening of the Qing Dynasty, invasion by foreign imperialists and civil war. The Taiping Rebellion (1850-1864) is thought to have caused around 20-30 million deaths. Some observers have referred to it as the bloodiest civil war in world history. However, as a percentage of China's then population, the toll appears barely over 5-6 per cent - although there are estimates of 70 million and 17 per cent. Banister calculates that the recorded population grew from about 429.5 million in 1851 to 582.6 million in 1953, an annual average growth rate of just 0.3 per cent - lower than it is today. Bearing in mind that the 1953 census was more complete than the 1851 population registration, the growth rate was probably below 0.3 per cent.

Despite this halt in population growth, a significant school of thought believed that policy intervention was necessary. Nineteenth-century intellectuals such as Wang Shiduo, Yan Fu and Kang Youwei had interventionist, if differing, approaches to the seemingly threatening demographic picture. Wang, for example, felt that China could do without 'the short and slight, ugly, mean-eyed, short-stepped, garrulous, effeminate, stupid people'; he also believed it could benefit from drowning female babies, especially from lower-class families.

Surprisingly, such thinking did not end with the reduction of population growth in the late nineteenth century but continued during the Republican period (1911-1949). There was a wave of interest in eugenics and a Malthusian-inspired desire to influence population outcomes. Writers such as Pan Guangdan and Zhang Junjun advocated various eugenic policies to achieve specific racial goals. This thinking continued and blossomed in the communist era.

As Banister notes,[12] figures for the period from the mid-nineteenth century to 1949 are not easy to come by, nor very accurate, but between 1929 and 1931 significant amounts of data were collected as part of a survey of land utilization. Although data were not collected on urban areas or from rural families not engaged in agriculture, the surveyors were still able to collect detailed information from more than 46,000 agricultural families in 119 locations. The findings were remarkably consistent. Over 99 per cent of people surveyed were married and the average age for women marrying was just 17.5 years - compare this to the figures for 2018 when the average actual marriage age for women was 27.4 - a near 14-year difference from the imperial minimum age. For men it was 21.3 years. Fertility was far below the number of theoretically possible births, with a total fertility rate (TFR) of 5.5 children per woman and 41 per thousand population. This compares with a TFR of 10.8 and crude birth rate of 55 per thousand population seen in high fertility populations.

The chaos of the warlord period following the collapse of the Qing Dynasty may in part explain the comparatively low fertility - although we should note that this level is actually high compared to modern levels. Other traditional factors may have affected fertility, including a long period of breastfeeding for babies, long separations between married couples and a ban on the remarriage of widows at a time when both men and women tended to die young. High death rates for men and women mean that life expectancy fell as low as 23.7 years for women and 24.6 years for men. Infant mortality was particularly high, with some estimates suggesting that 30 per cent of babies died in their first year.

The ageing of a population is characterized by fewer babies and at the same time greater longevity. In recent decades, longevity has increased. During the Qing Dynasty in the eighteenth century typical male life expectancy was 37.5 years, and this barely changed for several hundred years. During the Northern Qi Dynasty (550-557), the death penalty would be levied on families if girls were

---

12   Banister, *op. cit.*, p. 12.

not married by the required age. Throughout the dynastic period
- 770 BC–1911 AD - the average legal minimum marriage age
for a female was 13.6 years old. There was also a maximum age
(averaging 19) by which a girl was required to be married. In fact,
research shows that between 1174 and 1875 up to 38 per cent of
marriages involved girls below the legal age.[13]

The contrast with the modern era is stark. To summarize, at the
beginning of the twentieth century, marriage among China's large
agricultural population was universal and took place early, fertility
was moderately high, but mortality for all ages was extremely high.
Subsequent research by the Chinese government in the 1980s
suggests that fertility in China fell slightly during the Second World
War (1940-45), but rebounded after the defeat of the Japanese, even
during the civil war years. However, change was on the horizon.
Despite almost six centuries of continual population growth, new
high-quality agricultural land for the expanding rural population
was beginning to run out. Marginal lands were also in short supply
and producing enough food required greater inputs of expensive
chemical fertilisers. More people no longer meant more food.

With the accession of the communists under Mao Zedong to
power in 1949, China's population policies were initially unclear
and it would take another twenty years to bring them into focus.
Some party officials argued for population limitation and birth
control education. In 1953 Deng Xiaoping called for greater
emphasis on contraception. Ma Yin-chu, then president of Peking
University, asserted that population control could exist in a socialist
society. However, Mao favoured a growing population and the
alternative view was disdained as 'rightist'. Population increase was
seen as a sign of the strength of the new state. Ma was criticised as a
'bourgeois Malthusian' and dismissed as president of the university.

In 1949 Mao made his own thoughts very clear with the
statement, 'Of all things in the world, people are the most precious.'
Birth control was condemned, and the import of contraceptives
was banned. However, as early as 1953, following the introduction
of the First Five Year Plan, planners began to worry about increases
in the population. The census the same year showed that it was
growing by well over 2 per cent per year. Birth control policies

---

13 http://www.lse.ac.uk/Economic-History/Assets/Documents/
    WorkingPapers/Economic-History/2003/wp7603.pdf

began to creep in and by 1956 it was a firmly established strategy. By 1957 Mao was able to make his famous anti-natalist statement that the human race had been in a state of total anarchy in relation to procreation and had failed to exercise control.

Yet these early birth control policies soon came up against the harsh reality of the Great Leap Forward (the Second Five Year Plan), which relied on a large-scale rural labour force as the engine of industrial development through the establishment of people's communes. As is well known, the Great Leap Forward - which lasted from 1958-62 - was a huge disaster, with anything up to 45 million deaths, many by starvation, as the state seized much of the agricultural food surplus. The economy shrank and industrial development was set back. And birth control took a backseat.

From 1962 onwards birth control policies were gradually reintroduced. Contraceptives became available for the first time in several years and restrictions on abortion were lifted. In 1964 the Birth Planning Office of the State Council was set up. But this initiative also fell by the wayside with the advent of the chaotic Cultural Revolution in 1966 and during the next four years. Even then, it was not until the death of Mao in 1976 and the defeat of the leftist Gang of Four a few years later that more moderate policies, under the influence of Zhou Enlai, were put into effect. Birth control began to rise up the political agenda, with CCP chairman Hu Yaobang declaring in his report to the Twelfth Party Congress in 1983: 'In the economic and social development of our nation, the population problem is the most important problem. The implementation of the family planning programme is one of the basic national policies.'[14]

Data from the 1982 Census and the National Fertility Survey, which covered one in every 1,000 households, gave officials some indication of the direction policy should now follow. The Census showed that China's population had now reached 1.008 billion in mainland China, almost double the figure of 542 million for 1949. Annual average births had reached about 20 million a year from 1950-59; from 1962-70 they had reached an annual figure of 26 million. The introduction of birth control programmes from 1970

---

14   Quoted in Lee-Jay Cho, 'Population Dynamic and Policy in China', *Annals of the American Academy of Political and Social Science*, No 476, pp. 111-27. Reprinted in Poston and Yaukey, op. cit.

appears to have reduced annual births back to around 20 million, falling again to 18 million from 1976-81. Annual average growth fell from 2.6 per cent in 1970 to 1.5 per cent in 1982.

Thus from the 1950s until the 1970s, China's population increased by some 250 million. After the death of Mao in 1976 it became possible to consider birth control legislation. Various programmes having been tried rather unsuccessfully, the so-called 'One-child Policy' was enacted in 1979. In fact, in September the following year the Central Committee of the Party issued *An Open Letter of the Central Committee of the Chinese Communist Party of China to the General Members of the Communist Party and the Membership of the Chinese Communist Youth League on the Problems of Controlling Population Growth in Our Country*.[15] This stipulated that couples should have one child. Its aim was to stabilize the population at 1.2 billion by the year 2000. As vice-premier and head of the State Family Commission Chen Muhua noted at the time, 'Only if 95 per cent of the couples of reproductive age in urban areas and 90 per cent in rural villages give birth to only one child will the total population of our country be controlled at 1.2bn by the end of this century.'[16]

The new policy was not initially introduced as a law, but as 'guidance' to members of the Communist Party and its youth wing. Its aim was nothing less than to change by example China's population reproduction profile from one featuring high birth, low-death and high growth rates to one featuring low birth, low death and low growth rates, equalling those of moderately developed nations in a relative short period of time.

It is somewhat surprising that after the death of Mao, who is accused of complicity in the killing of as many as 50 million people, the leaders who succeeded him and removed his colleagues from power at gunpoint decided to install the most extreme intervention in family reproduction in world history. It is as if they disapproved of extremism which was not of their own making. The world was then absorbed with bureaucratic plans to lower birthrates. Infamously, India had already brought in a harsh birth control policy in 1976 that resulted in coercing people into accepting vasectomies for men and sterilization for women.

---

15   https://www.tandfonline.com/doi/abs/10.2753/CSA0009-4625240311
16   Lee-Jay Cho, *op.cit.*, p.63.

In China, the new measure coincided with transformative change in the urban areas where the 'opening up' policy was creating extraordinary opportunities for employment and prosperity. The effect was that jobs were prized and there was 'a greater opportunity cost to childbearing'. Partly as a result of this shift in direction, there was little urban resistance to the new policy.

It should be noted that the term 'One-child Policy' is misleading. It was never so simple. From the beginning, there were exceptions to the policy. Ethnic minorities, such as the Tibetans and Uyghurs, were excluded from the constraints, and separate, less restrictive, rules were applied to them. There were several adjustments to the 'One-child Policy' over the years. Partly in response to strong resistance, from as early as 1984 couples in rural China were allowed to have a second child (with a spacing requirement) upon meeting certain criteria regarding the level of wealth in the area and/or whether their first child was a girl. Gradually there was a liberalization in the cities for couples where both were single children if they met certain requirements. By 2002, all provinces except Henan had similar provisions.

At first the regulations were lightly applied. Later, diverse though the rules were, when imposed they were frequently applied with a cold bureaucratic severity. Substantial fines, forcible abortions, forced sterilization and seizure of unpermitted children for orphanages marked this long-lasting campaign. Many of those 'orphans' ended up being sold to couples in the United States. The enforcement of this policy demonstrated the moral vacuum at the heart of the Chinese state.

It should be stressed how each province and often each village had different ways of applying the birth control regulations. Even as far back as 2007, Yu Xuejun, spokesman of the National Population and Family Planning Commission, stated that only 35.9 per cent of the population was restricted to having just one child.[17] These were mostly urban, Han Chinese and government officials. However, the average number of births each year from 2007 to 2018 was only 16.4 million. The number of children per woman, or TFR, continues at less than 1.5, well below the necessary replacement rate of 2.1.

---

17   http://www.chinadaily.com.cn/china/2007-07/11/content_5432238.htm

The imposition of fines of up to $50,000 for those breaching the one-child policy became an end in itself. Provinces were asked to declare their receipts of fines in 2013. Of the 31 provinces and cities, 24 did so, declaring a total revenue over $3 billion in the previous year. Such fines have become a major source of local government finance. The National Audit Office believes the figures are understated as the family planning network, which has directly employed at least a million officials, is riddled with corruption.[18]

This harsh approach has certainly caused fear among large sections of the population. Yet the Chinese government reiterates the claim that if it were not for the birth restriction policy, there would have been 400 million further births. Later we will examine whether or not this is true.

Gender Disparity

China's long history means it is no stranger to most phenomena. It has experienced both gender disparity and steep falls in population. The novelty now is ageing. But none of these past experiences compares with the scale of the issue that we see today. The population decline - not to mention gender disparity - will be longer and steeper than has ever been seen. The following chapters will examine China's population in more detail, looking at ageing, gender disparity and the impact of a declining population on China's economy.

Gender disparity is nothing new. In the late Ming period at the end of the sixteenth century many regions showed extreme imbalances of men to women, with ratios as high as 2:1. We cannot assume these figures to be accurate. Female children were often under-counted or missed out. There are, however, numerous contemporary accounts of female infanticide, which has a 2,000-year history in China. Weather conditions were difficult and harvests volatile. We can probably assume that there was a material gender imbalance.

In the nineteenth century male surplus was frequent, mainly due to female infanticide. The Qing Dynasty sought to address the problem by encouraging young single men to engage in the

---

18   http://www.globaltimes.cn/content/988298.shtml

colonisation of Taiwan.[19] Gender disparity was a major cause of the Nian Rebellion in Jiangsu during the Qing Dynasty in the mid-nineteenth century (1851-68). It stemmed from unhappiness with incompetent public service delivery from Qing officials and long-term female infanticide, both of which resulted from disastrous famines that occurred when the Yellow River burst its banks and flooded northern China. It has been estimated that around a quarter of the young men in the affected area were unmarried. This 17-year conflict, contemporaneous with the even more bloody Taiping Rebellion, resulted in around 100,000 deaths.

There is some evidence that the male-to-female sex ratio during the Qing Dynasty was 1.17:1. It is not clear if this refers to the ratio at birth or across the whole population. Subsequently, it reportedly rose to 1.22:1 for the first decade of the Republican period. These figures - if correct - would make the Qing and early Republican period as skewed as China since 1982. Indeed, if they are correct and refer to the entire population, then the Qing and early Republican period were even more distorted than China today.[20]

In more modern times, there have been similar issues. Several sources suggest that during the 1930s and 1940s the sex ratio at birth (SRB) in China was higher than normal as a result of excess female mortality associated with female infanticide. This was a time when there were severe natural disasters and the nationalist government had to deal simultaneously with a Japanese invasion and a communist insurrection. It led to many policy malfunctions.[21]

Gender disparity returned to China in the early 1980s. It grew substantially and, as we shall see, is still material today.

19   http://documents.worldbank.org/curated/en/498661468221674913/pdf/776250JRN020090UBLIC00Missing0Girls.pdf

20   Kent G Deng, Re-examination of Chinese Premodern Population Statistics, LSE Department of Economic History, July 2003, http://www.lse.ac.uk/Economic-History/Assets/Documents/WorkingPapers/Economic-History/2003/wp7603.pdf

21   https://pdfs.semanticscholar.org/5b10/00bb7329e52c1f063521bc7f3762128cb3ac.pdf

2

AGEING

Ageing is one of the major issues facing China. What is an ageing society? It is one where there are fewer births and the elderly become an increasing proportion of society. The impact is that there are fewer working citizens to support the non-working elderly. This circumstance can be exacerbated by the elderly having a longer life owing to better health and diet. It is clearly an irony that this unwanted situation is a combination of good and bad news: greater longevity but also fewer children. Although it is less of a problem currently in China than in many other countries, the situation is changing rapidly and China will be one of the most affected countries within a few decades. Here we consider what affects longevity, what increasing ageing can lead to and the implications of an age imbalance.

What Affects Longevity?

As a result of China's falling birthrate, the proportion of elderly people in the population is rising. According to the World Bank, 'East Asia is aging more rapidly than any other region in history.'[1] Many factors affect longevity in China. A 2013 study by Chinese and international scientists blamed air pollution for cutting individual longevity in North China by an average of 5.5 years.[2] With more than 500 million people living in North China at the time of the survey, the researchers estimate that industrial pollution has caused the region 'to lose more than 2.5 billion years of life expectancy'. The study concludes, "these results may help explain why China's explosive economic growth has led to relatively anaemic growth in life expectancy". Given sufficient political will, this is reversible.

---

1   http://www.worldbank.org/en/region/eap/brief/rapid-aging-in-east-asia-and-pacific-will-shrink-workforce-increase-public-spending

2   https://www.sciencedaily.com/releases/2016/04/160426215327.htm

This area is one where longevity could be improved.[3]

While noting recent improvement in Beijing's air quality, a 2019 official eight-year survey confirmed a 'significant correlation' between excessive pollution and miscarriages. Reduced pollution levels were still five times those recommended by the World Health Organisation (WHO). The researchers observed that pollution affected the birthrate and that 'foetal health affects the fate of a family and even a country'.[4]

US research has shown that obesity has a severe impact on illness and reduces longevity. It has also been linked by Cambridge University with poor cognitive skills. Unfortunately, obesity is rising sharply in China. In 2016, Professor Joep Perk, cardiovascular prevention spokesman for the European Society of Cardiology, said that 'It is the worst explosion of childhood and adolescent obesity that I have ever seen… China is set for an escalation of cardiovascular disease and diabetes, and the popularity of the western lifestyle will cost lives.'[5] This represents a serious threat to Chinese longevity.

Starting life obese is one route to being obese for life. One solution could be to encourage breastfeeding, which not only increases the gut's protection against malignant bacteria but also sharply reduces obesity in children. Recent research refers to the positive medical impact of breastfeeding 'with the benefits actually extending beyond infancy'.[6] China has one of the lowest breastfeeding rates in the world.

Nor is that the only reason for increasing obesity in China. One of the reasons Southern Europe has more than double the child obesity of Northern Europe appears to be the decline of the 'Mediterranean diet'. We should note the rise in obesity in China has to some degree followed dietary changes there towards greater consumption of highly processed fast food.[7]

A pharmaceutical firm, Evolve Biosystems, states that challenges to the auto-immune system such as eczema and allergies,

---

3   https://www.pnas.org/content/pnas/110/32/12936.full.pdf
4   https://www.scmp.com/news/china/politics/article/3033090/breathing-polluted-air-may-put-women-greater-risk-miscarriage
5   www.sciencedaily.com/2016/04/160426215327.htm
6   https://www.mdpi.com/2072-6643/10/10/1355/htm
7   https://www.ucd.ie/newsandopinion/news/2019/may/01/breastfeedingcutschildhoodobesityrisknewwhostudyfinds/

which have arisen in East Asia, coincide 'with the rise of formula feeding, C-section deliveries and excessive use of antibiotics'.[8] In the United States, it says, 90 per cent of babies have a 'disrupted gut microbiome'. The company aims to re-establish functioning immune systems. It claims to achieve an 80 per cent reduction in 'potentially harmful bacteria that have been linked to various diseases later in life'. Again, ailments suffered by infants can link through to illness in mature adults.

Poor diet is linked to childhood obesity, which in turn often leads later to cardiovascular disease and diabetes. Breastfeeding cuts childhood obesity with lifelong benefits. It also leads to a stronger gut and immune system. These narratives illustrate the essential point that what happens in childhood can affect old age. Current lifestyles threaten longevity for as long as 60 to 80 years.

While fitful in its provision, China's medical care at its best is now substantially better than in the past. Beijing's successful efforts to bring hundreds of millions out of poverty have contributed to extended life. However, as China develops it faces the prospect of introducing typical 'first world' diseases such as diabetes, cancers, cardiovascular conditions, depression and obesity. The nature of illness has changed in China. In recent history infectious diseases primarily caused death. However, according to Harvard's Program on the Global Demography of Aging, by 2004 'non-communicable diseases, such as cardiovascular diseases and cancer, accounted for 59% of all deaths'.[9]

China has moved from experiencing contagious illnesses to largely internal and chronic ones; from the illnesses of poor countries to those of the rich. Some might say that Chinese people seem to have acquired the illnesses of prosperity more quickly than they have acquired prosperity itself. The China country chairman of pharmaceutical company Novartis told the *Financial Times* that 'Beijing must cope with ... facing a surge in chronic diseases as its population rapidly ages'.[10]

There are other possible contributory factors. For example, even though suicide is diminishing worldwide, rates among the elderly

8   https://www.scmp.com/business/companies/article/3008922/biotech-start-backed-li-ka-shing-and-bill-gates-launch-its

9   https://core.ac.uk/download/pdf/6518505.pdf

10   https://next.ft.com/content/f1f8c034-9a80-11e5-be4f-0abd1978acaa

are rising, and particularly in Asian countries. High rates for late sixty- and seventy-year-olds appear to have been a feature in China for at least the last twenty years. Recently the suicide rate for the over 70s in China was twice that of Hong Kong and Singapore.[11] Despite this unfortunate trend, the proportion of the elderly in the total population of China continues to grow. However, when we note the traditional Asian custom of respect for the elderly, there is clearly something wrong.

Trends in Longevity

Longevity, while not at developed world levels, has been steadily rising in China. In 1800, during the Qing Dynasty, a male at birth had an estimated life expectancy of 28 years, rising to 42 if he lived until ten, such was infant mortality. For women it was 27 and 41. In China in 2017 average life expectancy was 76.5.

Longevity has changed differentially. An American born in 1960 has a life expectancy of seventy. A Chinese person born in 1960 would already have died. But the facts are changing. An American born in 1970 would expect to live until around 71. A Chinese born at the same time could now expect to live until the age of 69. In 2040, an American born in 1980 would be 60 and expecting to live a further 14 years. A Chinese would expect to live another seven years.[12]

Significantly, according to the World Bank, improvement in longevity has dramatically slowed since 2010 for major countries such as the US, Britain, Germany and China.[13] In the case of the US and Britain it has actually gone negative and life expectancy has fallen. An exception has been Eastern Europe, which saw little improvement in life expectancy from 1960 to 2000 but managed some modest improvements after 2010. Even so, Hungary saw lower life expectancy in 2016.

---

11   World Health Organisation, *Preventing Suicide: A global Imperative*, Geneva, 2014. Accessed at http://apps.who.int/iris/bitstream/10665/131056/1/9789241564779_eng.pdf?ua=1&ua=1
12   https://data.worldbank.org/indicator/SP.DYN.LE00.IN?locations=CN
13   https://data.worldbank.org/indicator/sp.dyn.le00.in

World Longevity Changes Pace

1980-2016

	Longevity Each Year							Change in Longevity		
	1980	1990	2000	2010	2012	2014	2016	2016/1980	2016/2010	2010/1980
Germany	72.678	75.228	77.927	79.988	80.539	81.09	80.641	11%	0.80%	10%
China	66.843	69.293	71.955	75.236	75.602	75.932	76.252	14%	1.40%	13%
US	73.61	75.215	76.637	78.541	78.741	78.841	78.69	7%	0.20%	7%
UK	73.676	75.88	77.741	80.402	80.905	81.305	80.956	10%	0.70%	9%
Hungary	69.1	69.3	71.2	74.2	75.1	75.8	75.6	9%	1.90%	7.40%
Bulgaria	71.2	71.6	71.7	73.5	74.3	74.5	74.6	5%	1.50%	3.20%
World	62.867	65.435	67.685	70.683	71.215	71.694	72.035	15%	1.90%	12%

Source: World Bank   https://data.worldbank.org/indicator/sp.dyn.le00.in

Since 1840, the average lifespan in the developed world has increased by three months annually. Since 2010, China's has increased by less than one month a year and the other major countries have fared worse. In Britain, Germany and the US, one would need a microscope to view the increase. For example, in both Germany and China, since 2010 the annual rate of increase in longevity at birth has almost halved.

Not only has US life expectancy decreased recently but its 'healthy life expectancy' - the time one might expect to live without serious illness - has now been surpassed by China. According to 2016 data, the WHO estimates that US healthy life expectancy is 68.5 years while in China it is now 68.7. The US still has ten years of further life expectancy whereas China has 7.7. However, it is not clear to what extent the WHO has yet factored in the future effects of the increasingly sedentary and unhealthy contemporary Chinese lifestyle.

Healthy Life Expectancy			**2000-2016**
(years)	**2000**	**2016**	**Increase**
Britain	69.0	71.9	2.9
China	64.8	68.7	3.9
India	53.5	59.3	5.8
US	67.4	68.5	1.1

Source: World Health Organization 2018[14]

We should note the impact of changing longevity on corporate pension funds. An IMF paper in 2012 estimated that 'each additional year of life expectancy increases pension liabilities by about 3 to 4 percent ... but also ... would increase private U.S. DB [defined benefit] pension plan liabilities by as much as $84 billion.'[15] Pension schemes in the West are already in danger of being substantially underfunded. By 2016, analysts calculated that one additional year of longevity can more than double the world's total pension underfunding. This suggests that for those who survive

---

14   http://apps.who.int/gho/data/view.main.HALEXv?lang=en
15   https://www.imf.org/external/pubs/ft/wp/2012/wp12170.pdf

there may be a silver lining to the reduced longevity improvement.[16]

Nonetheless, taking increased life as a good, Shanghai has a consistently higher longevity than China as a whole, although its lead is steadily shrinking. National longevity in 2017 was 76.5 years. The central leadership has set a goal to reach 79 by 2030, despite the national and, indeed, global slowdown. It is a practical objective. Shanghai's was 83.2 in 2015. It would be useful to examine the evolution of life expectancy in the city. The development from infectious diseases to non-infectious diseases is happening across the country but is probably more clearly developed in Shanghai.

Why Has Life Expectancy Growth Slowed?

It is not clear why the longevity increase is slowing. There may be a connection with the recent slow rate of new drug discovery. Chronic disease creates enduring demand for drugs, but infectious diseases are often curable and thus create only short-term drug demand. The affluent world with advanced medical care systems tends to suffer predominantly from non-communicable diseases related to lifestyle. This has tended to discourage pharmaceutical companies from investing in drugs to address infectious diseases.

There are two complications to this picture. First, nearly all disease-bearing bacteria have gained at least some immunity against antibiotics - in the West as well as elsewhere. This is partly driven by excessive antibiotic prescription. Thus, despite most illness now being chronic rather than infectious, bacteria is still a very serious health risk. Second, the elderly everywhere are highly vulnerable to infections. Failure to address antibiotic resistance could cause a regression in the health of over-65s.

Two facts have a bearing here. It costs over $2 billion to bring a new drug to market. And ten of twelve antibiotics launched in the United States in the decade since 2008 achieved annual US sales of under $100 million. It is not surprising that funding for new drugs is elusive. In the year 2018 alone, pharmaceutical majors Sanofi, Novartis and Allergan terminated their antibiotic operations.

In 2017, the US stated that a principal driver of its own reduced longevity was an increase in the death rate of white females and males, linked by many analysts with the opioid crisis which has led

---

16   https://www.ft.com/content/0066d01c-1e74-11e6-b286-cddde55ca122

to an upsurge in overdoses and deaths, particularly among working-class whites. In Britain, the fall in life expectancy has been associated with a rise in obesity and diabetes. Longevity improvement faces more severe threats than we have seen for a long time.

We have yet to see the full impact of Covid-19 on the ageing process. Already it is clear that the viral disease disproportionately affects elderly people. The risk to those in their seventies and older from the virus is many times that faced by younger people.

An Ageing Society

Today, China does not stand out as an ageing society. In 2019 around 12 per cent of its population was over 65. This compares with Finland at 22 per cent and Japan at 29 per cent. By 2030, South Korea - 15 per cent in 2019 - is likely to have twice the proportion of elderly as China. The crucial point is that trends are developing differently in every country and China will have a later deterioration.

Of course, a society does not age solely owing to greater longevity, but because both the elderly live longer and parents do not have many children. The growth in China's elderly comes at a time when the population as a whole is experiencing almost no growth - barely 0.5 per cent a year. In fact, during the late 2020s it will peak and begin its decline. As a result, by 2040 nearly a quarter of the population will be over 65. As the World Bank has predicted, countries like China 'are in the midst of or will soon experience a pace of ageing that is unprecedented, transitioning from young to old societies in 20 to 25 years—a transition that took 50 to more than 100 years in OECD countries.'[17]

Currently, a country with more than seven per cent of its population over 65 qualifies as being an ageing society. To have over 14 per cent makes a country by some definitions a 'super-aging society'. Others say 20 per cent. China became the first by 2002 and is officially expected to become the second between 2025 and 2035. Academic research declares firmly that we can anticipate much of the future from the immediate past. Research from the Max Planck Institute in Germany concludes: 'The extremely rapid pace of population aging in the first half of this century is the

---

17   http://www.worldbank.org/en/news/infographic/2015/12/09/live-long-and-prosper-aging-in-east-asia-pacific

most important and worrisome development in China. This rapid population aging process results from the steep fertility decline since the 1970s.'[18] Similarly Guo *et al* declare that 'the future level of population aging is decided by the current fertility... We are thus ensured of a rapidly aging period for as long as 40 years.'[19]

One UN research paper has projected that if trends cannot be changed, by 2060 China will have seventy over 65s to every 100 people of working age. This compares with about 14 in 2015. In comparison, in the same period the US will move from 24 to 44. Thus, China faces the prospect of a steep rise to overwhelming old-age dependency and the consequent pervasive fiscal stress.

One of the key features of an ageing society is that the median age keeps rising. The demographer Yi Fuxian has argued that 'China's median age was 22 in 1980. By 2018, it was 40. That will rise to 46 in 2030 and 56 in 2050. In the US, the median age was 30 in 1980 and 38 in 2018. In 2030, it will be 40, and 44 in 2050.' Yi believes that median age is critical to economic vitality and innovation.[20] Japan's median age was 47.6 in 2019 but will be only 43 in 2050.[21] Thus China will go from younger than Japan in 2019 to older than Japan in 2050. Despite the stalling of life expectancy, the collapse of births makes China a rapidly ageing society.

March of the Elderly

In 2010, the UN Population Division forecast that the over-65s in China would grow from 110 million in 2010 to 317 million in 2040. This implied an annual growth rate of just over 3.5 per cent compound while the working population is actually falling. Since then the UN's 2017 revisions have increased the number of elderly expected in 2040. This raises the expected annual growth rate in the number of elderly between 2010 and 2040 to 3.7 per cent, almost 50 per cent faster than the global ageing rate of 2.5 per cent.

---

18 https://pdfs.semanticscholar.org/dd2a/ e38afae9bac8947d6fd4cdb5dec769d08c2c.pdf

19 Guo Zhigang, Wang Feng and Cai Yong, *China's Low Birth Rate and the Development of Population*, Routledge, 2018, p. 205.

20 https://www.scmp.com/comment/insight-opinion/asia/article/2180421/ worse-japan-how-chinas-looming-demographic-crisis-will

21 https://asia.nikkei.com/Opinion/Emerging-Asia-should-learn-from-Japan-s-demographic-experience

The Ageing of Society   2015-40

	2015	2040
UN		
65+	135.2m	337.9m
Total	1,397m	1,417m
%	9.7	23.8
USCB		
65+	137m	327m
Total	1,367m	1,365m
%	10	24

Estimates updated in 2017 by the UN and the USCB[22]

Unofficial vs Official Forecasts 2015-2050 for over-65s

UN/USCB		Unofficial		Source
354m	2050	370m	2016	CKGSB[23]
228m	2029	300m	2015	Novartis[24]
136m	2015	150m	2015	Novartis[25]

Independent forecasts for the future size of the elderly population seem consistently higher than the official ones. In 2016, the Cheung Kong Graduate School of Business (CKGSB) in Beijing produced a forecast of 370 million for 2050, against the UN/US Census Bureau estimate of 354 million.[26] The National Bureau of Statistics reported that by the end of 2017 the over-65s totalled 158 million. This implies that since the 2010 NBS estimate of 119 million was made, the number of the elderly has not grown at 3.5 per cent a year but at 4.2 per cent. If this trend were to continue, we would not expect 110 million elderly in 2010 to become 317 million, but 119 million in 2010 to become 398 million in 2040.

---

22   https://esa.un.org/unpd/wpp/Download/Probabilistic/Population/
www.census.gov/data-tools/demo/idb/informationGateway.php
23   http://knowledge.ckgsb.edu.cn/2016/10/17/demographics/silver-age-
      chinas-aging-population/
24   https://next.ft.com/content/f1f8c034-9a80-11e5-be4f-0abd1978acaa
25   Ibid.
26   http://knowledge.ckgsb.edu.cn/2016/10/17/demographics/silver-age-
      chinas-aging-population/

The China chairman of Novartis, whose research is mentioned above, gives a number for the elderly in 2015 which was higher than that estimated by the UN or US Census Bureau (USCB) and higher even than was reported by the National Bureau of Statistics. He estimated 150 million in 2015 and predicts a rise to 300 million by 2029. This implies a growth rate of over five per cent and is above the growth rate shown by the NBS figures for 2010-17. Furthermore, if the Novartis estimate of 300 million in 2029 continued growing at just the same USCB/UN low rate of 3.3 per cent during the following 11 years, it would reach 430 million by 2040.[27]

Of course, none of these calculations is currently verifiable. We know data are frail, and particularly so in China. However, two things seem true. The unofficial estimates are higher than those from the UN or USCB and the UN appears to raise its estimates frequently.

Furthermore, the UN had looked at the elderly in the context of society. In 2002, they made up 7 per cent of the population, a manageable proportion. On these figures, by 2040 they would have been 317 million or 23 per cent - a very different proposition. The population was not expected to exceed 1.36 billion. Now, if we think the elderly by 2040 might reach 400-430 million - and this is the result of people living longer than expected - then a forecast could even be 415 million elderly. If births continue to be overestimated and - despite longevity stalling - the elderly underestimated, they could constitute as much as 30 per cent of the total population.

It has been suggested that global ageing can levy a huge economic cost and for some rich countries will cut economic growth rates by a third to a half. Peter Peterson, a former CEO of Lehman Brothers, US Secretary of Commerce and Chairman of the New York Federal Reserve Bank, stated as long ago as 1999 that global ageing is a 'threat more grave and certain than those posed by chemical weapons, nuclear proliferation, or ethnic strife'. [28]

---

27   https://next.ft.com/content/f1f8c034-9a80-11e5-be4f-0abd1978acaa
28   Judith Banister, David E Bloom and Larry Rosenberg, *Population Aging and Economic Growth in China*, Program on the Global Demography of Aging, March 2010, https://core.ac.uk/download/pdf/6518505.pdf.

A Working Estimate

Given that, as usual, we really cannot know whether the raised USCB projection of 327 million elderly in 2040 will be correct or if the elderly will reach some higher figure such as 430 million as mentioned above, it would be as well to have a working forecast and maybe 400 million is as good as any.

Consequences of Societal Ageing: Pension Issues

There is nothing wrong with - and much to be said for - the numbers of the elderly growing as a result of the benefits of modern medicine. The problem comes only when total national population contracts at the same time. This is happening in China because people are choosing to have fewer children. Growing longevity and the reduction in births have together created a rising proportion of the elderly in society. While the improvement in longevity has been clear - and is to be welcomed - it is a fact that China's increased ageing is overwhelmingly the result of sharply falling fertility and is a severe negative. A fall in the total fertility rate (TFR) from over six to well under two is far more important than the increase in lifespan in increasing the percentage of the elderly in a given population. This makes it hard for those remaining in work to support those who have retired.

With this growing proportion of older members of society, we need to consider how their retirement will be funded. Traditionally in China children support their parents, but this system is breaking down for two reasons. The new norm of preferring smaller families has led to parents often having only one child to bear all the costs of old age. This does not work well financially. The second reason is that today's young adults are much more consumer-oriented and may not even want children themselves. As a result, they often begrudge contributing to their parents' retirement.

The conventional international approach to providing for the old is to introduce pension systems. China was late in introducing pensions. It has been a brave effort continually embroiled in titanic headwinds. Issues frequently raised are lack of portability, poor pay-outs, limited coverage and even the threat of huge deficits. In recent years the academic and official focuses have both moved straight from the introduction of pensions to the urgent need for reform of the new pension system.

The 1990s campaign to make the Chinese state-owned enterprises (SOEs) profitable so they could be listed on the stock market and thus market-financed came at the cost of them ceasing to provide social services to their workforces. Tens of millions of the SOE workforce were jettisoned or put on low-paid early retirement. As a result, the state is wrestling with social provision to a degree with which it was unfamiliar in earlier generations. Instead, creches, clinics and staff housing ceased and unemployment ballooned. SOEs became - just about − capable of listing. The state had to conjure health provision, unemployment pay and pensions from nowhere. This was an enormous undertaking, and it is no surprise that it is not yet a success.

According to the Shanghai Academy of Social Sciences, at the end of 2013, 63 per cent of China's urban workers and less than 20 per cent of rural workers had a pension. Problems include high contribution levels that are unaffordable for many workers or their employers, lack of portability for those who are highly mobile and the poor relationship between contribution and benefits.

Furthermore, cash deficits will arise across the board in Asian regional pension schemes over the years to 2040. Public health spending will rise almost as much as pension costs and well over a third of this will be due to ageing. Such factors can create an upward debt spiral, particularly if the debt needs to be incurred in foreign currency.

At a time when couples have fewer children to support their old age, the rapid ageing of China's population will create a burden on public finances and raise the spectre of unsustainable budget pressures. As pension deficits rise, there is a danger that the state will not be able to care for its swelling numbers of elderly. Migration to urban areas is hitting the provincially organized pension-funding system, through weakening the rural provinces. Unfortunately, urbanization is actually encouraged by government. The current limited coverage itself creates a financial weakness. If more workers joined, the system would be sounder.

A further serious problem is the development of 'informal work', which is outside the supervised labour market. Around 54 per cent of urban workers are now informal and fewer than half of them are enrolled in a pension scheme. This means that the demographic pressure on the pension system is compounded by non-participation by over a quarter of all urban workers, suggesting that for policy purposes we need to think about the ratio in future of retirees to pension-contributing workers.[29]

The Financial Prospect for the State Pension System

China's current pension and healthcare system is inadequate in that it is partly under-funded and partly insolvent. Dai Xianglong, then chairman of the National Council for Social Security Fund, stated in 2013 that pension reserves accounted for only 2 per cent of China's GDP, compared to 83 per cent in Norway, 25 per cent in Japan, and 15 per cent in the US.[30]

The 2016 pension fund deficit was officially put at $65 billion. Wang Dehua, a researcher at the National Academy of Economic Strategy in Beijing, estimated that, without reform, this would reach $100 billion by 2018 and $140 billion by 2020. Another state organization forecast that the deficit would reach $192 billion by 2019.[31] The Chinese Academy of Social Sciences (CASS) has estimated that the deficit in 2020 will have reached $540 billion.[32] Ma Jun, who later became the head of the People's Bank of China research department, estimated the deficit from 2012 until 2020 at $1 trillion.[33] The finance minister said in 2019 that China 'faces a shortfall of about 56.6 trillion yuan (US$8.4 trillion) in the basic pension scheme of urban workers between 2018 and 2050'.[34]

Professor Hu Jiye, a professor at China University of Political Science and Law, wrote in 2016 that 'according to actuarial forecasts, China's current social security system will have a financial gap of RMB 86 trillion ($14 trillion) in the future'.[35] The Prudential, a

---

29 https://www.sixthtone.com/news/1004594/why-informal-workers-are-opting-out-of-chinas-welfare-system

30 http://thediplomat.com/2013/11/population-aging-in-china-a-mixed-blessing/

31 http://www.scmp.com/news/china/economy/article/2132236/chinas-ageing-population-creating-new-debt-crisis-beijing-pension and http://www.fmcoprc.gov.hk/eng/xwdt/jzzh/t1322841.htm

32 https://www.scmp.com/business/china-business/article/3003066/china-faces-us540-billion-pensions-shortfall-and-must-do

33 http://www.ft.com/intl/cms/s/0/3141eb64-9c97-11e4-a730-00144feabdc0.html?siteedition=intl#axzz3OrtymCKA

34 https://www.msn.com/zh-hk/news/other/china-transfers-usdollar47-billion-of-picc-shares-to-state-pension-fund-part-of-a-programme-to-shift-assets-to-make-up-for-shortfall/ar-BBUHrHY

35 http://knowledge.ckgsb.edu.cn/2016/10/17/demographics/silver-age-chinas-aging-population/

major international insurance company in London, stated in 2018 that 'the pensions funding gap is already sizeable in Asia's largest markets and is set to rise to US$119tn in China by 2050'. The World Economic Forum has made the same estimate.[36] The reality is, of course, that nobody knows, but we can be reasonably sure that the financial outlook is severe.

The government announced a plan in 2017 to put 10 per cent of the equity of state-owned enterprises - estimated in 2018 at maybe Y4 trillion ($570 billion) - into the National State Superannuation Fund to limit deficits. Despite this, forecasts continue to be gloomy. CASS forecast in 2019 that the principal state pension fund's reserves would attain $1 trillion in 2027 but have a zero balance by 2035. Their research showed that the shortfall between receipts and expenditure could reach $1.64 trillion by 2050.[37]

China's civil servants were not previously required to contribute to their pensions but are now expected to do so. This will substantially refinance the state scheme. However, these officials are likely to demand an increase in their low salaries which will ultimately have the same impact on the public finances.

There are also signs that individual savings are rising due to growing concern in China about the financial stability of the state pension fund.[38] Other workers, particularly in the informal sector, prefer to avoid the state pension system as it pays out little and is hard to access. Some affluent employees simply buy private insurance.[39]

From these figures, there is no agreement on the deficit figure and we are anyway looking at a moving target. What is clear is that forecasts of China's 'looming deficit' are very high and rising. The impact of the UN's updated, higher, forecasts of the over-65s by 2040 will put massive further stress on projected deficit.

---

36   https://www.prudential.co.uk/~/media/Files/P/Prudential-V2/
     presentations/2018/investor-conference-transcript.pdf

37   https://www.scmp.com/economy/china-economy/article/3005759/chinas-
     state-pension-fund-run-dry-2035-workforce-shrinks-due

38   https://www.scmp.com/economy/china-economy/article/3028138/chinas-
     workforce-saving-more-retirement-amid-concerns-about

39   https://www.sixthtone.com/news/1004594/why-informal-workers-are-
     opting-out-of-chinas-welfare-system

Budgetary Effects

The fiscal impact of the original UN estimate of the elderly was enormous. It is difficult to see how Beijing could balance a budget of soaring welfare demand while at the same time funding growing military and domestic security requirements. This is despite the shaky assertion by a Beijing professor that all China's military spending is funded solely by the tax on cigarettes.[40] Although the numbers may be roughly correct, what they miss is that this tax is a large part of total tax revenue and that revenue spent on the military cannot then be spent on welfare or education. The strains began to appear in 2019 with internal debates about the rationale for projects such as the naval shipbuilding programme in the context of a slowing economy.

The latest estimate for the size of the elderly community raises the prospect of a yet further swollen welfare need. In 2016 the central government had to subsidize the pension fund system with $65 billion.[41] The scale of projected extra funding may already be enough to rock the national finances but when we consider growing numbers of aged, the situation is likely to deteriorate even further.

A World Bank study tells us that 'projections of pension … spending reveal significant fiscal pressure in coming decades in the absence of reform', and that projections in Asia-Pacific Economic Cooperation (APEC) member countries through 2070 'show economies converging to ratios of pension spending to GDP that are 8 to 12 percentage points higher than current levels.'[42] One Chinese report states that the 'pension deficit will take up 10 per cent of the country's annual expenditure by 2050 even if the government raises the retirement age'.[43]

There is also a lively global debate about the effect of an ageing society on interest rates. French bank BNP has argued that it brings them down and Charles Goodhart, the respected LSE economist, has proposed that it pushes them up. So far Paribas might appear

40   https://today.line.me/id/pc/article/China+s+military+build+up+just+starting+a+lot+more+to+come+expert+warns-XWl2q9
41   https://www.bloomberg.com/news/articles/2018-02-05/china-s-next-debt-bomb-is-an-aging-population
42   http://www.worldbank.org/en/news/infographic/2015/12/09/live-long-and-prosper-aging-in-east-asia-pacific
43   http://www.china.org.cn/business/2012-06/15/content_25654231.htm

to be winning but the effects are unlikely yet to be visible. What is likely to be true is that by the time we are sure we will ourselves be aged.[44]

Elderly Care and its Funding

The ageing dilemma is knocking on the door of diverse countries. The World Bank, in its 2015 *Live Long and Prosper* report, noted that Thailand provides a case in point: 'Although it has enjoyed solid growth in recent decades, the pace of aging is outstripping per capita income growth. It is following a path closer to that of Poland, which is now struggling with fiscal pressures from aging. Mongolia is experiencing stagnant GDP per capita and rapid aging.'[45] China is not alone but the scale is bigger, and the speed will accelerate.

In 2009 it was reported by China's Ministry of Civil Affairs that there were only 2.5 million beds in care homes for the elderly and there were only 220,000 staff in care facilities, 90 per cent of whom were underqualified.[46] Of the 126 million elderly in 2013, 40 per cent were 'diagnosably depressed'.[47] In 2014 Dou Yupei, the deputy Civil Affairs minister, said the three problems the government had in caring for the old were lack of money, lack of land and lack of nursing staff.[48] The staff shortage is particularly important both for government and the private sector. Consultants Deloitte put it bluntly, noting that 'the extreme insufficiency in both quality and quantity of elder care practitioners, scarcity of mature talents and the high turnover rate make it difficult to establish professional teams that can provide steady and high-quality service.'[49]

However, there are higher estimates now for available beds and very importantly the Ministry of Civil Affairs has been using the age of sixty as the definition of elderly. Sixty-five is probably much more realistic in today's climate. There has also been a steady

44   https://www.bis.org/publ/work656.pdf

45   http://www.worldbank.org/en/region/eap/brief/rapid-aging-in-east-asia-
      and-pacific-will-shrink-workforce-increase-public-spending

46   http://www.terradaily.com/reports/More_than_12_pct_of_Chinas_
      population_over_60_state_media_999.html

47   http://www.ibtimes.com/chinas-rapidly-expanding-elderly-population-has-
      much-smaller-safety-net-more-1287175

48   http://www.scmp.com/news/china/article/1431405/15pc-mainland-
      chinese-now-over-age-60-official-says

49   https://www2.deloitte.com/cn/en/pages/life-sciences-and-healthcare/
      articles/china-senior-housing.html

build-up in new beds. By 2017 there was an estimate of 6.7 million available beds and a forecast of 9.9 million by 2020. This is a sector on the move.

All these facilities will need trained and competent staff, of which there is little sign at present, and this could be a factor in how practical or financially attractive the business of care will become. It could be that there may be beds and facilities constructed but there may not be the skills to operate the facilities. This may make it impractical or unattractive to use a significant percentage of those available.[50]

As noted above, Chinese families have customarily cared for their elderly. In 2019 it was reported that 54 per cent of the elderly had the majority of their costs paid for by their adult children. However, this tradition is being eroded by lack of siblings to share responsibility, internal migration moving workers to faraway locations and even a perceived lack of filial piety by today's young people. The problem is exacerbated by the view that single children when young tend to be spoilt and when older are less empathetic to others. As one report put it, there is 'an intensifying conflict between young Chinese and their parents regarding their obligations to care for their parents'.[51] As a result, 'the elderly have unwillingly changed their care philosophy which in turn requires an increase in social elder care facilities.'

A survey in 2018 discovered that only 5 per cent of Chinese expect support in old age from their children and only 1 per cent expect to inherit anything meaningful from their parents. This is a dramatic change. All income groups are saving below the levels needed to meet their expectations, the average savings are $200 a month and yet the Central Bank says that household debt hit 60 per cent of GDP by the end of 2018.[52] Indeed, laws have been passed obliging sons and daughters to visit and provide for their elderly parents. Unfilial behaviour - not visiting or looking after elderly

50 https://www.dbs.com.sg/treasures/templatedata/article/generic/data/en/
    GR/032017/170313_insights_china_senior_housing_an_attractive_trap.
    xml#

51 https://www2.deloitte.com/content/dam/Deloitte/cn/Documents/life-
    sciences-health-care/deloitte-cn-lshc-seniorhousing-en-080616.pdf

52 http://www.fidelity.com.cn/en/chinaretirementreadinesssurvey2018/index.
    html#16/z
    https://www.ft.com/content/8c95a21c-0ff6-11ea-a7e6-62bf4f9e548a

parents - can result in family members being punished through losing access to credit. In 2019 Shanghai introduced a regulation requiring people to visit their elderly parents in nursing homes.[53] Since 2013, the Chinese authorities have been advocating equity release as a way for the property-owning elderly to fund their old age. There may, however, be 'Weimar fears' that a fixed income may not last the course in paying bills if the national finances weaken.[54]

For the moment the number of elderly people in state care is barely more than 2 per cent, with maybe another 1 per cent in private care. Yet - for the reasons given above - we may confidently anticipate the proportion in state care to rise closer to half by 2040. This will raise several serious questions. Masaaki Shirakawa, former Governor of the Bank of Japan, has observed that 'it is inevitable for the elderly to prefer the status quo and support income redistribution favoring them, not growth-friendly public expenditure with benefits which materialize after a long time.'[55] We should appreciate that political pressure is not only exercised by countries with elections. Furthermore, cadres also grow old.

As discussed above, by 2040 China's over-65s may have tripled from 2015's 136 million to 400 million. If we assume that falling births, cultural behaviour change and internal migration will reduce in-family care for the elderly, then perhaps half - or 200 million - will need state care. The annual cost could be (in today's money) around $530 billion, or the cost of building 100 aircraft carriers every year (China currently has two in the water). Not all over-65s will need care, indeed some will be working. Furthermore, the figure given for care excludes any serious health costs. It is likely that rising welfare burdens will cramp Beijing's budgetary decisions in other areas. As noted above they will probably demand to have their 'fair share' of the budget. Guo *et al* tell us that 'population aging will also impede generational relationships, even the concordance of the entire society and the nation's fate'.[56]

It is worthwhile comparing the challenge for China to that for Japan. The Japanese government has to try to manage downwards

53   https://next.ft.com/content/d33fdde0-ffc9-11e5-99cb-83242733f755
      http://time.com/5523805/china-aging-population-working-age/
54   http://www.chinadaily.com.cn/cndy/2013-09/24/content_16988824.htm
55   https://asia.nikkei.com/Opinion/Emerging-Asia-should-learn-from-Japan-s-demographic-experience
56   Guo Zhigang *et al*, *op. cit.*, p. 252.

public expectation for pensions when there are ever fewer future taxpayers being born. China has to raise the pay-outs when it is difficult to even manage the current levels and there are fewer taxpayers arriving.

International Implications of an Ageing China

The Chinese Academy of Social Sciences forecast in 2010 that China would overtake Japan in 2030 to have the largest proportion of elderly in the world. This is certainly not close to Japanese expectations. The National Institute of Population and Social Security Research in Japan published estimates in 2017 stating that the over-65s would make up 31 per cent of total population by 2030, whereas the UN and the USCB both carry an estimate of 17 per cent for China. Japan is more aged than China. However, we should have higher expectations for ageing than the multinational agencies as they tend to overestimate the rate of China's births.

Even though UN projections probably overstate China's future total population, the proportion of the over-65s should remain below that of Japan until 2050. But the result in 2050 and beyond is not so clear. What makes ageing in China so special? It is the fact that it is the world's most populous country and - unlike Japan - not yet a developed country, which makes the financial pressure of rapid ageing much harder to handle. There is also the fact that under Xi Jinping China has made itself an anti-status quo power. Thus, ageing and associated budgetary pressure become strategic factors as they could have an impact on foreign policy stance, military policy and expenditure and power projection.

Global Times quotes the CIA as estimating that the average age of India's population is 27.6, whereas China's is 37.1. Yi Fuxian, the US-based demographer, has made a very important statement that 'as the median age gets older, the national mentality will become more closed'.[57] This deserves serious attention, and though it may not be correct, it requires consideration.

If the Chinese mentality becomes increasingly closed as it ages, this has implications for its foreign policy and military strategy as well as for its ability to innovate. This scenario suggests a less friendly country, less cooperative with its neighbours and maybe less

---

57   http://www.globaltimes.cn/content/1050069.shtml

willing to make compromises. It could also suggest a country more willing to take risks. The national character is currently imbued with shades of autism in its global posture. Any deterioration is a cause for concern. Yi's research stresses that the ageing, which might normally be seen as positive for international affairs, could potentially be a negative. His comment about an increasingly closed mentality seems to point in a worrying direction. Perhaps relief might be provided by the thought that zeal and fanaticism are often the prerogative of youth? Senescence can lead to mellowness and reflection. Perhaps we should be more worried about the increasing youthfulness of Chinese leaders.

To Retire or Not?

If citizens are living longer and there is no sound social security system, there is a strong argument to continue work beyond the conventional retirement age. Indeed, there are several arguments that work keeps one engaged and is thus a positive force in life and health. Retirement makes many lose purpose, identity and confidence. In 2016, 19 per cent of Americans over 65 were working. These figures are at a fifty-year record high. Reportedly another 25 per cent are actively looking for work. We should question the concept of retirement and, in particular, compulsory retirement.[58]

Hong Kong's over-65s will double between 2016 and 2036, from 16 to 30 per cent. Lam Ching-choi, chairman of Hong Kong's Elderly Commission, has said: 'Retirement is basically an insane thing, a threat to health, leading to many ailments. It's pushing people to be unhealthy and lonely. We need to unlearn our ideas about retirement.'[59]

We have already touched on several developments among Japan's elderly. There are now more crimes each year by the over-65s than by those between 14 and 19. One-fifth of prison inmates are over sixty. The elderly crime rate doubled between 2003 and 2013. This is partially explained by the fact that the lowest cost of living is 25 per cent above the basic state pension annual income of Y780,000 ($7,358). A further point is that 40 per cent of the

---

58 http://www.pewsocialtrends.org/2009/09/03/recession-turns-a-graying-office-grayer/

59 https://amp.scmp.com/business/article/2166357/how-succeed-100-year-life-start-young-save-more-and-eschew-

elderly now live alone and rarely see anyone. Some actually want to go to prison, which is often configured for the elderly, to have company. Recidivism is rife. From 1991 to 2013, the elderly jailed for repeating the same offence six times rose by 460 per cent. In certain respects Japan might be seen as a precursor of China and thus worth examination. This point is underlined by the rising crime and recidivism amongst the elderly in Korea and also in China.[60]

Retirement is being cramped by pressure on welfare entitlements. This is less through cuts, which have so far proved politically difficult, and more through lack of increases. Governments are giving thought to delaying retirement age for the dual benefit of reducing calls on pension income and supporting workforce numbers. In fact, Shinzo Abe, Japan's prime minister until 2020, has suggested that people should be allowed to defer their pension beyond seventy.[61] Why not? After all, Japan is now discussing the 100-year life.

The growth of ageing in China is unparalleled in its history and also a severe threat to its financial system. It is difficult to believe that it will not at some point change the flow of state expenditure.

---

60 See the report here about a raid by 200 police in 2018 to bust a dogfight-betting ring in Guangdong province organized by a group of retired people: http://www.scmp.com/news/china/society/article/2142422/chinese-police-break-underground-dog-fighting-ring-run-pensioners
61 https://www.ft.com/content/702de9c8-b001-11e8-8d14-6f049d06439c

3

GENDER DISPARITY

Gender disparity is the statistical difference in numbers between sexes in a given country or location. It has nothing to do with income. Such disparities can arise through wars or other disasters but nowadays usually because of the birth of more babies of one sex than another. This affects the national sex ratio at birth, or SRB, commonly expressed through a ratio of male babies to 100 female babies. Today the World Health Organisation (WHO) says that a normal SRB ratio is 105, in other words, 105 male children to 100 female ones.[1]

The reason for this natural disparity is believed to be a natural biological reaction to the higher infant mortality in male babies. However, it has been observed that since 1970 there has been a reduction in the differential impact of infant mortality on male and female babies. Nonetheless 105 or 104-107 is viewed as the globally normal ratio today. It has been the observed norm since at least the seventeenth century.[2]

Throughout the Qing Dynasty (1644-1911) China had a strong bias towards producing male babies, in part due to the practice of female infanticide. There was, for example, an unusually high (male) sex ratio of babies in the 1930s and 1940s due to this practice.[3] In one survey, the 1950s was also a decade of uncommonly high SRB of over 109 - although other data suggest 106.7, closer to normal small male surpluses. Even so, if we accept the data suggesting normality, 'the normal SRBs over these periods stood at around the upper limit of the normal range', according to one group of

1   http://www.searo.who.int/entity/health_situation_trends/data/chi/sex-ratio/en/
2   http://www.pnas.org/content/pnas/105/13/5016.full.pdf
3   https://pdfs.semanticscholar.org/5b10/00bb7329e52c1f063521bc7f3762128cb3ac.pdf

researchers.[4] Since the early 1980s we have again seen almost 40 years of unbroken very high SRB. In other words, for 65-75 per cent of the last ninety years we have seen excessively high male surpluses.

This is a prolonged period of unnaturally high male surplus. Worryingly, the evidence suggests that the period of the 1960s to 1980s when there was a male surplus, but of internationally normal dimensions, was actually the exception in the last 100 years, not the norm. This turns conventional historical analysis on its head. We might have assumed that extreme male surpluses are rare - and rare worldwide - so when will normality resume? In fact, faced with the evidence of twentieth-century China, we may be seeing something closer than we want to normality in the male baby surplus of today's China.

As we have noted, the world average SRB for male children to female is around 103-107:100. China burst up through this level in 1982 and has stood at grossly elevated levels from the 1990s until now. By 1990, the ratio was over 111 boys to every 100 girls and by 2000 it was over 116. Through the next few years, the ratio varied between 115 and 121. It has reportedly fallen slowly in each of the past eight years. In 2016 it reportedly fell to 113. However, the World Bank's data show no more between 2010 and 2017 than a small reduction from 116 to 115. This represents almost 40 years of grossly distorted SRB figures. The condition is predominantly in the ethnically Han provinces in the south and east, where there is a strong cultural preference for boys. There now seems to be a slight downward trend in the figures but at a very slow rate. Even so, the problem has already taken effect, the level is still extreme and even if the condition has eased it has definitely not ceased.

SRBs vary considerably between individual provinces. Tibet's has been very low and Anhui's very high. Chen Wei at Renmin University in Beijing has observed that 'some of the provinces, whose populations are comparable to the large countries in the

4   Zhongwei Zhao, Yuan Zhu and Anna Reimondos, 'Could changes in reported sex ratios at birth during and after China's 1958-1961 famine support the adaptive sex ratio adjustment hypothesis?', *Demographic Research*, vol. 29, article 30, pp. 885-907, October 2013, retrieved from https://www.demographic-research.org/volumes/vol29/33/29-33.pdf
     https://pdfs.semanticscholar.
     org/5b10/00bb7329e52c1f063521bc7f3762128cb3ac.pdf

world, probably have produced SRBs unprecedented in human history.'[5]

Gender Ratio at birth in China (1970-2014)[6]
the number of males born for every 100 females

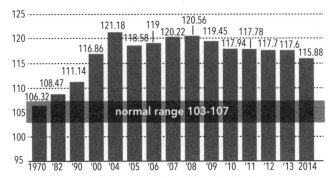

Source: the National Health and Family Planning Commission

Why is the Ratio so Distorted?

Why are Chinese families now having such a disproportionate number of male children? It is not accidental. First, there are evolutionary biological theories that innate will can influence sex ratio at birth amongst mammals and humans. The Trivers-Willard hypothesis advances two views. 'First, that a mother in good condition should bias the sex ratio of her offspring towards males (if males exhibit greater variation in reproductive value). Second, that a mother in good condition should invest more per son than per daughter.'[7]

A recent paper by Veller, Haig and Nowak, evolutionary biologists at Harvard, strongly suggests that the first proposition is credible; the second less so. On that basis we would see a strong determination - conscious or not - by well-placed families to choose male children and this being translated into physical effect at birth. Demographers seem not yet to have encountered this biological thesis to support or reject it.[8]

5   https://pdfs.semanticscholar.
     org/5b10/00bb7329e52c1f063521bc7f3762128cb3ac.pdf
6   http://www.chinadaily.com.cn/china/2015-09/17/content_21901190.htm
7   https://www.ncbi.nlm.nih.gov/pubmed/27170721
8   https://www.ncbi.nlm.nih.gov/pmc/articles/PMC4874707/

Rob Brooks, Professor of Evolutionary Biology at the University of New South Wales, has described the Trivers-Willard effect as 'one of the most original and powerful ideas to emerge from modern evolutionary biology'.[9] He illustrates the thesis by noting that 60 per cent of billionaires' children are boys and junior wives of polygamous marriages in Rwanda produce mostly girls. He further mentions research indicating that in pre-industrial Germany landowning families' sons were more likely to survive their first birthday than their sisters. The opposite was true of the poor.

If we subscribe to this theory, we could assume that when the Chinese social environment is normal and positive, a mother in a dominant social position would wish her children to be male. A mother in a more precarious situation would prefer her children to be female. The social characteristic called hypergamy, where women tend to marry upwards to partners who are wealthier, brighter or better-looking, allows less-advantaged women to marry better-endowed males. This suggests - rather loosely - that if the verdict on modern China by its inhabitants is positive then the SRB is likely to be one of notable male surplus. However, mothers from poorer areas are likely to produce a surplus of females. We are getting the national male surplus, denoting a positive view of the future, but among the Han people those in poorer areas are often more prone to this than those from richer areas.

Chen Wei advances the opposite thesis: that from the 1980s China has experienced a wrenching socio-economic experience of 'marketization' where tens of millions were laid off by state factories, unemployment was rife and people had the disorientating experience of entering private-sector employment where results are important. This period of uncertainty caused a preference for sons.

The fact that there is a worldwide male surplus at birth of 4-7 per cent is, of course, already a question of nature taking a hand and compensating for the effects of infant mortality which has historically affected male infants more than females. China is a rare exception where excess female mortality has been the rule for over 20 years. However, infant mortality has been falling for decades. In the US it fell by 73 per cent between 1969 and 2016

---

9   https://theconversation.com/little-china-girls-how-historys-worst-famine-shifted-the-sex-ratio-6312

and in Germany by 85 per cent. In China in the same period it reportedly fell by 90 per cent and in India by 76 per cent. This is a global phenomenon.

And yet male surpluses have remained static. In a large, developed country such as the US and a large developing country such as Indonesia, SRBs have tracked each other from the mid-1960s until now with little variation. The same applied to India until it began a decisive upward breakout from the 1970s and has now risen sharply. The world's SRB from 1962 until 2015 varied modestly between 1.055 and 1.076.[10]

Within the trend of infant mortality, we need to look specifically at the development of male infant mortality. There seems always to have been excess male mortality. However, research in developed countries indicates that since the eighteenth century, male babies have suffered a rising share of infant mortality.[11] They represented an excess mortality of 10 per cent in the 1750s and over 30 per cent in 1970. Subsequently there has been an abrupt fall in excess male mortality to the point that boys after 2000 have a broadly 20 per cent greater chance than girls of death before their first birthday.

The reasons for these changes within infant mortality are usually put down to improvements in medical treatment as the leading causes of infant death shifted from infectious diseases, congenital conditions and complications of childbirth and premature delivery.[12] A fortunate side effect of this undoubted improvement is that infectious diseases were gender-blind. Nonetheless, male babies are 60 per cent more prone to be premature and have a tendency to have large heads or be otherwise sizeable which can create a difficult birth. Thus the odds shifted decisively away from male infants through the first part of the twentieth century. After the 1970s, the growing popularity of C-section deliveries and intensive care units redressed the balance back to a smaller surplus of excess mortality for boys.[13]

Male excess mortality has diminished since the 1970s, but overall infant mortality has collapsed during the last half-century. The latter is even more important than the former. However,

---

10   https://data.worldbank.org/indicator/SP.POP.BRTH.MF
11   http://www.pnas.org/content/pnas/105/13/5016.full.pdf
12   https://www.sciencedaily.com/releases/2008/03/080324173552.htm
13   https://pressroom.usc.edu/baby-boys-are-more-likely-to-die-than-baby-girls/

modest male surpluses at birth continue to be the global norm. These trends suggest that nature works to a different calendar when adjusting for fundamental improvements in global health. It also underlines the view that demographic change comes very slowly.

There is also a widespread theory that the prevalence of hepatitis-B has a deleterious impact on female births, but this has been much disputed. Emily Oster of Chicago University, whose 2005 paper supported this view, subsequently retracted it in 2008. Interestingly, the late Dr Baruch Blumberg, winner of the 1976 Nobel Prize for Medicine, argued in 2006 that parents who are carriers of the hepatitis-B virus have lower fertility than parents who are not carriers due to the birth of a smaller number of live female children. In general, however, scientists seem not to accept this thesis.[14]

In his paper, Chen Wei also cites British research indicating that female vegetarians are substantially more likely to have male children. Improvements in foetal mortality have had a slight impact on increasing SRBs as it is male foetuses which have traditionally been more at risk prior to and at birth. Declining fertility is in itself a factor. Fertility is falling for a variety of reasons which can be unplanned and unconscious. This means that those who prefer a son will not necessarily naturally be successful. As a result, measures might be taken to change the odds. Chen observes that racial differences play a part. He cites research indicating that 'oriental SRBs tend to be higher than white SRBs which are higher than those of blacks'.[15]

The most important factors are conscious and deliberate anthropogenic causes. These are a combination of motive and opportunity. The motive has been that China is a substantially Confucian-influenced society with an historic rural heritage. This predisposes families to want male children for reasons such as farming the household plot, caring for parents and grandparents and perpetuating the clan and family name. With families since the 1960s gradually having fewer children - now scarcely over one on average - they prefer the child to be male.[16]

---

14   https://pdfs.semanticscholar.org/cf29/
      ac083146f576233302fcd10477a9c986c25c.pdf
      https://www.astrobio.net/origin-and-evolution-of-life/does-hepatitis-b-affect-
      human-gender-ratios/
15   https://pdfs.semanticscholar.
      org/5b10/00bb7329e52c1f063521bc7f3762128cb3ac.pdf
16   https://www.ncbi.nlm.nih.gov/pmc/articles/PMC5152891/

The opportunity has been the availability of modern technology since 1984, in the form of ultrasound equipment, at affordable prices. This has meant that - although it is illegal, with fines of up to US$10,000 - families can discover the gender of an unborn child and if contrary to their desires they can abort the foetus in order to try again. While understandably against the law since 2002, this access to modern science nonetheless gives choice to parents. There are estimates that a million unborn girls have been aborted each year. As this activity is illicit, it is difficult to quantify but consistent with the reported sex ratios at birth.

As a sign of changing customs, the burgeoning sex selection industry in Hong Kong and Macau is showing some evidence of being used to respond to the government's liberalization of birth policy by using modern technology deliberately to select girls. However, the numbers are small compared to China's nationwide trends. While there have been numerous crackdowns on such use of science since 2002, it has simply led to a brisk illegal cross-border trade in blood samples from pregnant women in China for analysis in Hong Kong and Macau laboratories. In 2010, it cost $640 for a tube of blood to be taken across the border, with a report to be issued the next day. By 2019, the price of this illegal trade had fallen to $440-600. It is especially interesting that three years after almost everyone was allowed to have two children, the decision to abort females actively continues.[17]

Since the 1990s there has been an explosion in the private-sector workforce. Not only are these people much better paid but they have also been freed from the constraints of the work unit, company housing and social policing. This helped in taking decisions on sex-selective abortion. Research in 2008 indicates that those regions where birth control policy was most rigidly enforced have experienced the highest SRBs, but this is perhaps only another way of saying - as we have done earlier - that lower fertility (voluntary or involuntary) leads to difficult choices being made on children's gender.[18]

Nicholas Eberstadt of the American Enterprise Institute (AEI) in Washington writes that the problem results from 'the fateful collision

---

17 https://www.scmp.com/news/hong-kong/health-environment/
    article/3008893/high-mainland-demand-tests-identify-sex-babies
18 http://jhr.uwpress.org/content/45/1/87.refs

between overweening son preference, the use of rapidly spreading prenatal sex-determination technology and declining fertility'.[19] In 2005 Chen Wei put the balance of factors in proportion. He first refers to some of the natural, external influences: 'the greatly elevated SRB in China (as well as in Taiwan and South Korea) over the last two decades has gone well beyond the forces of these historical changes even if they could have served to raise it…' Then he draws the conclusion that 'an SRB that substantially deviates from this normal range implies deliberate interventions'.[20]

That most people were allowed to have at least two children from 2015 is important. Research suggests that the first child ratio has not been particularly skewed for gender, but second and subsequent child ratios are highly imbalanced, indicating that that is usually the moment when those with a daughter apply self-selection to aim for a boy. It is largely the better educated, and thus affluent, who have a boy as a second child. This is doubtless related to the ability to pay for ultrasound and other support.

While this narrative might emphasize surplus males, an alternative is to reference 'missing girls'. The meaning differs little. Yet what is more important is that from the latter perspective there has been a literature proposing that further baby girls were born but unreported and only somehow merged into mainstream documented society in their teens when school and other social constraints required it. This alternative narrative is undermined by widespread official references to gender disparity and its effects in various parts of China.

Further evidence of the rising gender imbalance includes an increase in the introduction of foreign brides to counter a shortage of domestic brides. The trafficking of young women across the border from Vietnam and other neighbouring countries is a well-known phenomenon. Third, there is also the rising 'bride price' which rural husbands pay on marriage to their brides or their families, which can exceed $30,000. This shortage of domestic brides strengthens the hand of the bride's family. An example is the widespread expectation that a potential husband should already have an apartment before marriage. Chinese state media refer to

---

19   http://www.economist.com/node/15636231
20   https://pdfs.semanticscholar.
    org/5b10/00bb7329e52c1f063521bc7f3762128cb3ac.pdf

bride prices as 'skyrocketing' and local officials frequently try to enforce limits, with no evident success.

Regional Trends within China

The SRBs have, as noted, varied across the regions of China and where high, the reasons have also varied. The minority areas have been largely unscathed by high SRBs. This may reflect a variety of factors. Until recently Tibetan Buddhists and Muslims had generally been freer from fertility controls, they do not subscribe to Confucian conceptions of son preference and education levels are often lower than the national average.

In the 1990s the cities saw a marked increase in SRBs. This was more pronounced among the non-migrant population. As urban residents are not associated with working the land or rural tradition, this may be linked more with a pronounced desire for smaller families and thus any male child preference being magnified. Female equality seems to have regressed in the half-century to 2000. It also certainly seems true recently. This could have led to a greater maternal desire for sons.

Chen Wei cites earlier research in saying that of the 30 characteristics that affect a child, social class and social status of parents are two of the most important in determining SRB. He does not explain whether he means in the active sense of employing sex-selective abortion or in an alternative sense that a mother's wishes may in practice lead to the engendering of a male child. If the latter, it seems to support the Trivers-Willard thesis. He could also mean that care and nutrition could be better.[21]

Urban, educated, young, ethnically Han women with senior-level occupations tend to have very high SRBs. Uneducated women in Western China tend to have lower SRBs. South-central and East China have high SRBs. Chen notes that 'parents of upper social classes are more likely to have higher SRBs than the parents of lower social classes'. This suggests that linking the issue of high SRBs with traditional farmers in poor provinces misses the point. As in India, high birth ratios are often associated with high status. Therefore, more education will not necessarily banish the issue.

---

21   https://pdfs.semanticscholar.
      org/5b10/00bb7329e52c1f063521bc7f3762128cb3ac.pdf

Changing Trends in SRBs

Speaking in September 2010 at a Beijing seminar marking the thirtieth anniversary of the Family Planning Association of China, Prime Minister Li Keqiang said that the government would launch measures 'to narrow the widening ratio of men to women'.[22] The Five-Year Plan in 2011 set out the target to bring the SRB - standing at 118.0 in 2010 - to 112/113 by 2016. The achieved result by 2016 was declared to be 113. The World Bank, however, recorded it as only falling from 116.4 in 2010 to 115.2 in 2016.[23] In 2013, the authorities forecast the national SRB would 'drop below 112 by 2020 and 107 by 2030, according to the National Population Development Outline'. There is considerable caution about these goals. In 2011 Professor Yuan Xin of Nankai University echoed the authorities, saying he expected it would take 10-20 years or more to end this extreme ratio. Others think he is an optimist.[24]

Wang Peian, deputy director of the National Health and Family Planning Commission, said in 2016 that although reported SRBs have been steadily declining, 'maintaining that momentum will remain extremely difficult ... it will be more challenging to continue'.[25] In 2017, the NHFPC echoed Wang's thoughts when it announced that the target in the 13th Five-Year Plan for 2020 is 112, a less than 1 per cent fall over four years. This was less optimistic than the 2013 target 'to drop below 112 by 2020'.[26] Furthermore, as the World Bank says the ratio only fell from 117 to 115 in ten years from 2007 to 2017, for the level to fall from 115 to 112 in the subsequent three years seems unlikely.

With the officially-announced weakening of the elevated SRBs, Prime Minister Li could believe success is at hand. But scientific evidence suggests that it may not be possible easily to achieve the desired ultimate result. Furthermore, the government

---

22 http://mastertheblaster.blogspot.hk/2010/09/china-will-coordinate-family-planning.html
23 http://www.chinadialogue.net/article/show/single/en/4702-China-s-gender-crisis
    https://data.worldbank.org/indicator/SP.POP.BRTH.MF?locations=CN
24 http://www.chinadaily.com.cn/cndy/2017-01/27/content_28064836.htm
25 http://www.scmp.com/news/china/policies-politics/article/2027122/boys-vastly-outnumber-girls-china-years-population
26 http://china.org.cn/china/2017-02/20/content_40322126.htm

forecast might be attainable but there will be a very long-term consequence from the prolonged gender mismatch which has happened already.

The UN Family Planning Association (UNFPA) in 2012 produced two scenarios for the future direction of SRBs. They said that 'simulations based on a rapid sex ratio transition indicate that 15 per cent of Chinese men … will not be able to find a wife by 2050, even if SRB is assumed to return to normal in 2020. In the less optimistic scenario of no change in the current levels of SRB, the male surplus in the marriage market would reach 90 per cent in both countries after 2050, which means that there would be about twice as many men ready to marry as women.'[27]

If the National Plan is met and SRBs return to normal in 2030, it means another decade of abnormally high male births until then. Many estimates are up to 2020 or before and so we need to add on the likely surplus from 2020 or earlier until 2030 to those estimates. According to the UN database this is a further 10.2 million births. Of course, some observers do not think 2030 is a realistic date for SRBs to return to normality. Jiang and Feldman in 2013 did not expect a normal ratio until 2040. In 2012 the UN did not anticipate normality in this century.[28]

The Question of Under-reporting

A research study published by Shi and Kennedy in 2016 generated a lot of publicity after it suggested that China's gender disparity had been exaggerated.[29] The general view has long been that Chinese families produce a surplus of male babies at birth and this surplus has been rising since around 1982. It rose to achieve 121 boys to 100 girls in both 2004 and 2008, probably a world record high for an entire individual country. In recent years it has fallen somewhat but is still way above almost every other country. Shi and Kennedy propose that, owing to the Chinese birth control regulations, families declined to report the births of daughters so

27 https://www.unfpa.org/sites/default/files/pub-pdf/Sex%20Imbalances%20
    at%20Birth.%20PDF%20UNFPA%20APRO%20publication%202012.pdf
28 http://www.chinadaily.com.cn/china/2017-01/27/content_28064356.htm
    https://link.springer.com/article/10.1007/s11113-013-9283-8
29 Yaojiang Shi and John James Kennedy, 'Delayed Registration and Identifying
    the "Missing Girls" in China', *The China Quarterly*, 2016; 1 DOI: 10.1017/
    S0305741016001132

they might later have the chance of bearing sons. It is only much later that parents would apply for papers for their undocumented daughters, maybe when teenagers. Shi and Kennedy argue that the gender disparity is largely an imbalance in birth registration and, for example, from the 2010 census it is clear to them that there had been no gross imbalance in the sexes at birth in 1990. The problem, they say, was that girls were not registered when born.

One of the specific tasks expected of the 2010 census was to establish how many 'missing children' there actually were. Since then we have also had a 'mini' census in 2015 which covered 1.55 per cent of the population. So, if we multiply up the findings by 1.55 per cent, we can have data for five years after 2010 as well.

What comes across from the censuses is that there was some lowering of the sex ratios after the age of 15, as Shi and Kennedy proposed. However, it was not caused by more women entering the system but by male numbers going down. Second, the births for the period 1980 to 2010 are a consistent 550 million in both censuses but well below the 570-575 million in the UNPD and USCB birth data. Hence roughly 25 million reported births may have failed to trouble the census collectors. In other words, it is not the original birth data which seem to omit people but the census afterwards. These inconsistencies, where the subsequent census shows fewer children alive than the original birth data, make it difficult to accept Shi and Kennedy's argument that there are substantial numbers of girls alive whose births were not recorded.

Third, the 2015 census carries a noticeably higher estimate of male surpluses than the 2010 census for the years 1980-1995. This is mainly due to an increase in the estimated number of males in this age group. Estimates of females rose by 400,000, but males by 1.7 million.

Neither census gives a higher estimate than the UNPD or the USCB for any population group until the birth cohort of 1975-80, which is before the mass male surplus emerged. The two censuses show materially higher SRBs for the period 2000-2015 than do the UNPD or the USCB. That means that if they are to reduce later, they will be falling from higher levels.

Hence the 2010 census, despite being expected to confirm the actual situation of the 'missing girls', did not produce a new higher population total but in fact finished with a population total even smaller than the precursor birth data would have implied. Unless we think there is a rational reason for people year after year to report births which never took place, it is difficult not to conclude that the 2010 census came nowhere near totalling the population. There are suggestions of inaccuracy and even falsification in government birth data, but this is not proven. The reason would presumably be to give a mistaken impression that the country is not facing a demographic crisis.

We should not overlook the possibility of girls, being traditionally disdained, not being registered with the authorities in order to permit the chance of a subsequent boy. However, the requirements for education, marriage licences and simple identity papers suggest that eventually girls must enter the documented world. This should surely happen - at the latest - by the age of 20-24. Moreover, census officials are aware of the possibilities and have been clear that the data they gather are confidential and not to be shared with local officials, in the hope of gaining a full understanding of the population base. These facts limit the potential for there being large numbers of undeclared females.

Shi and Kennedy accept that censuses show a substantial gap between male and female births in the early years, saying that 'when examining age cohorts and backward projections for the 1990, 2000 and 2010 censuses, we find that the sex ratio decreases after the age of 15 and tends to become more normal after the age of 20.'

Here is a table showing the numbers of women shown in Chinese government censuses and age range data from the UNPD and the USCB: (Reference?)

Reporting of Women   Aged 10-24

Born	1995-2000	1990-95	1985-90
Censuses	'000		
2010 Census	34642	47985	63404
2015 Census	34793	48109	63561
Increase	0.40%	0.26%	0.25%
UNPD			
2010 data	38016	48212	62990
2015 data	37864	47942	62668
Decrease	-0.40%	0.60%	-0.50%

USCB

2010 data	40247	48906	62780
2015 data	40069	48546	62373
Decrease	-0.40%	0.70%	-0.60%

The simple fact is that there is no emergence of missing women at the age of fifteen or 20. No source of data shows such a trend. If Shi and Kennedy mean that the census is a more accurate tool of measurement than the birth data, then it must be said that the 2010 census actually shows a male surplus of 18.2m for the years 0-14 which is actually higher than the UN birth data, which shows 17.2 million. This census then goes on to show only 4.5 million male surplus for the age group 15-24 against the UN at 10 million. So far, so good.

The 2015 census is not so obliging. It shows 18.4 million against 18.7 million for male surpluses up to fourteen. However, in the all-critical 15-24 age range, it shows 9.7 million against the UN birth data of 10.5 million. This is not even an 8 per cent reduction.

As mentioned earlier, those undeclared may include a large number of girls, but in the context of the population the growing number of references by official sources suggests strongly that the sizeable male surplus is a real and very substantial fact. The evidence for disagreeing with the view that delayed birth registration of girls who are actually living is the major reason for the 'apparent' male surplus rests on the following facts:

a. Chinese government, UN and US Census Bureau birth estimates since the 1980s all concur on a large male surplus at birth.

b. The 2010 census and the 2015 mini-censuses do - as Shi and Kennedy said - show a lower sex ratio for those aged fifteen and above in 2010 but the principal reason for this is that they show fewer males than expected. They do not find more females.

c. The fact that the two censuses have substantially smaller total populations in these age groups suggests that either the censuses or the birth data are very wrong. The inconsistency between the 2010 and 2015 censuses on the number of excess males suggests that the 2010 census is a particular outlier.

d. The continuing references in government documents since the censuses suggests that they are aware of the implications in the census data for male surplus but continue to believe in the higher figures, uncomfortable reading though they are for government.

e. If the censuses are deemed more accurate than the birth data, then we should note that they carry higher SRBs than the birth data for recent years. This adds up to an extra excess of one million males between 1995 and 2010.

f. If we look at the two censuses or the data from the UN, the NBS or the USCB, in all cases there was no increase between 2010 and 2015 in the numbers of women in the 0-25 age range, despite the suggestion of substantial unreported births.

Hence there are different views on this subject. Shi and Kennedy suggest that many of the females who would have been born in a normal gender ratio society were born and are alive, but undocumented. Accordingly, the issue of surplus males is not serious. The proponents of the surplus male problem would say the surplus is very serious. The UNFPA, for example, says flatly, 'a vast majority of these missing girls were in fact never born'.

I would share this view. There may be in the region of 5 million undocumented girls but not 30 million. The girls in most cases do not exist. The male surplus - net of undocumented girls - could peak at above 50 million. For such a large part of the population to be unhappy and angry, unable to marry, is destabilizing. This phenomenon has already been observed to be raising urban crime rates.[30]

How Many?

As there will clearly be a large number of single males, it is worth making an effort to estimate the scale. To illustrate the issue, we have compiled a table below of twelve forecasts made over the last fifteen years of the size of the surplus male population. There is also a discussion of two forecasts extrapolated from scenarios outlined by the UNFPA. This provides fourteen forecasts in total.

---

30 *Sex imbalances at birth, Current trends, consequences and policy implications*, UNFPA Asia and the Pacific Regional Office, Bangkok, 2013. Retrieved from https://www.unfpa.org/sites/default/files/pub-pdf/Sex%20Imbalances%20at%20Birth.%20PDF%20UNFPA%20APRO%20publication%202012.pdf

There are several problems with these forecasts. One is that they are for different years and thus not strictly comparable. Another distinction is that the age ranges for which the forecasts are made can be widely different. Some estimates take males of marriageable age defined as up to the 30s/40s. Others take all unmarried males of any age. Some start with males aged 20. An alternative is to take all single males up to fifty as potential marriage partners. A further iteration is to take excess males as single males (however defined) but fewer undeclared girls, on the grounds that there are substantial numbers of unreported girls.

Sometimes forecasts of the male surplus are accompanied by the phrase 'marriage age' or the word 'bachelors' and/or 'young' without any ages mentioned. One cannot legally marry in China before 22. Can we then use the term bachelor for a 21-year-old man? It seems everyone has their own idea of what constitutes marriage age. Is it best used up to 39, or 49 or at any age? This makes it difficult to compare forecasts with 'mainstream' data (USCB, UN etc.). Where there is doubt, I have usually interpreted marriageable age as 25-39. 'Young' is cut off at 49.

The result of these permutations, where all the elements are not necessarily declared, is that we cannot accurately compare one forecast with another but merely treat each one on the strength of what we know about it. I have compared the forecasts with the estimates provided by the UN and the USCB, as members of the group of official or mainstream organizations with the unenviable role of producing an annual dataset of demographic detail which is internally consistent. The USCB and the UN are chosen because their data are available annually and are easily accessed. They do not always agree. Indeed, as will be noticed, there can be up to a 35 per cent difference in their numbers.

Table of 12 Forecasts of Male Surpluses Compared with USCB and UN Forecasts

Made	For Year		Author	Estd Years	Term Used	Range 2
2004	2020	30m	NPFPC	25-39	'marriage age'	
		9.6m	USCB		20m	20-50
		12.4m	UN		22.5m	

2005	2020	28m	Hudson, den Boer	25-39	'young adult males'		
		9.6m	USCB			20m	20-49
		12.4m	UN			22.5m	
2009	2020	24m	CASS	25-39	'marriageable age'		
		9.6m	USCB			20m	20-49
		12.4m	UN			22.5m	
2010	2020	30-40m	CASS	0-19			
		23m	USCB				
		23.8m	UN				
2012	2020	51-55m	Poston, Yang	0-37	Born since 1983		
		39m	USCB				
		40m	UN				
2015	2020	35.3m	Yao MX	0-29			
		34.1m	USCB				
		34.2m	UN				
2017	2020	15m	CASS	35-59			
		8m	USCB				
		10.8m	UN				
2004	2025	30m	Y Chen	20-49			
		22m	USCB				
		25m	UN				
2015	2030	30m	UNPF	25-45	'young, involuntary bachelors'		
		18m	USBC				
		19.8m	UN				
2004	2040	40m	Y Chen	20-49			
		30m	USCB				
		33.2m	UN				
2017	2047	30m	Zhai ZW	25-39	'marriageable age'		
		14.3m	USCB			27m	20-49
		17.2m	UN			27.8m	

2017	2050	30m	CASS	35-59
		24m	USCB	35-59
		26.7m	UN	

Where the selected group is not defined by age the term is cited. If the result looks too unlikely another age range is shown.

NB

- Two more forecasts are extrapolated below from UNFPA scenarios.
- Professor Poston's higher forecast in 2012 was conditional on nothing being done to change the trend in SRBs. The 2011 SRB was 117.6. By 2016, it was 113, a fall of 3.9 per cent. To achieve 107 would be another 5.3 per cent fall, which we are told is hard to achieve.

As we can see, there are many estimates as to the scale of the imbalance. These usually rely on expectations of how quickly the highly abnormal SRB can be normalized. There are several problems in measurement. First, we cannot be confident of the historic population data. Both Chinese and foreign academics have criticized data inaccuracy. Some have gone as far as stating that there is frequent falsification. If we knew where we are now, we would next like to estimate how long it will be before sex ratios at birth become 'normalized'. We should also ask ourselves whether China has a particular proclivity for more than averagely skewed ratios. There is some evidence of this during the twentieth century. Some academic opinion suggests that there is an inherent Chinese racial bias towards male surplus.

Even if we discard these points, it is a matter of debate how quickly we should expect SRBs in China to regress to a global mean. As has been noted, the UNFPA gives two scenarios for this. One is for a rapid transition to normality by 2020 and the other is for no change in the current levels. The fact that as sober a body as the UNFPA has decided that these two are the scenarios of choice is a good enough illustration. It is perhaps telling that the second alternative is merely described as 'the less optimistic scenario'.[31] Poston and Yang do the same but come up with different results.[32]

---

31   https://www.unfpa.org/sites/default/files/pub-pdf/Sex%20Imbalances%20
     at%20Birth.%20PDF%20UNFPA%20APRO%20publication%202012.pdf
32   http://www.ios.sinica.edu.tw/dicgf/abstract/p-9-1.pdf

An alternative view came from the researchers Tucker and Van Hook in 2013. They calculate three scenarios and estimate in the middle one that a gradual fall in SRB of about 1 per cent annually would not cause the number of surplus males to change before 2060 - 40 years away.[33]

It will be necessary to make some judgments on these matters in order to form a view as to what is more likely.

NPFPC Estimate 2004

NPFPC is an old name for what is now China's National Health and Family Planning Commission (NHFPC or HFPC). As they are policymaker, agency and statistician, they have an interest in the results appearing to justify their policies and have the ability to make this happen. As a result, there are frequent disputes over their data.[34]

Their forecast in 2004 was that 'males of marriage age would outnumber females by 30 million by 2020'. What we do not know is the definition of marriage age. Given that the minimum legal age for a man to marry is 22 and around 40 per cent of young people go to university in China and many others abroad, a guess of the 'marriage age' implied might be 25-39. If so, there is a deviation from generally accepted estimates. In 2018 the USCB expected the gap between males and females of 25-39 years in 2020 to be 9.6 million. The only way to get close to the forecast is to assume the NPFPC forecast was framed loosely and should count males from 20 to 50. Even then the forecast is 10 million over the USCB estimate. Ironically for the policymaker, this forecast looks quite pessimistic.

Hudson, den Boer 2005

Professor Valerie Hudson of Texas A&M University and Dr Andrea den Boer of the University of Kent are longstanding researchers in this field. In a paper they wrote in 2005, they forecast 'substantial numbers of "bare branches" (by 2020, 28 million in India—the

---

33   https://www.ncbi.nlm.nih.gov/pmc/articles/PMC3873140/
34   https://www.thechinastory.org/chinas-gender-imbalance-and-its-economic-performance/

same or more in China)'.[35] We have taken 28 million. They defined 'bare branches' as the number of young adult males who exceed the number of young adult females in China. As with the NPFPC forecast above, we can compare it with the USCB estimates of 9.6 million for the 25-39 age group or 20 million for the 20-49 age group. On both bases Hudson and den Boer are forecasting above the mainstream.[36]

CASS Forecasts 2009 and 2010

The Chinese Academy of Social Sciences published two forecasts quite close to each other in December 2009 and January 2010. According to *Xinhua*, the December report 'estimated that China's male population at marriageable age will be 24 million more than female counterparts in 2020'.[37] *The Economist* reported that in the January report CASS stated that 'China in 2020 will have 30m-40m more men [of 0-19] than young women'.[38]

Marriageable age starts at 20 and ends when the writer wishes it. Thus, all in that category were born in the years before 2000. Those aged 0-19 in 2020 would clearly be born after 2000. Therefore, we are probably comparing male births between 1980 and 2000 with those between 2000 and 2020. The two statements simply suggest that excess males continued to be produced after 2000 and the number was 6-16 million.

This suggests an annual average male surplus of 600,000-1.6 million. The USCB estimates that during the five years 2014-2018, there was a declining average annual male surplus of 1.11 million. This suggests that CASS could have been correct with both its projections. If it was too low with its 2020 estimate of excess marriageable males - and clearly the other two available forecasts for 2020 think they were - then the number could have been 30 million instead of their 24 million. The available data since their January 2010 forecast of births 2000-2020 look to be reasonably accurate.

---

35 https://www.scribd.com/document/106272292/Missing-Women-and-Bare-Branches-Gender-Balance-and-Conflict
36 Ibid.
37 http://www.womenofchina.cn/womenofchina/html1/opinion/10/3614-1.htm
38 http://www.economist.com/node/15636231

Poston and Yang 2012

Professor Poston of Texas A&M University remarked in January 2012 that 'already, 41 million bachelors will not have women to marry. If nothing is done to change this trend ... by 2020 there will be 55 million extra boys in China.'[39] Poston claimed that there were already 41 million bachelors, presumably as at the end of 2011. As he uses both the term 'bachelors' and 'boys', conservatively these are probably of any age from 0 up to let's say 50. He also proposes that eight years later - in 2020 - this figure could be 55 million 'if nothing is done'.

Some actions are in fact being taken, although it is debatable how effectively. The Care for Girls programme, pensions for daughters' parents and laws against sex determination are measures, although often weakly applied. However, SRBs have only fallen modestly. Poston and Yang in 2013-14 estimated a range of 51-55 million 'extra boys born between 1983 and 2020 who will not be able to find wives to marry'. This is in the age group 0-37. The range is based on 51 million if SRBs fall steadily from 120 in 2010 to 107 in 2020 and 55 million if there are 'no changes in China's SRB by 2020'.[40]

If we compare the 0-37 age range estimated by USCB for 2010, it is 28 million against Poston's 41 million. The USCB forecast for 2020 is 39 million against Poston and Yang's 51-55 million. The 400,000 average difference in excess male births between 2010 and 2020 implied by these forecasts of 51-33 million is quite reasonable. What is questionable is the 2011 starting point of 41 million. As a result, we might regard the Poston and Yang forecasts as an outlier in the estimates.

Yao Meixiong 2015

The deputy census director of Fujian province, Yao Meixiong, has made a forecast of the surplus of up to 29-year-old males in China by 2020, noting that they will be more than the population of Australia. The term 'extra men' is used in place of excess or surplus men. He specifically estimates the 0-9 age group as being

---

39   http://www.prb.org/Publications/Articles/2012/china-census-excess-males.
     aspx
40   http://www.ios.sinica.edu.tw/dicgf/abstract/p-9-1.pdf

12.6 million and the 20-29-year-old group as being 9.5 million. The USCB estimate the surpluses in these groups by 2020 as 11 million and 11 million. Here there is no apparent difference.[41]

Y Chen 2004

Chen Yei of Nanjing University made a multiple forecast in a 2004 paper that 'the number of surplus males between the ages of 20 and 49 will continue to increase, reaching 20 million by 2015, 30 million by 2025, and 40 million by 2040.'[42] This forecast is very much in the mainstream. It largely refers to births in 1995, 2005 and 2020. To grow the number by 10 million in the first ten years is not so difficult. A further 10 million in the subsequent 15 years is also not so demanding. What it requires is that the number of unmarried single men passing the milepost of 49 is exceeded by 666,000 annually by the number of surplus young men becoming 20. If the latter is, say, 1.22 million annually and the number ageing past 50 is 555,000, then that works. For the moment reported births support this estimate.

UN Population Fund 2015

In 2015, the UNPF presented a document forecasting 'an estimated 30 million young men as involuntary bachelors by 2030'.[43] This is a somewhat subjective expression and sounds as if it is not an estimate of all single males or even those up to 50. We might reasonably say that you cannot be an involuntary bachelor at 20-24, when the minimum marriage age is 22. And, you cannot be young at 50. Thus, we might be talking of excess males aged 25 to 45. According to the US Census Bureau, there would be 199 million men aged 25-45, and 30 million bachelors would be 15 per cent of those young men in 2030. The USCB estimates a surplus of 17.7 million males aged 25-45 in 2030. So the UNPF's is a high forecast.

The conventional estimates for excess males could be too low and there could easily be 12 million women not marrying at all by 2030. Given these factors, 30 million male involuntary bachelors

---

41   http://www.scmp.com/news/china/society/article/1854545/its-raining-men-single-males-china-exceed-entire-population
42   https://link.springer.com/article/10.1007/s11113-013-9283-8
43   https://www.unfpa.org/sites/default/files/portal-document/China%20CPD%20-%20ODS.pdf

is not improbable. However, such a forecast is not based solely on gender imbalance.

Zhai Zhenwu 2017

Professor Zhai of Renmin University wrote in 2017 that the accumulated effects of high SRBs 'will lead to a 30 million surplus of men at marriageable age over the next 30 years'.[44] If we take marriageable age as 25-39, the US Census Bureau says the number in 2047 will be 14 million. However, if we stretch the definition to 20 (below marriage age) to 50, then the USCB would estimate 27 million. So, on a loose definition of marriage age, this forecast is fairly mainstream.

CASS 2017

In 2017, Wang Guangzhou from CASS made forecasts for 2020 and 2050 that predicted 'the number of unmarried Chinese men between 35 and 59 will reach 15 million in 2020 and 30 million in 2050'. (ref?) It is interesting that these forecasts were for age groups different from the CASS forecasts of 2009 and 2010. They covered the 35-59 age group rather than those of marriageable age or the 0-19-year-olds. Hence, we cannot directly trace any evolution of thinking - and in any case different teams at CASS may come to different conclusions.

The USCB has estimates for male surplus in the age group of 35-59 of 8 million and 23 million as opposed to CASS at 15 million and 30 million. As a result, we should say that these forecasts from CASS are substantially above the official projections. However, Professor Yuan Xin at Nankai University agreed that 'the number will likely exceed 30 million in 2050'.[45] Thus the CASS forecast is another example of estimates well above the mainstream and yet seen as credible by Chinese academics.

We should note here that unmarried males and surplus males are treated as interchangeable concepts, as if, were there parity, all men and women would be married. This assumption ignores several contemporary features. One is the growing interest in living a single life. As these singles are often middle-class and well-educated, they are not interchangeable with peasant workers in

---

44   http://europe.chinadaily.com.cn/china/2017-02/13/content_28184326.htm
45   http://www.globaltimes.cn/content/1032677.shtml

rural China. They are female as well as male. As such, they increase the likely unmarried numbers.

UNFPA 2012

We should also include in here the work in the UNFPA book published in 2012: *Sex Imbalances at Birth*.[46] This included both the above-mentioned UN scenarios for SRB trajectory and an estimate of the gender gap in 2010. On the gender gap for 2010, the UNFPA calculates 'missing girls'. 'Estimates of missing women have been computed for the population below 20, i.e. born after 1990... China's missing girls number 24 million.' Thus there are 24 million from 1990 to 2010 who were either un-reported or not born. In the view of UNFPA, 'a vast majority of these missing girls were in fact never born'. I will take the liberty of interpreting 'vast majority' as 80 per cent, or 19.2 million. This suggests undocumented girls at 5 million. The UNFPA forecast of a 25 million gender gap in 2010 among the 0-20 age group compares with an estimate of 24 million from the USCB.

The scenarios propose (a) a fast normalization in which SRB falls to 105 by 2020. In such a case, '15 per cent of Chinese men ... will not be able to find a wife by 2050'. It seems reasonable to take this as the age group of 25-49. The USCB estimates that in 2050 there will be 198 million males in this cohort. Fifteen per cent of this number is 30 million. There would be 175 million women. This is a male surplus of 22 million. So the first UNFPA scenario is noticeably above the mainstream view. This is despite the fact that the UNFPA implies it is an 'optimistic' approach.

UNFPA also proposes (b) a less optimistic scenario, in which 'the male surplus in the marriage market' would reach 90 per cent over available women. For consistency I again translate this as referring to the 25-49 age range. This assumes SRB staying around 120 throughout the period. In such a case, unmarried men should be 47 per cent of all men. Taking the USCB estimate of males, this implies a surplus of 93 million. There would be 105 million women. (Alternatively - and much less likely - if we take the USCB estimate of females in 2050, there would be 175 million women and thus a male surplus of 158 million.)

---

46   UNFPA, *op. cit.*

For the two extreme UNFPA situations to occur, there could be noticeable changes to the number of males and/or females of marriageable age. However, we must use what we have. The most cautious rendering of the UNFPA second scenario is that millions of women will not be born and the male surplus is 93 million.

The UNFPA scenarios for sex ratio at birth over the next 30 years are clearly rough estimates. The numbers of excess males they might produce are a wide range of 30 million to 93 million. SRBs have fallen below 120 but are unlikely to have reached 105 by 2020. We should expect that the ultimate UNFPA estimate number will be somewhere in between the two implied estimates.[47]

We should also be aware of the opinions of Professor Yuan Xin, Catherine Tucker and Professor Van Hook and the NHFPC itself that reduction of SRBs from now on could be or will be slower than hitherto. Thus a 'middle ground' reduction in SRBs could be a very slow process and may not yield a middle number between 30 million and 93 million for 2050 excess males. Instead of 62 million, let us therefore assume that it will be 62-77 million. We could estimate 70 million surplus males of 25-49 by 2050.[48]

Summary of Estimates

What at first seemed to be a random jumble of forecasts of different numbers for different years begins to assume a clearer shape when we note the different dates and consider the differing age groups for which each forecast is constructed or implied. The high estimates seem less demanding when placed in their appropriate context. Every forecast is well above the conventional view of the US Census Bureau, with one exception which is broadly in line. The estimates vary in source from domestic official bodies through Chinese academics to overseas academics and international organizations. Of the 14 forecasts, nine are from Chinese sources and five from overseas. Twelve of the 14 forecasts are materially higher than the USCB estimates based on official data. One is about 10 per cent over and one is more or less the same. These are the principal forecasts available.

---

47   https://www.unfpa.org/sites/default/files/pub-pdf/Sex%20Imbalances%20 at%20Birth.%20PDF%20UNFPA%20APRO%20publication%202012.pdf

48   https://www.ncbi.nlm.nih.gov/pmc/articles/PMC3873140/

It seems that those non-governmental researchers who ponder these questions conclude - more or less universally - that the total of excess males will be substantially higher than the official numbers. These researchers include CASS, the government research institute. Ironically, their ranks even include the National Health and Family Planning Commission (NHFPC), the government demographic agency.

How are SRBs Declining?

I think there is a consensus that distorted SRBs have declined. However, this appears to be from extreme to severe. There are different views on current SRB levels, as well as how fast they will decline. For the five years from 2013 to 2017, the USCB shows births which imply that SRBs fell by 2.3 per cent. For the same period, the World Bank says SRBs fell by a mere 0.7 per cent.

China's NHFPC reports that the SRB crashed by 3 per cent in just two years to 113.5. These projections suggest it will have reached 112 or less by 2020 and 107 by 2030.

	2013	2014	2015	2016	2017	2018	2020	2030
USCB	116.3	115.6	114.9	114.3	113.6	112.9		
WB	115.8	115.6	115.4	115.2	115			
NHFPC	117		113.5				112	107

It is very important to the Communist Party to be seen in control of major social developments such as births. However, we should note three points:

a. There are different opinions about where SRBs are now and how they have declined.

b. Chinese academics and officials suggest that it will become increasingly difficult and slow to reduce SRBs from these less extreme levels.

c. China has a history of inaccurate, contradictory and even false population data.

What we do know is that there are now maybe 40 million surplus males already born, SRBs are declining but surplus males are still being born at a rate of around one million a year. No-one - not even the government - is forecasting normal gender ratios before 2030.

A Rational Expectation of Surplus Males in Future

If we ask what the excess male total will be by 2040 and set the parameters with the same top age limit of 59 as did CASS, we will be using the age group 0-59. The 2017 0-37-year-olds, according to the USCB, have a male surplus of 37.3 million. We should note that there are several higher calculations for this number. This cohort, or age group, will be the 23-60-year-olds in 2040. We then need to hazard an estimate of the births over the period 2018 to 2040, to provide the cohort of 0-23-year-olds in 2040.

It is a widely held view that SRB normalization is likely to slow down. Let us assume the male annual birth surplus falls to an average of one million for 2018-2027, 750,000 for 2028-2037 and 500,000 for the last three years (2038-2040). This totals 19 million surplus males born between 2018 and 2040. When forming these assumptions, we should note that when 'normality' resumes at, say, 107 male births to 100 female ones, annual births might be down at around 12 million. There would then be about 420,000 annual male surplus births anyway.

We might ask: what about infant mortality? Surely it is skewed against male children? Certainly this has been the case historically, as discussed earlier. Does this not mean that a male surplus at birth will be reduced by adulthood? Research suggests that from 1975 to 1987 male infant mortality fell 42 per cent but female mortality only fell by 23 per cent. Those falls brought the rates down to 36.6/1,000 and 35.2/1,000 respectively for males and females. This is a difference of less than 4 per cent. If recent research shows male excess mortality falling sharply and the long-range recent history also shows the same, I am going to assert that now, in the early 2020s, there is probably no effective difference.[49]

I propose a reasonable estimate for 2040 might be a surplus of 55 million males between 0-59 and a total of 5 million undisclosed girls. These excess girls will have been born since 1990, although by 2040 they will probably be in the national database. This implies a likely net number of surplus males of 50 million, which compares with a USCB estimate of 42 million surplus males, before netting off any missing girls. The main reason for the difference is that I am more cautious as to how quickly the sex

---

49   https://www.ncbi.nlm.nih.gov/pubmed/12345193

ratio at birth will normalize. USCB estimates that the SRB will fall from the (presumably known) 114.3 for those born between 2010 and 2015, to the normal 106.9 for those born between 2045 and 2050. This is a reduction of 6.5 per cent. I think this rate of reduction is implausible and thus I anticipate a continuation of excess males for rather longer.

An estimated net 50 million excess males of 0-59 by 2040 would be less than implied by Poston and Yang or the pessimistic forecast of the UNFPA but it is close to the more optimistic UNFPA forecast. (The gross 55 million estimate is 30 per cent over the comparable USCB forecast, which is appreciably less than most of the other independent forecasts). Both the early estimations before 2010 and the most recent ones are consistent with a surplus in China of over 50 million males by 2020. Only three of the 14 independent forecasts are close to the official thinking.

The Data are Highly Confusing

Reported SRBs have been falling since 2008/9. However, there are questions over the quality of the official data. Jiang and Yu from Xian Jiaotong University observe that 'generally there is misreporting in such data. But as no other reliable data source or method were available to adjust systematically the data employed in this paper, the data were incorporated directly from the survey or census without any adjustment.'[50]

As Lutz and Scherbov from IIASA in Vienna have noted, the data are confused. They have already been cited remarking that 'fertility is not the only uncertain demographic condition in China today. Estimates for the sex ratio at birth range from 113 (Wang 2003) to 123 (Ma 2004). This is a remarkable difference that will significantly influence the future proportion of men to women in the adult population and hence population dynamics.'[51] They imply quite correctly that if we do not know the present, it makes the future even harder to predict. That leaves us to consider that there is a very large and growing number of surplus men - likely to reach the region of 50 million.

---

50   https://www.cambridge.org/core/journals/journal-of-biosocial-science/
     article/changes-in-sex-ratio-at-birth-in-china-a-decomposition-by-birth-order
     /51D48C611E5176A042FF28684041D997/core-reader
51   http://www.austriaca.at/0xc1aa500d_0x0017f0d7

It seems we might expect a decline in SRBs but this is complicated by not knowing for sure where we have been, where we are now - as well as being unclear about the speed of any change. We are reasonably clear that the unbalanced SRBs have been excessive for a prolonged time but that there is a reasonable chance of a reversion to less distorted levels eventually, albeit at an unknown speed.

What Happens?

The afore-mentioned sociological concept of *hypergamy* indicates that women make marriage decisions, by way of acceptance or rejection of approaches, and most women 'marry upwards'. They prefer to marry men who are more intelligent, more affluent or better-looking, than other men. As the UNFPA remarked in 2012 in the context of the current mismatch of the genders, 'it is also clear that men from underprivileged sections will suffer disproportionally from this marriage squeeze'.[52] They state that the proportion of poorer men who are unmarried is likely to be twice the national average of unmarried men.

In the conditions that China is facing in coming decades we can project that male marriage will not occur randomly. It will occur between women in general and men who possess a mixture of desirable features. We can accordingly draw the sobering conclusion that some 50 million men, substantially more than the total male population of Germany, will not marry and they will be largely discarded by being deemed among the poor, the stupid and the unattractive. This creates fertile ground for instability.

Research shows that in the 1980s, only 1 in 200 college graduates was unmarried by the age of 40 compared to 1 in 7 of the illiterate and semi-literate. In 1990, 1 in 5 poor farmers was unmarried at 40. The 2000 census reveals that of never-married males of 40-44, 1 in 3 were illiterate. Marriageability seems very closely correlated to literacy and education.[53] We have already noted the statement that 'in China, for example, 94 percent of unmarried people aged 28 to 49 years old are male and virtually all of them have not completed high school'.[54]

---

52 http://www.unfpa.org/sites/default/files/pub-pdf/Sex%20Imbalances%20at%20Birth.%20PDF%20UNFPA%20APRO%20publication%202012.pdf
53 https://link.springer.com/article/10.1007/s11113-013-9283-8
54 http://www.passblue.com/2016/09/28/six-asian-nations-lead-in-seriously-skewed-sex-ratios-at-birth/

Research in 2014 by Jiang, Feldman and Li, three demographers from the Institute for Population and Development Studies at Xi'an Jiaotong University, China and from Stanford in the US, estimates that 'in 2020, the sex ratio will be 150 never-married males for 100 never-married females, so three never-married males will compete for two never-married females, and this ratio will rise to 180 males for 100 females in 2030… The sex ratio is close to 200 males for 100 females between 2045 and 2050.' This thesis is reflected in the authors' chart below:

Ratio of Never-married Males to Females[55]

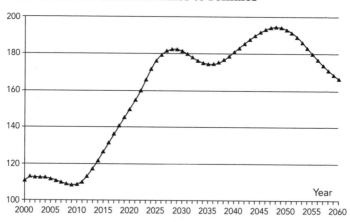

One palliative proposed by the UNFPA is that men could delay their marriage a few years and thus marry younger women. This can partially address the issue over time but not eradicate it. The vast majority will simply not be able to marry. The UNFPA admitted in 2012, 'we have still no idea of the coping mechanisms likely to emerge when marriage postponement or bachelorhood affect millions of men in China'.[56] Society must anticipate and address the implications of this issue. Joseph Chamie, formerly of the UN Population Division, has said that this situation could 'incite more child marriages'.[57]

---

55   https://link.springer.com/article/10.1007/s11113-013-9283-8

56   http://www.unfpa.org/sites/default/files/pub-pdf/Sex%20Imbalances%20 at%20Birth.%20PDF%20UNFPA%20APRO%20publication%202012.pdf

57   http://www.passblue.com/2016/09/28/six-asian-nations-lead-in-seriously-skewed-sex-ratios-at-birth/

What Happens to Marriage?

In 2012 the UNFPA recalculated sex ratios using instead the age at which men and women actually marry.[58] The ratio rises extremely rapidly after 2010 and peaks in 2025 at 121. It will then stay around 120. The UNFPA then pointedly states that 'in the optimistic scenario of a rapid SRB decline, this weighted sex ratio [across age groups] in China will remain above 110 until 2035 and will reach almost normal levels only during the second half of the century.' In this situation by 2050 there will be 15 per cent of Chinese men who cannot marry. If there is no change in SRB, then by 2050 almost half of Chinese men will be unable to marry.

In 2012, the academic Christophe Z Guilmoto stated that 'the number of prospective grooms in both (China and India) will exceed that of prospective brides by more [than] 50% for three decades in the most favourable scenario. Rates of male bachelorhood will not peak before 2050 ... the proportion of men unmarried at age 50 is expected to rise to 15% in China by 2055.' He has further predicted that 'over 21% of Chinese men would still be unmarried at 50 in 2070'.[59]

Urban bachelors with dim prospects can often find poorer rural women living in the cities. In the countryside it is much harder. It is quite normal for a rural bridegroom to pay a 'bride price' to the family of his bride. This figure has been 'skyrocketing' since the 1980s and faster than the economy itself. It can currently reach over $30,000. The reasons for the rise are various including 'economic development and rising incomes, but oversupply of males has been an important determinant'.[60] Rural bachelors often resort to using agents to buy women from poorer rural areas, for which the cost can be lower. Other solutions are also practised.

Many brides now expect, in addition to the bride price, to receive a car and a village house or apartment in a town. At 2016 prices a groom might expect to pay around $50,000. It is no surprise that many young men have simply given up thinking of affording such a cost. Many families will save for years and even incur debt in order to marry their son. For poorer men, there is an

---

58   https://www.unfpa.org/sites/default/files/pub-pdf/Sex%20Imbalances%20
      at%20Birth.%20PDF%20UNFPA%20APRO%20publication%202012.pdf
59   *The Economist*, 18 April 2015.
60   https://cpianalysis.org/2017/09/21/bride-price-in-china/

active Chinese internal coercive traffic in women but it is, of course, frequently from the poor areas to the richer areas and thus yet more disadvantageous to the poorer rural Chinese bachelors.

One theme which has attracted some attention is the stark powershift within couples due to the changing gender ratios. Women occupy a much stronger position in a relationship as a result of the increasing shortage of adult females. New York academics Trent and South have noted, bluntly, 'the positive effects of a numerical abundance of men on women's likelihood of engaging in premarital, multi-partnered, and extramarital intercourse'.[61] An increase in such behaviours is likely to weaken marriage, raise the divorce rate and delay - and thus reduce - childbirth. This suggests that those marriages which do happen in a grossly distorted gender environment are likely overall to have fewer children.

We should additionally consider four other contemporary trends among young Chinese women. There is a rising disenchantment with marriage among women, a frequent preference of career over marriage, discontentment with 'spoiled' male single children and a failure to meet 'the right man'. Surveys indicate many young women find large numbers of contemporary men unattractive marriage partners. This may stem from a form of personality spoiling, born of the low birthrates, large numbers of only children and widespread 'son preference'. Even young men with attractive income, intellect and features may be spurned on grounds of character.

A Single Life

Reference is frequently made to the tendency by young men and women to live alone. It often becomes conflated with the story of gender disparity and low birthrates. Living alone has become increasingly common and is rising rapidly. There are reportedly almost 200 million single people in China. By 2015 they totalled around 15 per cent of the population, up from 6 per cent in 1990.[62] The number of single women over 30 doubled from 2000 to 2010. This is quite shocking - for China, but not for the world. In the US

---

61   K Trent & SJ South, 'Too Many Men? Sex Ratios and Women's Partnering Behavior in China', *Social Forces; a scientific medium of social study and interpretation*, *90*(1), 2011, pp. 247-67. https://doi.org/10.1093/sf/90.1.247.

62   https://qz.com/1019300/in-china-single-women-are-looked-down-upon-regardless-of-their-success/

and Britain about half the population is single. In China marriage has traditionally been entered young. This is gradually ceasing to be the case.[63]

The ratio of single women to single men is about 80 million to 115 million or 1.4:1. There is a surplus of about 35 million men. However, they are not distributed uniformly across the country. The rural areas have a large male surplus; the cities have a substantial female surplus. The large cities are particularly skewed towards single women. It is estimated that in Shanghai the number of single men is about a quarter of the number of single women.

Since 2016 there has been a female university student majority despite the country having a pronounced male majority. This should lead to the phenomenon we see in the US where at marriage age there are four female graduates to three males. Most graduate American women will not marry a non-graduate and the result is that they delay marriage. Similar ideas are arising in China.

Joseph Chamie said in 2016 that '94 percent of unmarried people aged 28 to 49 years old are male and virtually all of them have not completed high school'. This mirrors the US where the unmarried tend to be working-class males and female graduates - the top women and the bottom men. Working-class men cannot marry as women from their stratum can marry upwards but men cannot. Female graduates have choices to marry but often dislike the options they encounter. Unmarried men are unmarried involuntarily; unmarried women are usually unmarried by choice.[64]

These facts lead to unusual results. Gaps of 10-20 years are now not uncommon in Chinese marriages. Young women who are waiting years to find a suitable partner often travel abroad to freeze their eggs. Interesting though the travails of the single young may be, it does not directly affect us unless delayed marriage eventually becomes no marriage. There is now clearly an increasing risk of this happening.

Leftover Women

A smaller problem is the reverse one of unmarried women. This is that group of women - often referred to as 'left-over women', who

---

63   http://www.globaltimes.cn/content/1032677.shtml
64   http://www.passblue.com/2016/09/28/six-asian-nations-lead-in-seriously-skewed-sex-ratios-at-birth/

are so involved with their career that they prioritize it to the point of missing courtship at conventional age only to find that men are no longer interested when they are older. The solution proposed in the Chinese media is that leftover women should marry expatriate men: 'Expat men are ideal mates for China's leftover women' is a typical headline, highlighting the fact that the government has made it easier for expats to extend their green cards and for foreign students to stay and work in China after graduation.[65] The author, though, goes on to criticize almost every element in the equation: 'This can also lead to more "leftover" women who, having been rejected by Chinese men, turn to less-discriminating foreign men. Ironically, in the Chinese women's eyes, expat men are the true "leftovers".' It seems as if no one should feel good about their situation in this solution. It is simply the only one offered. The - seemingly non-Chinese - author goes on to point out the long-term risk of diluting the Chinese gene pool but a solution is at least found to a topical problem.

The fact that young women choose not to marry in an environment of massive male surplus tells a story. However, the narrative of women 'left over' or 'on the shelf' at 28, poignant though it may be, is a small story compared with 50 million single men not getting married because there are simply not enough girls. What all of this misses is that China's contemporary problem in sex imbalance is not leftover women. It is a vast plurality in males of marriageable age. However, any women who do fail to marry for whatever reason - and clearly the number is not negligible - are adding to the dilemma of the men who would like to marry but cannot.[66]

The Implications for the Surplus Males

We will see the formation of an underclass of men reverse-selected on grounds of poverty, illiteracy, weak intelligence and unfortunate looks to become lifelong bachelors. This is not a voluntary and romantic brotherhood but a mandatory life sentence from society. Let us just consider one stark condition. The Chinese Academy of Social Sciences forecast in 2010 that 20 per cent of young men

---

65   http://www.globaltimes.cn/content/1011215.shtml
66   http://www.aljazeera.com/indepth/features/2015/10/china-leftover-women-151029141452444.html

would not get married. China has twice as many birth defects per capita as the US.[67] Like bachelorhood, birth defects are showing a significant uptrend. This strongly suggests that, as one in 18 Chinese (5.6 per cent) has one, it will become a distinguishing feature of the unmarried, unwanted males, a form of perverse stigma. Between 2000 and 2011 they rose by 40 per cent per capita.[68] We should expect that there will be large communities of males excluded but living on the fringes of society.

The Social Problem of Unmarried Men

China's legions of unmarried men are likely to make their way to the cities, will probably be angry and could be increasingly prone to violence. Research indicates that single men are more prone to crime. Indeed, there is already some evidence of property crimes and crimes of violence being disproportionately committed by young single males. This is extensively covered most notably in the research of Lena Edlund et al. In their 2013 paper, Sex Ratios and Crime: Evidence from China, they state that crime has seen a marked rise since the mid-1990s, one-seventh of which they attribute to elevated SRBs.[69]

Cameron, Meng et al also point out that 'Crime rates in China have increased dramatically - from 7.4 per ten thousand in 1982 to 47.8 per ten thousand in 2014.'[70] They go on to say that 'more than two-thirds of violent and property crimes in China are committed by men aged between 16 and 25 years'. They also point out that there is a considerable tendency of young men towards high-payoff crimes such as theft and drug-dealing in order to raise the money to attract women.

Professor Yuan Xin, with the Institute of Population and Development at Nankai University, corroborated this in his comments on the 2014 census that 'men may have difficulties finding partners and getting married, with relationship stability suffering as a result. This could lead to social problems such as sex-

67   http://www.economist.com/node/15636231
68   http://www.scmp.com/news/china/article/1759828/china-urged-fund-genetic-tests-birth-defects-mothers-get-older
      https://www.ncbi.nlm.nih.gov/pmc/articles/PMC4728203/
69   http://www.columbia.edu/~le93/EdlundLiYiZhang13.pdf
70   ttp://ftp.iza.org/dp9747.pdf

related crimes, human trafficking and even children trafficking.'[71] Yuan said at the same time that 'a great imbalance in gender would lead to … dramatic increases in cases of sexual violence'.[72]

We should anticipate urban crime continuing to rise with the possibility of increased social instability. Research in 2013 identified surplus young males as a material factor in China's rising crime rates. Young men have been described by sociologists as 'the most homicidal demographic category'. A mainland academic warns that 'a great imbalance in gender would lead to a high divorce rate and dramatic increases in cases of sexual violence. It would also become a fiscal burden to the government, which had to care for bachelors after they retired.'[73]

Cameron, Meng *et al* suggest that young single males will have a higher tendency to crime for two separate reasons. The first is through frustration at not being able to marry and also through the need to raise money for the 'bride price'.[74] There is also the potential for such young men to create social instability or become involved in some form of terrorism as they will feel outside society and rejected. This may make them fodder for anti-state activity. Another risk is that bachelors may not be suitable providers of care for their parents through lack of income combined with mental stress and other problems. This can also contribute to increasing the state's fiscal burden.

In other societies in history where surplus males have been a problem, military draft has been a strategy. However, China has been trying to reduce its military headcount in favour of a more lean and professional force. The idea is challenged further by the psychological assessment that single children tend to be less comradely, and by rising rates of obesity. The rejection rate of candidates for the military seems to have been rising, particularly on grounds of physical fitness.[75] Increasing reliance on AI for military systems will also reduce the need for large numbers of soldiers.

---

71   http://www.globaltimes.cn/content/903085.shtml
72   http://www.scmp.com/news/china/article/1683778/chinas-workforce-shrinks-nearly-4-million-amid-greying-population
73   http://www.psy.cmu.edu/~rakison/dalywilson.pdf
74   http://ftp.iza.org/dp9747.pdf
75   http://www.straitstimes.com/asia/east-asia/want-to-be-in-the-chinese-army-then-stop-masturbating?utm_source=Sailthru&utm_medium=email&utm_campaign=New%20Campaign&utm_term=%2ASituation%20Report

Other less attractive mitigations of social risk include proposals for state-sponsored prostitution. Professor Xie Zuoshi said in 2015 that an answer may be polyandry, or the sharing of wives, as happens in similar circumstances in India, particularly among brothers.[76] It is, of course, not at all clear that policymakers will find such strategies acceptable.

Overseas Brides and Trafficking

Some assume that the looming gender imbalance could be solved by importing women from neighbouring countries. It is difficult, however, to imagine largescale successful unions between English-speaking Filipinas or Vietnamese, Burmese or Cambodian girls and under-employed farm labourers in areas such as Anhui province. There are few Asian societies so deprived that there is a significant incentive to avoid marrying within one's own (relatively gender-balanced) culture and instead choosing from amongst the rural poor of China. Moreover, there are competitors in Asia for the affections of such women, including Korean and Taiwanese bachelors. There is certainly regular cross-border voluntary inducement as well as involuntary trafficking of women from neighbouring countries, but not on a scale which can materially address this issue. Reports of the trafficking of Vietnamese women into China for forced marriages state that the practice has spread from northern Vietnam down into the south and involves a growing number of women. The women can sell for over $10,000. As we have noted, this can be less than paying a bride price for a Chinese wife.

There are estimated to be up to 200,000 North Koreans in China, most of whom are female. They are in China informally and are mostly in prostitution or sold to Chinese bachelors. During 2019, gangs were reported to be enticing Pakistani girls into dubious roles in China. The US Department of State's annual *Trafficking in Persons* reports categorize countries for their action on this issue.[77] 'Tier 2 Watchlist' and Tier 3 are the weak countries. Tier 2 Watchlist is defined as countries making efforts to improve but either there are numerous cases, there is no explanation of the steps being taken or action will be taken in the future. They included Burma, Laos and Thailand. China and North Korea were in Tier 3, which is defined

76   http://www.bbc.com/news/world-asia-china-34612919
77   https://www.state.gov/wp-content/uploads/2019/01/282798.pdf

as 'Countries whose governments do not fully meet the minimum standards and are not making significant efforts to do so'.

Vietnam has managed to get into Tier 2 but has been regularly criticized for insufficient action. Countries mentioned as sources for forced marriage and prostitution include Burma, Laos, Cambodia, Vietnam, Mongolia and North Korea 'as well as … Africa and the Americas'. Specific trends include the increased trafficking of women from Burma for forced marriage and domestic servitude in China. The situation of women from the Kachin region is notable due to their vulnerability through the fighting and displacement from their homes.

Not only Southeast Asian, but also South Asian and even African women are being trafficked into China 'for forced and fraudulent marriage' at fees of up to $30,000. Chinese men and their parents are engaged in contracting fraudulent marriages to confine Southeast Asian women in order to oblige pregnancy. However, trafficking can also be domestic. Chinese women are frequently trafficked overseas for the benefit of large overseas Chinese communities or remote sites such as construction, logging or mining camps. Within China, there is a clear trend to recruit women from rural areas to attract them to urban areas. Both of these movements will further distort the gender imbalance in rural China.

The Outlook

The definitive observation on this subject came in 2013 from Tucker and Van Hook who stated that 'our projections show that any change in policy, even if enacted immediately, would come too late to ameliorate the problems caused by China's unbalanced sex ratio at birth.'[78] It certainly seems the case that in the coming years there will probably be around 50 million men in China who will not be able to marry and who will accordingly be angry and unstable.

---

78   https://www.ncbi.nlm.nih.gov/pmc/articles/PMC3873140/

4

VOLUNTARY POPULATION COLLAPSE

Of all the demographic challenges facing China, the most profound will be the coming long-term and deep fall in the total population. What will cause this and how dramatic can it get? In the 1970s it was very fashionable to worry about the growth of the world's population and to urge governments somehow to limit it, ideas popularized by the Club of Rome think tank and its 1972 report *The Limits to Growth.*[1] China rather characteristically arrived late and responded excessively. Socialist governments believe that the state ultimately owns everything, even if it chooses not to exercise such rights. Property, income, assets - people - are all deemed to be legitimately within the gift or control of government. Rarely has this thinking been applied so extensively or intimately as in China's birth control regulations, where the state has asserted the right to decide how many children a woman, or a family, could have.

In 1979 draconian limitations were imposed on childbirth to control the country's population growth. The rules differed from district to district. However, from 1980 the family planning enforcers habitually terrorized villages and towns with compulsory sterilization, forced abortions and child abductions. Despite now largely allowing two children per family, there is still a widespread legacy in China from the ill-considered and harshly administered family planning measures. Moreover, even in 1979 there were alternative policies - less extreme - available to the government. As academics have said rather emolliently, 'if the alternative proposal had been adopted, the intense relationship between the cadres and the masses brought by execution of the one-child policy would have been avoided.'[2]

---

1   The book, which sold 30 million copies, argued that economic growth could not continue indefinitely because of resource depletion.
2   Guo Zhigang, Wang Feng and Cai Yong, *China's Low Birth Rate and the Development of Population*, Routledge, 2018, p. 146.

Even as late as 2017 Chinese state media boasted that 90 per cent of migrant workers had access to family planning - usually a euphemism for methods to limit having a family. As we will see, this is the last thing China needs, but several controls remain in place; for example, there are still limits preventing most families from having three children. This is a country where - following the extreme policy reverse - in 2018 the Communist Party newspaper, *People's Daily*, felt it appropriate to say, 'to put it bluntly, the birth of a baby is not only a matter of the family itself, but also a state affair'.[3] The state has not only intervened in an unprecedented way in family life, but it also believes it is right to do so. The causes of China's future challenge seem clear.

All is not exactly as it seems. The story actually begins not with the policy change in 1979, but much earlier. Births peaked in China in the 1960s. Since then births have been on a jagged but downward trend. Let me explain. The technical term 'total fertility ratio' (TFR) describes how many children the average woman in a specific society will bear during her life. In order simply to replace the existing population in any given society - barring any major catastrophe - each woman on average should have 2.1 children i.e. a national TFR of 2.1. This is termed, globally, the 'replacement rate'. Two children replace the two parents and 0.1 is a precaution to cover eventualities such as infant mortality. If the national TFR is 2.1 or above, the population will grow. If lower, it will shrink. China's TFR is one of the world's lowest.

China's TFR has been falling since 1965-70, when it stood at 6.3, i.e. each woman on average had just over six children. By as early as 1975-80, as industrialization took off in China and people began moving in large numbers from the countryside to the cities, the TFR had more than halved to 3. So a rapidly falling population was the context in which in 1979 Beijing introduced regulations which almost immediately had the effect of limiting much of the population to one child. Let us just note that point. By 1980 the birthrate had more than halved from its peak but the birth control legislation was rolled out that same year. Thenceforth China's birthrate continued to fall, but more slowly than the average of its neighbours in the rest of East Asia, which had no such legislation.

---

3   https://cn.nytimes.com/china/20180813/china-one-child-policy-birthrate/zh-hant/dual/

China and East Asia TFR Compared 1950-2015[4]

	1950-55	1955-60	1960-65	1965-70	1970-75	1975-80	1980-85	1985-90	1990-95	1995-2000	2000-05	2005-10	2010-15
PRC	6.11	5.48	6.15	6.3	4.85	3.01	2.52	2.75	2	1.48	1.5	1.53	1.55
Taiwan					2.64				1.79			1.26	1.07
Thailand	6.14	6.14	6.13	5.99	5.05	3.92	2.95	2.3	1.99	1.77	1.6	1.56	1.53
S Korea	5.05	6.33	5.63	4.71	4.28	2.92	2.23	1.6	1.7	1.51	1.22	1.23	1.26
Singapore	6.61	6.34	5.12	3.65	2.82	1.84	1.69	1.7	1.73	1.57	1.35	1.26	1.23
HK	4.44	4.72	5.31	3.65	3.29	2.31	1.72	1.36	1.24	0.87	0.96	1.03	1.2

---

4   http://esa.un.org/unpd/wpp/Publications/Files/Key_Findings_WPP_2015.pdf   http://esa.un.org/unpd/wpp/DVD/

Regarding the introduction of the new birth control regime in China, it seems odd to note that there was never a general government order about it nor was it written into national law. Incredibly for such an important initiative, it started with a letter to members of the Communist Party and the Communist Youth League that advocated a limit on births. Each province was reduced to finding its own way to address the policy, led by the example of party cadres.

We must be very clear here. Beijing initiated extreme and strict birth control regulations in 1979 and started unwinding them in 2013 - a period of 34 years. However, China's birthrate had already collapsed between the mid-1960s and 1979. From 1980 until 2015, the fertility rate fell by a further half in China - and by the same or more in Hong Kong, Thailand, Taiwan and Korea, none of which had a one-child policy. Additionally, over both the long haul (since before 1965) and short (since 1995), Singapore saw its fertility rate fall by more than that of China. We can thus say that China's birthrate closely reflected that of most other East Asian countries from 1980 until 2015 and therefore Beijing's regulations appear to have had no visible aggregate effect.

Despite this, the policy was one of the most brutal social engineering policies in history, scarred by mandatory fostering, compulsory sterilization and forced abortions. It had a terrible impact on families throughout the country and yet at the national level it did not change anything. Tens of millions suffered for a failed policy.

What happened from the early 1970s until now is that births fell. Although we must bear in mind the inherent weakness of Chinese data, it is possible to see some aggregate trends. As Jiang Quanbao and Liu Yixiao, researchers at Xi'an Jiaotong University, noted in 2016, 'the fastest fertility decline did not coincide with the most stringent implementation of this birth control policy ... the most rapid decline in China occurred during two periods. One period is from 1970 to 1979 when China advocated the "*wan-xi-shao*" policy (literally "later-longer-fewer", referring to later marriage, longer spacing between births, and fewer births). The other period is after 1987, when China experienced fast economic development, rising income and improved living standards.'[5]

---

5   Quanbao Jiang & Yixiao Liu, 'Low fertility and concurrent
     birth control policy in China', , 21:4, 2016, pp. 551-77, DOI:
     10.1080/1081602X.2016.1213179

Until the early 1970s, annual reported births regularly totalled over 25 million. After that it only happened in one further year. The initial reason for this was greater voluntary individual contraceptive action (or abortion) in the 1970s. The second reason is evident from the 1980s, as China re-joined the world. It involved a fall in infant mortality, resurrection of graduate education, emergence of widespread female tertiary education, later marriage, increased longevity, prosperity and urbanization, both in China and in East Asia in general. In such a climate - and evidently in China - families usually choose to have fewer children.

It seems extraordinary that after ten years of its One Child Policy, China did not notice that its population was reproducing below replacement level and therefore continued the same policy for a further 25 years. Part of the problem was that the population officials did not believe the ultra-low TFR rates that their surveys were producing. Jiang and Liu explain that China's Population and Family Planning Commission repudiated its own data, suggesting instead that fertility was being underestimated: 'Therefore, the … Commission inflated these data. China's National Bureau of Statistics raised the number of births reported annually in the 1990s and early 2000s, though no details of their adjustment methods were exposed.'[6] Citing the work of fellow Chinese demographers, Jiang and Liu point out that 'there was under-counting and concealing of births in the census, but a dramatic upward adjustment without solid evidence is unacceptable'.[7] Peking University's Professor Guo Zhigang supports these views, criticizing past population studies which were 'largely biased and overestimated the fertility level by exaggerating the magnitude of under-reported births'.[8]

So, perhaps being fed inaccurate information and analysis by their senior staff who had a vested interest in fabricating their success explains why China's leaders failed to react swiftly to the evident emerging catastrophe. Moreover, party leaders are more likely to believe news which tells them they have succeeded than that which suggests they have failed. That the policy failed to bring birthrates down - and scrapping it isn't putting them up - is unpalatable. The Chinese Communist Party believes its policies work and that the

---

6   https://www.tandfonline.com/doi/full/10.1080/1081602X.2016.1213179
7   Ibid.
8   Guo Zhigang *et al*, *op. cit.*, p. 4.

'One Child Policy' did bring down the birthrate and so it should have concluded: job done, time for new policies.

Why Did They Do it?

After the death of Mao Zedong in 1976, Deng Xiaoping emerged yet again from having been purged to become *de facto* leader of the country. He astutely manoeuvred through the 'second generation' of leaders. He did not claim a senior post but focused on concentrating power. Gradually, and with varying degrees of enthusiasm, his contemporaries accepted him as the natural leader. After the chaos of radical ideology, Deng made his priority economic recovery and development. He introduced the objective of quadrupling annual per capita income by 2000. He had in the past been an advocate of population control when the population was growing rapidly. In the late 1970s he still saw population growth as a threat to his economic development policy and did not want it to undermine his economic reforms and per capita income.

By the end of the 1970s, not just Deng, but all of China's top leaders were committed anti-natalists, in part due to sustained lobbying from scientists led by Song Jian, the missile specialist and cybernetics advocate, who many would say was the architect of the one-child policy.[9] Coming from a strict party and PLA background, Song had attended the Seventh World Congress of the International Federation of Automatic Control in Helsinki, Finland, in 1978, where he was introduced to cybernetic-based population control theory, which held out the prospect of a scientific approach to demographics and the perceived impending population explosion. The same theories lay behind many of the over-pessimistic, neo-Malthusian, conclusions of the Club of Rome.

Despite his lack of knowledge of demographics - there were no demographers in China at this time - Song and his group of military scientists decided that China's optimum population target was 650-700 million. On his calculations, that required one child per couple for up to 40 years, before slowly raising the limit to 2.1 children per couple i.e. the replacement level. Without such limits, the scientist argued, China's population would rise to 4 billion by 2080. Song was backed by the Chinese Academy of Social Sciences

---

9   Mara Hvistendahl, 'Of Population Projections and Projectiles', *Science*, 17 September 2010, vol. 329, issue 5998. DOI: 10.1126/science.329.5998.1460

and by vice-premiers Chen Muhua and Wang Zhen. In September 1980, the third session of the Fifth National People's Congress approved the policy in general terms. The fact that it was a scientist with a specialism in ballistics who was behind this important social policy did not appear to matter.

Over the following years China's huge army of birth control enforcers set about ensuring that everyone followed the party line. In her book *One Child: The Story of China's Most Radical Experiment*,[10] writer Mei Fong explained how it worked. In one village of just 500 inhabitants, for example, there were 15 people involved in full-time family planning. In total some 85 million people were employed part-time, with another half-a-million full-time employees at the National Population and Family Planning Commission. The Commission itself had its own archives and statistics departments, affiliated centres for research, film production and publishing and a consulting company.

The military and police have their own internal family-planning units, as do all state-owned companies. Throughout the 1990s women were often compulsorily sterilized after the birth of a second child. In 1983 alone China sterilized over 20 million women and gave vasectomises to 4 million men. Millions of women were forced to have abortions. Parents of children born without permission were fined up to ten times their annual disposable income. Often goods were taken instead of cash and sold at auction to benefit the local authority. These 'social compensation fees' (*shehui fuyangfei*) have become a major source of income for many counties, as the fees did not have to be handed over to central government. In 2013, for example, it was calculated that total income from such fees amounted to at least $2.7bn.

Faced with a backlash in rural areas from families where tradition dictated that a male child should inherit property, the CCP introduced Central Document 7 in April 1984, giving provinces more power to adopt the policy to local conditions. Even though it made the policy more difficult to understand, it meant that places like Tibet and Yunnan, with large ethnic minorities, had much more liberal policies than more populous provinces such as Sichuan and Henan. Meanwhile, the campaign against second

---

10   Mei Fong, *One Child: The Story of China's Most Radical Experiment*, Houghton Mifflin Harcourt, 2016.

births continued unabated. Incredibly, in 1983 the UN's first-ever Population Award medals were conferred on Indira Gandhi - famous for her forced sterilizations policy – and Qian Xinzhong, China's minister of population planning. As recently as 2010 a mass sterilization campaign for around 10,000 women was held in Puning City, Guangdong. When there was little enthusiasm shown, almost 1,400 relatives were detained to pressurize couples to take part.

One-Child Households

Because of the lack of a formal policy and the changes introduced by Central Document 7, prior to 2013 China had a patchwork of varying local birth regulations which meant that less than 37 per cent of the population was held strictly to any one-child policy. This is why the term is unhelpful. It has been observed that 'one-and-a-half child policy' might be a more accurate description.[11] Although most Chinese people were not restricted to having only one child, nevertheless one child has become increasingly an accepted social norm. In other words, Chinese social practice - in aggregate - voluntarily deviated by undershooting the government rules.

In 2009 it was estimated that 145 million homes had only one child. Sadly, by 2015 researchers had discovered that in about one million homes the sole child had died and the mother was beyond reproductive age. They estimate that the number of such households will reach 11 million by 2050.[12] A shortage of children in a one-child society has many impacts, including the erosion of support for the elderly. It has been stated that 'the vast number of one-child families in China will bring great pressure on these families, and will become the biggest and long-lasting risk for China in the twenty-first century.'[13]

Reaction to the 2012 Birth Control Relaxation

After a lengthy and violent nightmare in which families' natal choices were persistently and brutally overridden, the CCP finally awoke to

---

11   See, for example, Ju-hua, Yang, 'The "One-and-A-Half Child Policy": An Analysis from the Perspective of Gender and Social Policy', *Collection of Women's Studies*, 2009.
12   https://paa2015.princeton.edu/papers/150372
13   Guo Zhigang *et al, op. cit.*, p. 252.

the fact that the problem was not endless population growth but possible unstoppable shrinkage. In 2012, important changes were announced to the birth control regulations. From November 2013 couples in which one was an only child could apply for a permit to have a second child. Officials forecast that this policy liberalization would lead to at least an extra two million births a year, raising the annual level from over 16 million to in excess of 18 million. Twenty demographers and economists published an official report in 2012 forecasting that the first envisaged liberalization would bring over three million extra births each year.[14]

We should clarify what this policy relaxation meant. These couples could apply for permission for an extra child, but it was not guaranteed that their application would be accepted. If accepted, they would not all necessarily try for a second child. And even if they did try, they would not always be successful as there is significant infertility.

In the event, the take-up rate was derisory. After two years, only 13 per cent of those eligible had applied for permission. After even the first three years, only 2 million couples out of an eligible 11 million in total applied for permission for another child. In 2014, Beijing announced 16.87 million births, up 2.9 per cent. Births in 2015 did not rise at all, but fell from 16.87 million to 16.55 million. By late 2016, even *China Daily* was reduced to citing a May 2015 report - written over 18 months earlier - to say that by that date only 13 per cent (1.45 million out of 11 million) of eligible couples had applied. This does not tell us if they received permission, later chose to attempt conception or successfully gave birth. By the end of 2016 the number was still only around 2 million, or 18 per cent of those eligible. This means that 82 per cent of families appear to have declined even to apply. The modest fluctuation in births suggests that not all the applicants went ahead.

Despite having forecast a million extra births in 2015, officials said that the fall was predictable as it was the Year of the Goat in the Chinese zodiac, an unpropitious year, particularly in the north. Surprisingly, they had not anticipated this outcome. Although the Chinese New Year does not coincide with the end of December, but takes place in either January or February, we can broadly equate

---

14   Jiang & Liu, *op. cit.*

a calendar year with a zodiac year. Years which are particularly pronounced in birth lore in Taiwan and Singapore are the Year of the Tiger (for avoiding) and the Year of the Dragon (to be sought). Hong Kong seems to like both the Tiger and the Dragon. However, China's birthrates seem historically impervious to the image of individual years. It seems that the influence of the zodiac on birth decisions only arose in recent decades as Chinese families in the region moved from wanting large families with children born in any year at all to preferring small families where a good year could confer advantage.

Second Liberalization

After the failure of the 2012 reform, a further adjustment was made in late 2015 to allow almost anyone to have two children. China's National Health and Family Planning Commission said in October 2015 that about 90 million families could qualify under the new two-child policy, out of the 140 million women of child-bearing age who had had one child already. From early 2016 all couples subject to the one-child restriction could have two children, but not three. This is clearly not the same as allowing families to have as many children as they choose. Parents also needed to gain approval before acting.

Again, officials forecast that over three million extra babies would be born in each of the following five years, bringing the births at times up to over 20 million a year. In 2014, Professor Zhai Zhenwu, president of the China Population Association, forecast that the second proposed liberalization would lead annual births to peak at 50 million. Later he reduced his expectation to 31 million.[15] However, 60 per cent of these mothers were over 35. In China, 90 per cent of births are to women between 20 and 29.

Despite the relaxation in regulations, not all regions of China were reading off the same song sheet. In early 2016 Liaoning province in China's north-east even drafted a law mandating severe fines for families which had a third child. This is a province which has recently experienced negative economic growth and a falling population. This example underlines the fact that birth controls have not stopped; they have simply been mitigated.

---

15 *Ibid.*

Although the National Bureau of Statistics no longer publishes TFR statistics, we can still look at the official birth data. In the six years up to 2013 when controls began to be relaxed, annual births averaged 16.16 million. In the subsequent six years (2014-2019), annual births averaged 16.40 million. The increase of 1.5 per cent is less than the slim increase in population in the same period. In other words, it looks as if birth control relaxation has no visible impact on births. There is no wall of pent-up demand waiting to be unleashed.

Effect of Liberalization on Births 2008-2019

Before

	2008	2009	2010	2011	2012	2013	Average
(million)	16.08	16.15	15.92	16.04	16.35	16.4	16.16m

After

	2014	2015	2016	2017	2018	2019	
(million)	16.87	16.55	17.86	17.23	15.23	14.65	16.40m

Author's chart,

Sources: NBS, *China Daily* and *People's Daily*

These birthrates will displease the authorities, who have slowly adopted a natalist position. They have consistently over-estimated the results of their birth control reforms. This massive rejection of the chance for a second child reflects other prior developments. It emphasizes the fact that China has had stubbornly low births for a long time, whatever policy was in place and that for a whole raft of reasons the falling rates are impervious to policy stimulation.

We should not be misled into assuming that Beijing is micro-managing a wholesale change in China's birth environment. The public reaction to liberalization of births is quite personal and largely uninterested. One early study in 2012 anticipated this, stating that 'raising fertility is probably an even more challenging task than reducing it'.[16] However, the almost inevitable result of having a ruling political party which believes in the Five-Year Plan is that officials receive a series of shocks from finding that not only

---

16   Feng Wang, Yong Cai and Baochang Gu, 'Population, Policy and Politics: How will History judge China's One Child Policy?' https://www.brookings. edu/articles/population-policy-and-politics-how-will-history-judge-chinas-one-child-policy/

did regulation not cut the birthrates more than elsewhere but that deregulating them does not raise them.

The combination of partial deregulation and lack of interest by couples reduces the role of the state's family planning enforcers. This host of 7.7 million officials - over 3.5 times the size of the Chinese army - found it had little to do. Ironically, the situation was reached where, according to Beijing's *Global Times*, some enforcers took time off to have a second child. Now cadres are reportedly being given new priority objectives which include raising the birthrate.[17]

China's authoritarian government has a reputation for ruthless efficiency. This certainly does not seem to apply in the field of demography. The country's birthrate fell below replacement rate at the beginning of the 1990s. It was only in 2012, after a quarter of a century, that the Communist Party dimly realized some of the damage being done and took half-hearted measures to change course. The idea of a political party governing with ruthless efficiency seems to appeal to many, but the idea of ruthless inefficiency would probably appeal to few.

The results from the liberalizations are explained by surveys of public childbirth preferences. Using a meta-analysis of 227 surveys, 606,000 people were accessed. In the 1980s, 59 per cent wanted two or more children. In the 1990s, 36 per cent did. In the early years of the twenty-first century (2001-13), 15 per cent did. Public preference has moved in a direction contradictory to that of public policy.[18]

One trend which is masked by the poor overall birth results is that second-child births are standing up quite well but the interest in having a first child is collapsing. In 2012, there were 11.45 million first children born (70 per cent of 16.35 million). Seven years later, in 2019, there were 5.87 million (40 per cent of 14.65 million) - a decline of almost a half. As we have noted, if this continues China will change from having a large population of one-child families and move towards a bifurcated situation of families with two children and families with none. This is likely to cause friction between those who would like more state child welfare spending and those who may prefer less tax on their own spending.

---

17   http://www.bschool.cuhk.edu.hk/faculty/cbk/article.aspx?id=71114452
18   Jiang & Liu, *op. cit.*

China's Fertility Rate

It is argued that China needs a replacement rate not of the global standard of 2.1, but of 2.3 owing to its distorted gender ratio. China has been below 'replacement rate' for over a quarter of a century. The actual rate of national TFR is disputed but agreed by all to be very low. Common estimates are in the range of 1.3-1.6. The 2010 census indicated a TFR of 1.18.[19] What is perhaps more interesting is that according to the *2016 China Statistical Yearbook*, the country's 2015 fertility rate was 'about 1.05'.[20] Even Chinese demographers refer to national fertility as 'ultra-low'.

These very low statistics naturally attracted attention, but officials chose to find excuses for disagreeing with them rather than seeing them as accurate and an alarm bell. Theories have been proffered that rates of childbirth are actually close to normal, but they were simply unreported owing to the birth control regulations. This is not credible. A major reason is that the number of first childbirths was depressed. There was no reason to hide a first child. Reported lower fertility in recent years is not related to inaccurate data but to delayed or reduced marriage and delayed or reduced childbearing. Births have not been unreported: they have not happened. We will examine this more later on.

For several years the picture was muddied because the near 300 million rural migrants - or 'floating population' - were blamed for travelling in order to flout regulations, for under-reporting births and effectively for artificially depressing the official birth numbers. However, demographer Christophe Guilmoto pointed out in 2015 that 'many careful studies (Chen and Wu 2006; Guo 2010) argued against this accusation by showing that the floating population tends to marry and have children at later ages and thus has lower fertility than the non-floating people who remain at the place of their household registration.'[21]

As noted above, the 2010 national census showed a TFR of 1.18, although government departments disagreed with it. While

---

19   http://www.niussp.org/article/breaking-down-the-decline-in-fertility-and-births-in-china/

20   http://www.scmp.com/news/china/policies-politics/article/2049477/call-china-further-ease-birth-control-policy-amid-fears

21   Christophe Z Guilmoto & Gavin W Jones (eds.), *Contemporary Demographic Transformations in China, India and Indonesia*, Springer, 2016, p. 103.

we should always recall the frailty of Chinese data, since hitting a reported TFR of 1.04 in 2011, Chinese authorities did not herald any recovery in TFR for some years. Guo Zhigang, who studies China's birth rate, stated in 2016 that 'the real TFR of China in 2010 should be no more than 1.5, and the average TFR in the decade from 2000 to 2010 should be even lower'.[22] When the government released the *China Statistical Abstract 2016* it gave a figure of 1.05 for 2015.[23] The National Health Commission claims that TFR recovered to 1.7 in 2016, but even this is contested. Jiang and Liu note that between 2000 and 2015, 'nearly all population censuses and annual sampling surveys indicate a very low TFR between 1.3 and 1.5, but these data have been questioned as being underestimated and adjusted by indirect estimation techniques to around 1.8.'[24] All this indicates that not only have births in the most populous country in the world been running below replacement rate for 25 years but possibly at close to half replacement rate for several recent years. The TFR figure of 1.05 for 2015 was lower than 199 other countries, according to the World Bank.

By 2019, China's TFR was anywhere between around 1.5 to almost down to 1. The data are suspect, contradictory and thus difficult to analyse. However, there is no mistaking the general position. Fertility rates fell steadily from the 1960s and now - whatever level they are - they are desperately low. China is in - or below - a group of states led by Japan, Germany, Thailand and Korea which have a TFR of under 1.5.

If everyone can apply for two children but almost no-one for three, then the likely permitted *and desired* aggregate outcome - of below two - will be adversely affected by families suffering fertility issues, families not wishing a further child, or indeed a child at all, singles who decide not to marry and rising gender disparity. It suggests that the net national TFR is almost certain to be well below the replacement rate, despite all the reforms which have been announced. Official data frequently vary. The National Bureau of Statistics in Beijing used to publish TFR data which differed from that of the Family Planning Commission. The NBS was widely thought to be more reliable. As already noted, they have now ceased to publish.

---

22   *Ibid*, p. 110.
23   http://www.globaltimes.cn/content/1019792.shtml
24   Jiang & Liu, *op. cit.*,

China is not unique in having a below-replacement TFR. It is rampant in East Asia and common in Europe, mitigated only by the impact of immigration. According to research in 2019, well over half the world is living in countries with birthrates below replacement.[25] The same study showed that over one-third of all Muslim countries are at or below replacement fertility.[26] In fact fertility is falling in nearly every country in the world. However, China is the world's most populous country, and it is not just below replacement rate but 'ultra-low', with little sign of improvement.

Fertility Rates are Stubborn

In 2018, Zhang Chewei, vice-president of the official China Population Association, said that 'China's fertility rate is very low and there is no possibility that it will rebound greatly in the future.'[27] This is corroborated by Professor Guo Zhigang's observation that 'population progresses systematically, and it follows its own pattern strictly'.[28] Yu Ning, at the Shanghai Academy of Social Sciences, has commented that 'changes in total fertility rate follow its own laws and inertia, which is not completely subjected to policy control. It is difficult and slow to rise again after TFR drops down to ultra-low fertility rate… Since the population development is cyclical and population issues are long-term, if ultra-low fertility rate is mishandled, this will lead to irreversible long-term consequences.'[29]

Thomas Sobotka at the Vienna Institute of Demography has taken issue with the Panglossian UN view that TFRs will converge and stabilize around replacement rate. He said in 2017 that 'there is no obvious theoretical or empirical threshold around which period fertility tends to stabilize. Period fertility rates usually continue

---

25   See Steim E Vollset, Emily Goren *et al*, 'Fertility, Mortality, Migration and Population Scenarios for 195 Countries and territories from 2017 to 2100: a forecasting analysis for the Global Burden of Disease Study', *The Lancet*, 14 July 2020. https://www.thelancet.com/pdfs/journals/lancet/PIIS0140-6736(20)30677-2.pdf

26   https://www.thelancet.com/journals/lancet/article/PIIS0140-6736(18)32278-5/fulltext

27   http://www.chinadaily.com.cn/a/201808/11/WS5b6e22bca310add14f3852fb.html

28   Guo Zhigang *et al, op. cit.*, p. 185.

29   http://english.sass.org.cn:8001/u/cms/www/201610/081007066foa.pdf

falling once the threshold of replacement fertility is crossed, often to very low levels.'[30]

Sustained low births makes it very difficult for a society to break out and up into a replacement rate level. As the World Bank noted, 'you may get a temporary uptick in people who wanted to have a second child having one, but we don't see a big long-term impact there.'[31] Despite birth control liberalization, Joseph Chamie, a former head of the UN Population Division, has said that 'in urban areas couples may not be inclined to want a second child, given the costs of raising children and the work of a larger family'.[32]

One of the critical characteristics of demographic developments is their durability. Professor Guo Zhigang noted in 2018, 'the issues of population are characterized by long-term periods and lasting momentum'.[33] The norm in demography is that what has happened is more likely to persist than change. In the long term, low birthrates have the habit of engendering further lower birthrates. It is quite difficult to reverse this trend. Demography tends to take long pathways. Research for the UN in 2013 indicates that in countries such as China, Thailand, and Vietnam, the TFR is well below replacement and continues to fall.[34] As China has had low births for a very long time, this trend will entrench itself in the number of girls born now and thus the number of future children in successive generations.

Demography is a science with an extended gestation period. Secular factors in the twentieth century can produce profound consequences in the twenty-first. As Professor Guo Zhigang has said, 'the population structure in our country made it certain that the total population would be cut down by hundreds of millions in the twenty-first century'.[35] Similarly, there tend not to be any quick fixes.

---

30 https://www.cambridge.org/core/journals/journal-of-biosocial-science/article/posttransitional-fertility-the-role-of-childbearing-postponement-in-fuelling-the-shift-to-low-and-unstable-fertility-levels/87A525209AC856A1C279BDCDD310622E
31 https://www.ft.com/content/d6681cba-9e3c-11e5-b45d-4812f209f861
32 https://www.passblue.com/2016/09/28/six-asian-nations-lead-in-seriously-skewed-sex-ratios-at-birth/
33 Guo Zhigang et al, Yong, *op. cit.*, p. 5.
34 https://openknowledge.worldbank.org/bitstream/handle/10986/23133/9781464804694.pdf
35 Guo Zhigang *et al, op. cit.*, p. 212.

After citing all these specialists expressing gloom about the demographic outlook, it is essential to mention that I have not omitted an equal school of opposite opinion. The stark fact is that there simply do not appear to be experts who hold an alternative view. The most optimistic view is from the UN, which still hopes for a reversion to replacement rate but at a lower population level. These facts of life are naturally frustrating for politicians but once understood they provide a focus for policy.

How Accurate are Official Numbers?

During 2017 a narrative developed that the birth figures and indeed the total population in China have both been over-estimated. This even formed a debate in the Communist Party's *Global Times* newspaper. Professor Guo Zhigang and colleagues said in 2018 that their research 'represents a challenge to most past population studies which were largely biased and overestimated the fertility level by exaggerating the magnitude of underreported births, hence were misleading'.[36] This will be a recurrent theme throughout this book. US-based Chinese demographer Yi Fuxian gained serious exposure in *Global Times* in 2017 for his outspoken research on population. This is despite the conclusions making uncomfortable reading for the party leadership. In this respect *Global Times* again deserves praise for raising interesting and provocative topics.

There were two figures released for total national births in 2016. First, in late January 2017 the National Bureau of Statistics announced 17.86 million births, up 7.9 per cent. Then - 48 hours later - the National Health and Family Planning Commission declared a total of 18.46 million, up 11.5 per cent. Third, several provincial annual population surveys were released, which have shown either little rise in the crude birth rate in 2016 or even falls. This seems at variance with the two national announcements.

In Jiangxi and Shaanxi the rises were tiny; for Jiangxi, for example, the rate rose from 13.24 births per thousand people to 13.4 - still lower than all years before 2013. As early as 2013, Chinese academics predicted that Shaanxi would see its population start contracting by 2020.

---

36   *Ibid*, p. 4.

In Guangxi and Gansu, birthrates fell compared with 2015. Both have large ethnic minorities. In the view of the *Financial Times*, 'they are now assimilating the birth habits of the richer Han majority'. While this is quite possible, it varies from the census over the last two decades. From 1990 until 2010, the China state census suggested that the minority birthrate has been the same as the Han, as their relative percentages of the population have scarcely changed. The Han grew by 6.5 per cent and reportedly the minorities by 7.3 per cent (this is the difference between an annual growth rate of 0.3 and 0.35 per cent). As the ethnic minorities have been free from the birth control policy, it is surprising that in the last 20 years they have not outgrown the Han majority by much more.

Contradicting the census, the Communist Party has criticized the Uyghurs in Xinjiang, one of China's largest minorities, for 'worryingly high birthrates'. One is led to assume that if the party is correct about high Uyghur births, then the government censuses have deliberately understated the results. As we have already noted, despite relaxations elsewhere, in recent years the Communist Party has introduced draconian measures to limit the birthrate in this predominantly Muslim region.

Historically, the party has had no especial animosity towards Muslims. The Hui, for example, are ethnic Chinese, many of whom are Muslim. The problem for the Uyghurs is that they are Turkic, not Han Chinese, and thus have cultural and linguistic differences from Han China and are seen as possible separatists. Recently there have been signs of hostility by Beijing towards all religious communities, but this is relatively novel.

The demographers Basten and Jiang made it clear that 'there is considerable current debate over the "true" current fertility rate for China, not least between different government bodies'.[37] Yi Fuxian said that even the lower data issued by the National Bureau of Statistics 'could be overstated ... according to his own calculations the real number of new births in China might be at most 13 million'. He was joined by Huang Wenzheng, a birth and population researcher at the NGO Cnpop.org. Huang said, 'I think there is a difference of about 5 million people, [which means] that

37   https://pdfs.semanticscholar.
      org/76ad/0b776417afe818486feb2192bc5c0116223e.pdf

we have over-counted. The realistic number is maybe that we have 12 million new births each year.'[38]

Yi's point is that births in China have been substantially overstated for many years. The result is that the total population in 2016 was overstated. It was actually 1.286 billion. In May 2017, Yi calculated an overestimate in China's population of 90 million; by June it was reported as 96 million and by August revised up to 100 million to take account of emigration overseas by Chinese families. He noted that 'local authorities tended to inflate population numbers to get more central government funding for education, health and transport'.[39]

Whichever birth statistics were right for 2016, even the highest 18.45 million number means that fertility is way below the country's replacement level. Thus, this far after liberalization of birth policy we are not seeing couples respond with sufficient interest to regain replacement rate. Indeed, if Yi and Huang are correct about 12-13 million births rather than around 18 million as the authorities had suggested, it implies that the real national TFR is now under 1.

Yi Fuxian, as we have noted, has been very critical of official birth data in recent years; he cites provincial inconsistency, inconsistency with census data, widespread theft of blank birth certificates, hospitals' desire for increased subsidies and inconsistency with healthcare authority data. He has rejected the official birth total of 14.65 million for 2019. In his view the result is more likely to be around 10 million.[40]

The very fact that China's National Bureau of Statistics and the National Health and Family Planning Commission can within 48 hours release birth data which differ by 600,000 underlines the fact that China's data are always frail. However, Yang Yiyong, a researcher with the National Development and Reform Commission (NDRC), criticized Yi Fuxian's population estimate, saying that 'the estimate defied common sense... China's population data is much more accurate than its GDP [numbers].'[41]

---

38   https://www.scmp.com/news/china/policies-politics/article/2064219/
     china-sees-13-million-more-new-babies-2016-workforce
39   https://www.scmp.com/news/china/economy/article/2107685/chinas-real-
     population-total-100-million-fewer-official-mark
40   https://www.scmp.com/comment/opinion/article/3047798/how-chinese-
     officials-inflated-nations-birth-rate-and-population
41   Ibid.

There are two points we can draw from Yang Yiyong's assertion. One is that even the NDRC does not believe the country's GDP figures, with which many of us would wholly agree. The second point is that Yang could well be correct in asserting that population data may be less wildly imaginative than the GDP numbers, but this does not at all mean that they are correct.

The original calculation of a 90 million overestimate of population by Yi Fuxian was partly based on the belief that local authorities tended to inflate the figures. From simply reading state media in China we know that local officials frequently falsify data for a variety of reasons such as meeting targets and gaining promotions. Hence it is very likely that Yi is correct. What we do not know is his methodology for getting to 100 million rather than 50 or 200 million. These varying estimations corroborate both (recent) official and (long-term) overseas questioning of the quality and motivation of official data. Overall, Yi may be right with his estimates or the truth may lie somewhere between his conclusions and the official data. What is highly unlikely is that government population data are precisely correct.

Bountiful Births in Beijing

Recent birth announcements in Beijing are a story in themselves. In early 2017 Beijing city trumpeted a 62 per cent increase in 2016 births compared with 2015. This seems a very high increase in year-to-year terms and also in the context of a reported national increase of 7.6 per cent. First, it should be noted that the comparison with 2015 is flattering as it was the Year of the Goat, the least popular year for childbirth under the traditional Chinese calendar. Hence only 172,000 were born compared with a five-year average of 200,000. Chinese New Year 2016 until 2017 was the Year of the Monkey and very auspicious. We would expect a substantial rise in births for that reason alone.

Second, the state-run Beijing Medical Association had predicted that there would be 400,000 babies born in 2016. So, although they forecast a doubling of births from the five-year average of 200,000, the number only rose by 40 per cent to 280,000. This has been the consistent history of official forecasts of the result of the party liberalizing the birth control policies. In January 2015, a government official said the authorities expected two million extra births per year as a result of liberalization. That year total births fell. The following year they were reported as rising by 1.31 million from a particularly low point.

Furthermore, we could ask why the figure in Beijing was up 62 per cent when the national figure was up by only 7.6 per cent. One reason may be the continuing rise in urbanization and perhaps some liberalizing of the *hukou* (household registration controls on where citizens can reside), which may have allowed more migrant workers' wives to remain in the capital. There could even have been a boundary change. However, given the government's admission of widespread statistical manipulation, we should not necessarily assume the reported birth figures are wholly accurate.

Compare the situation in Shanghai, which shares some characteristics with Beijing; of all women eligible to apply for a second child under liberalisation in January 2015, only 5 per cent chose to do so. By March 2015 only 15 per cent said they intended to have a second child. Even so, they may not have applied. By January 2016 the Shanghai government was desperately offering extra holidays to women who had a second child - or even one. If Shanghai is not very interested, should Beijing be very different?

Deindustrialization and Resource-Depleted Cities

A wave of deindustrialization is sweeping through areas of China, particularly the north-east, due to the depletion of coal and other minerals. Cities face a series of problems: unemployment, falling revenues, environmental blight and huge clean-up costs. Frequently, subsidence results from the large-scale, uninspected, extraction of minerals. Often no suitable economic sectors arise to re-employ the redundant workers and the population begins to fall as people drift away to find work. In 2009, China had 12 'resource-depleted cities' - an official categorization that attracts funds. By 2013, there were 69 such cities and the number is doubtless growing. In 2016 the state planning agency announced it was providing more funds to these blighted cities. Beijing planned to initiate 130 further infrastructure projects in China's north-east to address these issues.

The north-east of China - the three provinces of Heilongjiang, Jilin and Liaoning - has around 110 million people, or something under 10 per cent of the country's population. Inner Mongolia, with 25 million, is often added as a fourth province. The region is showing a falling population.

China's poorest north-eastern regions

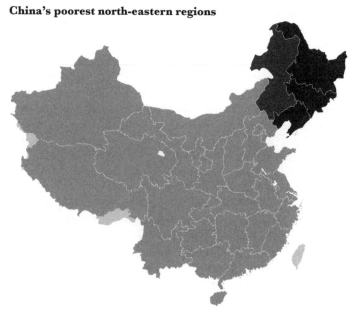

Source: Wikipedia

After the communist victory in the civil war in 1949, a large number of state-owned enterprises (SOEs) were developed in the north-east, partly owing to the proximity of the Soviet Union which in those years provided substantial assistance. This in turn attracted large numbers of migrants from other provinces. The economy of the north-east is heavily geared to SOEs, rather than private companies. SOEs constitute 50 per cent of the region's economy compared with about 30 per cent in China overall. Such firms generally perform in the slow lane. They have tended to be in heavy industry sectors and are today mostly old, dirty and inefficient. Redundancy is a huge challenge to yesterday's industries. It is clear there are serious problems redeploying workers from heavy industrial SOEs into the new service economy which Beijing would like to see.

In 2014 the three north-eastern provinces were among the five worst reported performers for economic growth. In 2016 it was said that 'over the course of … 35 years, China's northeast has gone from being the country's economic powerhouse to its most systematically troubled large region.' This deterioration has continued. Xinhua, the state news agency, has reportedly stated that 'excessive government intervention was also behind the lagging economy in the northeast'.[42]

The north-east remains rich in oil and coal. Beijing has been wrestling to cut coal production on grounds of overcapacity and environmental policy. As usual, the main burden will probably fall on private mine owners rather than SOEs, but there will inevitably be some damage to employment in the SOE-dominated north-east. When former Prime Minister Zhu Rongji made 30 million SOE workers redundant in the 1990s, one quarter were in the north-east. This kind of surgery is being proposed again. Even service sectors suffer when the main employing industries are troubled.

Liang Qidong, deputy head of the Liaoning Academy of Social Sciences, has said north-eastern China, an area about the size of France and the United Kingdom combined, has 'the most extensive planned economy in the world' and is struggling to find a way out.[43]

Beijing has been concerned about the lack of economic growth in the region and sent an inspection team there in 2014. One of its conclusions - of no surprise to those who follow China's GDP - was 'that the falsification of data was rampant'.[44]

The three provinces all border either Russia or North Korea. They have had a large Korean minority population, many of whom have contributed to the area's depopulation simply by moving to South Korea for better economic opportunity. Most of those who have moved away are the young, the middle-aged and the entrepreneurially inclined. The area is 'now known for mass layoffs, ailing economy and exodus of young talent'.[45] Most emigrants go to Beijing and other major cities. An estimated two million residents work in other parts of China. The departure of the young and redundancy of the non-re-deployable old explains why there are complaints that 'the lack of labour is getting worse, and on the other hand the jobless rate will keep increasing'.[46] In other words,

42 http://www.chinafirstcapital.com/blog/2016/12/01/chinas-depressed-northeast-not-officials-can-fix-ailing-state-owned-firms-south-china-morning-post/

43 https://www.scmp.com/news/china/china-economy/article/2162065/chinas-ailing-rust-belt-struggles-shake-reliance-state

44 http://www.economist.com/news/china/21637449-after-promising-signs-renaissance-chinas-old-rustbelt-suffers-big-setback-back-cold

45 https://www.scmp.com/business/commodities/article/2076401/human-cost-chinas-failing-industrial-soes

46 http://www.china.org.cn/china/2015-07/16/content_36074861.htm

this is a depressed economic area where labour shortages and unemployment co-exist.

However, a contributory factor to depopulation has been the unwillingness of north-eastern Chinese to bear children. Chinese media said in 2015 that the average woman in the north-east was having below 0.75 children, whereas the national average was 1.05. We need to remember here that China's one-child policy had multiple versions across different localities, but the TFR in the north-east is ultra-low even by China's low standards.

In 2014, Heilongjiang changed its birth policy to allow a second child for couples where one parent is a single child; 15 months later, only 1.6 per cent of those eligible had applied for a certificate to do so. This compares with the already dismal national average of 8.3 per cent. More recently, the province changed its policy again to permit certain families - those with a spouse who is overseas Chinese or from an ethnic minority, those living in 18 cities near the Russian border and those with disabled children - to have three children. However, the official All-Chinese Women's Federation cited a *China Business Journal* report claiming that women in the Heilongjiang city of Heihe, bordering Russia, did not want multiple children and found parenting very difficult.[47]

Population contraction is already appearing in some of the border areas. Although China has had - as noted - overall fertility rates of below replacement for 25 years, it will take some time for this to show through in the population level. It appears to be coming in the north-east first.

Low fertility and emigration are leading to depopulation of the north-east provinces. The party propaganda chief of Liaoning said in 2016 that the local media should not use 'pessimistic but inappropriate comments such as "economic lost track", "economic collapse" and "economic fall"'. However, state media in Beijing have referred to 'a potential population crisis'.[48] If the people of this region simply move and have children somewhere else, there is something of a loss to China through later, and thus reduced, marriage and births. However, the principal problem is the majority who stay put with

47   http://www.womenofchina.cn/womenofchina/html1/special/grassroots_
       women/heilongjiang/1608/2670-1.htm
48   https://www.scmp.com/news/china/policies-politics/article/1909204/
       censors-have-gone-too-far-influential-voice-deng

dwindling prospects and no impulse to raise children. If such areas multiply and hope falls further, they are likely to form zones across China of ageing, childlessness and despair.

The Real Trend in Births

I have noted independent demographers such as Yi Fuxian and Huang Wenzheng suggesting that annual births have been maybe 40 per cent overstated and that the real annual figure for births might be as low as 10 or 12 million. This is a shocking thought. However, there is more to consider. Liang Jianzhang, a professor of economics at Peking University, has looked at the lower female births in recent years and considered what this means for future births. He has formed a striking conclusion. The record low births of 15 million in 2018 'will not be surpassed for the next 100 years. China will never see more than 15 million newborns in the future.'[49] And Liang is premising his views on the supposition that government data might be accurate. If Yi and Huang are correct, he might lower his projection. Certainly, there is a 2020 forecast from Global Demographics in Hong Kong that annual births in 2028 will have fallen to 11.8 million.[50]

Annual Birth Progression from 1965 to 2019

(demonstrated by average reported annual births for 5-year periods from 1965 and then the year 2019)

1965	1975	1985	1995	2005	2015	2019
27.1	21.1	22.0	20.6	16.2	16.6	14.7

Author's table from official data

Let us just think about this:
  a. According to the National Bureau of Statistics 14.65 million has been the lowest birth total in the 70-year history of communist China.[51]
  b. Professor Liang Jianzheng says that China's birth totals will not exceed 15 million in the next 100 years. This is a standout call.

49 https://www.theguardian.com/world/2019/mar/02/china-population-control-two-child-policy
50 https://www.globaldemographics.com/
51 https://www.chinadaily.com.cn/a/202001/18/WS5e22494fa310128217271d58.html

We should note the US Census Bureau estimates that in the five years 2025-2029 average annual births in China will be 13.2 million. Low levels of fertility are causing researchers to explore and apply the scientific idea of 'half-life' to apply to the number of years in which a population would halve. We have seen official tallies of births at under half the 30 million level of 1963. And recent official birth data have been challenged as overstated and the steepness of the impending fall in births is being increasingly emphasized.

In 2019, consultancy Global Demographics brought its forecast for China's peak population forward five years to 2023.[52] In the same year Dr Yi Fuxian and Su Jian, an economist at Peking University, went further and argued that 2018 was actually the first year in China's impending total population contraction. This is another standout call.

Why are People Having Fewer Children?

There are two categories of reason for people having fewer children. The first encompasses involuntary reasons and the second voluntary reasons. First we will address involuntary reasons and these will include indirect factors which could be removed or reduced but their impact is not widely appreciated.

Involuntary Infertility

There is sometimes a thin line between voluntary and involuntary factors. Urbanization, television, unsuitable food, sedentary work and pollution can be thought of as involuntary as people rarely engage in them in the clear knowledge that they will reduce fertility but marrying late or choosing to have one child are clearly specific decisions. Tomáš Sobotka's 2015 work on global infertility has some relevance for Asia. He identifies several of the factors behind worldwide low fertility: population density, television 'soap operas', childbearing delayed until after 30, and lack of social trust.[53]

The specific reasons adduced for involuntary infertility in China are usually pollution, tainted food, abortion, smoking, lack of sleep - staying up late, working at night - and sedentary lifestyle,

---

52   https://www.globaldemographics.com/china-maternity-cliff
53   http://www.un.org/en/development/desa/population/events/pdf/
     expert/24/Presentations/Sobotka_EGM_02Nov2015

along with going to saunas. These affect the body directly. Air pollution does not help but there are some signs of improvement there.[54] General lifestyle is important. Indirect reasons for infertility are more expensive real estate, school fees, pollution and of course urbanization. Academics recognize urbanization as a global enemy of fertility. Unfortunately, China's policy is to turbo-charge yesterday's quite rapid pace of urbanization.

Urbanization

One reason for fewer children is that China is fast becoming more urban, examined in detail in our next chapter. City life is both expensive and disruptive. The cost of second and third bedrooms and also childcare and schooling costs are high. Second, a market economy where jobs are not guaranteed creates uncertainty for potential parents. Unlike in farming, there may be no pressing economic reason for an extra child in the city. When people migrate from rural areas to urban communities anywhere in the world, they tend to have fewer children. Rural fertility is higher than urban fertility in each of 83 developing countries, with the average difference between rural and urban TFRs being 1.5. China is one of the fastest urbanizing countries.

Trust

With reference to Sobotka's point, several surveys and research studies show that China is a 'low-trust society'. According to Ke and Zhang: 'we have to accept the fact that lack of trust is common and serious in today's China. It not only reduces the economic efficiency, but it's even threatening the existence of market and transaction.'[55] Niu and Xin in 2015 concluded that Canadians trust others more than Chinese do and trust their spouses more.[56] A 2012 survey by Tsinghua University and the Communist Party's *Xiaokang* magazine revealed that only 56 per cent trusted their spouse and only 39 per cent their siblings. Moreover, 'just over 41 percent of

---

54 https://uk.reuters.com/article/us-china-pollution-beijing/beijing-set-to-exit-list-of-worlds-top-200-most-polluted-cities-data-idUKKCN1VX05Z
55 http://papers.ssrn.com/sol3/papers.cfm?abstract_id=577781
56 https://www.researchgate.net/publication/233853058_Trust_discrimination_tendency_of_trust_circles_in_the_positive_and_negative_information-sharingdisclosing_domains_and_cultural_differences_between_Canada_and_China

those surveyed said that they could trust 1 to 3 people'. This is clearly not an environment conducive to fertility. In 2019 a research group reported on an experiment with lost wallets with and without money. Among 40 countries, China came in the bottom four for non-return of wallets with and without money.[57]

In China, trust used to be based on family networks but with people having fewer close relatives, there is a truncated network of family relationships. It is a society where official data are seen by the public as largely or definitely falsified and trust is so low that according to surveys in the state media, prostitutes are trusted more than government officials.[58] In a society where petty crime is practised almost ubiquitously, business cannot be trusted, families are small and wives and husbands barely trust each other, it is understandable that marriages are weak and children may be too long-term a project for many.

Does Unhappiness Reduce Child-raising?

Since at least 2012 there has been increasing interest among institutions such as the United Nations Development Programme and the OECD in happiness or subjective well-being (SWB) in contrast to economic growth, or GDP. This has given rise to tools such as the annual World Happiness Report. One of the key things about this scale is that it uses academic rigour to make its alternative points.

The 2017 World Happiness Report placed the US, Britain and Germany between 14th and 19th and Colombia and Saudi Arabia at 36th and 37th out of 153 countries. China was rated 79th.[59] (By 2020 it had fallen to 94th.[60]) The report included an extensive study led by Professor Richard Easterlin on Growth and Happiness in China 1990-2015. GDP growth was strong during this period, but using Chinese and US opinion surveys, Easterlin argues that SWB was very weak. Indeed the conclusion is that 'it is doubtful that the recovery in SWB by the end of the period reaches a value equal to that in 1990'.

---

57   https://science.sciencemag.org/content/early/2019/06/19/science.aau8712
58   http://newshub.nus.edu.sg/news/0908/PDF/TRUST-st-5Aug-pA16.pdf
59   https://s3.amazonaws.com/happiness-report/2017/HR17.pdf
60   https://worldhappiness.report/ed/2020/social-environments-for-world-happiness/

The researchers rationally assessed the various potential factors generating subjective well-being. They eliminated most possibilities and identified two or three which appear to have a high correlation with well-being. First, they discard the globally held view that GDP growth correlates with well-being. In China that is not true. GDP growth was high early and weakened later. However, employment, social security and, to a reasonable extent, trust all correlate well. China started well in 1990 on these criteria, saw them collapse and then improve.

The authors note that 'in little more than a decade (1992-93 to 2004) 50 out of 78 million lost their jobs in state-owned enterprises (SOEs), and another 20 million were laid off in urban collectives. Knight and Song aptly describe this period as one of "draconian … labor shedding".[61] Draco's influence seems quite pervasive in contemporary China. Surveys of well-being match this timing closely. If Chinese people are less happy than they were in 1990, might this bear on their willingness to bring children into the world?

Childcare

The ultra-slow rolling out of a welfare system for the elderly is undermining births. This is because many adults have their hands full with caring for their parents and are not always able to contemplate one or two children as well. The even slower provision of affordable kindergartens and affordable housing also reduces interest in bearing children. On the other hand, the gradual institution of a comprehensive, though modest, social system in the country somewhat reduces the traditional need for children to care for the elderly.

In the short term, the absence of siblings among adults reduces their ability to provide care to the rural elderly when so many young couples have gone to the cities for jobs. It also reduces the chance of adult family supervision of children left behind when their parents migrate to urban work. It has been estimated that one-fifth of all children in China are left behind by their parents to attend school in their rural home communities. Two million are living at home without the support of any close relatives. Misery and suicides proliferate in the countryside among such 'left behind' children.

---

61   http://conference.iza.org/conference_files/ICID_Renmin_2016/wang_
      f8757.pdf

People's Daily said bluntly in 2019 that 'the declining marriage rate is also closely correlated to the rising costs faced by married couples, especially the staggeringly high housing prices in some big cities and the increasing costs of childcare'.[62] I think we can safely say that the high price or complete absence of childcare is an involuntary constraint on childbearing.

Presence of Social Services

It is interesting that both the absence of certain social services and the presence of others are having a similarly prophylactic effect. In other words, for some couples, having no childcare can prevent work and therefore encourage childbearing. For other couples, the provision of state care for the elderly can encourage migration to the cities and thus lessen the ability of grandparents to provide childcare and so reduce the likelihood of birth.

Infertility

What is not voluntary is the effect of infertility. Fertility is low when people choose to delay or not consummate certain options. Infertility is when they have no choice; they cannot or their ability is impaired. China has both problems. Voluntary low fertility is endemic but infertility is also high. Here we address infertility.

Mascarenhas and Flaxman produced a comprehensive global study of infertility between 1990 and 2010.[63] Primary infertility has been falling except in Central Asia and East Asia. However, of all women who have had a child and might have a second, 10.5 per cent are infertile (secondary infertility). Secondary infertility has been growing everywhere except in Sub-Saharan Africa. In East Asia it has been growing at double the global rate. Hence East Asia is in a worse position than almost all other regions. The authors have little specific data on China but, as we have seen, East Asian countries tend to have many similarities in fertility.

Couples who have put off having children or having a second child or married late are in many cases thinking of having a child but finding it difficult. There is a price for taking postgraduate degrees or starting businesses before marriage or letting such

---

62   http://en.people.cn/n3/2019/0402/c90000-9563197.html
63   http://www.plosmedicine.org/article/fetchObject.
        action?uri=info:doi/10.1371/journal.pmed.1001356&representation=PDF

choices interfere with having children. Medical experts suggest that the most desirable age for having children is 25-29 but many Chinese cannot achieve this. Education, work and lack of money are the main reasons.

Secondary infertility, where a woman has a child but cannot have another, seems to be growing in East Asia at more than twice the global rate, according to the Mascarenhas and Flaxman survey. While China was omitted from the study, trends in East Asia can be indicative. However, we do know that there is a greater fall in the numbers of first births in China than in overall births. Therefore, any rise in secondary infertility is a particularly serious problem.

Media reports regularly suggest China's 'rising' infertility affects as many as 15 per cent of couples. This is somewhat misleading. As usual, we have conflicting data. According to one government survey by the China Population Association, infertility in China rose from around 3 per cent in 1992 to 12.5 per cent in 2012. Another study in 2016 concluded it was 13 per cent.[64] However, current levels - say, 12.5-15 per cent − are not so different from those reported in the rest of the world and the past figures may have been under-reported for cultural and social reasons. We cannot be certain that China has more infertility than other countries, but it does have fewer facilities for addressing the issue.

In the 20 years to 2010, reported global infertility was essentially unchanged but in China it apparently quadrupled from 3 to a more typical international level of 12.5 per cent. If there actually was an increase in the rate, rather than an improvement in recording, it was perhaps the result of unprofessional abortions and a deteriorating environment, which are both present. There is also evidence of rising cases of male infertility in Singapore, but again this may relate to a greater willingness to seek treatment than in the past in a conservative Asian society.

There are no clear data on infertility in China except that the authorities suggest it appears to be rising. One of the major global studies on infertility in 2012 included little data on China. Infertility is blamed on lifestyle, late marriage and pollution.

---

64   https://international.thenewslens.com/article/44982

Sperm Quality

A very specific form of infertility is low quality sperm. The definition of acceptable sperm has been steadily reduced through the last 20 years. Dr Joe Lee, consultant and director of andrology and male reproductive medicine at Singapore's National University Hospital's department of urology, says that the standards by which the WHO gauges the parameters for 'normal' sperm 'have been progressively lowered over the decades'. In 1999, the WHO assessed normal semen as 'containing at least 20 million sperm per millilitre of semen (the fluid containing sperm), with a motility rate of at least 50 per cent. By 2010, the standard required 'at least 15 million sperm per millilitre of semen, with a motility rate of at least 40 per cent'.[65] Recent academic research for 2008-14 on sperm bank donors in Shandong province, published in 2017 by Wang *et al*, proposes that semen quality has fallen more than in Europe and the US.[66]

In recent years European sperm concentration has fallen by 2.3 per cent annually against 0.8 per cent in the US. The WHO has reflected this by reducing its definition of quality. However, Wang *et al* found in their large study that the yearly rate of decline in China was 6.9 per cent. They say that this is a subject rarely researched but were able to refer to three other studies in China. Their conclusion stated that 'the decline of semen quality among sperm bank donors in our study may be alarming and should receive great attention'.

Wang and his colleagues surveyed preceding work in the field. Zhang *et al* in 1999 'proposed that sperm quality in China had declined significantly faster than that in Western countries during the same time period'. Jiang et al in 2014 decided that 'semen quality of adult men in Sichuan (China) declined'. Rao *et al* in 2015 proposed in a study in Wuhan 'that the yearly decline rate in sperm concentration in their study was even higher than that in [Wang *et al*]'. As was remarked by Wang *et al*, 'semen quality is known to be a well-recognized marker of fertility'. However, their scholarly conclusion on the speed of the decline was alarming. It seems that recent systemically falling male fertility in China is serious.

---

65   https://www.businesstimes.com.sg/life-culture/rise-in-male-infertility-in-singapore-mirrors-global-sperm-crisis

66   http://www.ajandrology.com/article.asp?issn=1008-682X;year=2017;volume=19;issue=5;spage=521;epage=525;aulast=Wang

The IVF support potentially available as a result of sperm banks is prejudiced as the latter are desperately short of sperm. This is not so much because there are millions of clients but because there are so few sperm banks - only 22 in the whole country - and a very keen but very small clientele. So we are talking of supply and demand in a small context. In 2011 there were 30 reproductive medicine centres in the country. For a then-estimated 132 million infertile people, this represented 4.4 million per centre. As they are not necessarily married to other infertile partners, if they know they are infertile and if the centres were open 365 days a year, they would need to see about 12,000 people a day - if they only came once. It is not surprising that for those who do turn up, the waiting time for donor insemination is long; in 2011 it was 1.5-2 years. This often makes couples abandon their quest. The customers are generally people who have left having children until very late or couples who have had other issues of infertility.

The course can last six months. The sperm banks have had to respond to the shortage by lowering the height and education requirements for donors. One estimate is that only 20 per cent are accepted because of quality screening. In Shanxi province in 2015 the sperm bank rejected 87 per cent of donors on quality grounds.[67] This is despite the fact that cash payments for donors have increased from $500 to $1,000 – even iPhones have been offered to donors.

State media announced in 2016 that 'from the year of 2003 to present, sperm donations in Shanghai cannot meet the high demand for quality sperm from barren Chinese couples.'[68] Similarly, sperm banks in Beijing, Shanxi and Hubei also announced that their reserves of sperm were at an all-time low. This means, broadly, that there is more infertility in China than there are willing, qualified donors. It seems reasonable to make an informed judgement based on such evidence that male infertility has increased in recent years and possibly more sharply in China than elsewhere.

Infant Mortality

Global infant mortality has more than halved in the last 30 years. In China it has reportedly fallen by over 80 per cent. China's national infant mortality rate was reported by the World Bank in 2017 as 8

---

67   http://www.globaltimes.cn/content/982324.shtml
68   http://www.globaltimes.cn/content/982324.shtml

per 1,000 live births. However, in Western China the situation is very different. Although the World Bank calculated China's infant mortality in 2009 at 14.6, the WHO in 2013 concluded that the national rural average for 2009 was 34 and in the western provinces was 65.[69] The latter is close to 69, the infant mortality rate in 2009 of Burkina Faso in West Africa, one of the world's most impoverished countries.[70]

The WHO strongly believes that breastfeeding, rather than infant formula, can shield a child from many of the diseases of infancy. China has one of the lowest breastfeeding rates in the world - 29 per cent. However, Western China has a 9 per cent rate of 'still breastfeeding at 20-24 months', almost the lowest in the world. 'In 2008, it was estimated that, globally, suboptimal breastfeeding in the first 6 months of life accounted for 10 to 15% of deaths in children younger than 5 years.'[71]

Thus, despite the normal appearance of the national average infant mortality rate, there are populated regions of China where a serious reduction in infant mortality would markedly increase the number of young people in the population. Even relatively affluent Guangdong province had an outbreak of infantile intestinal bacteria in 2019 which caused a series of new-born deaths. Research indicates that a mother's lifestyle and diet from conception affect the health of the infant she is carrying. China has little effective advice for expectant or new mothers.

Another issue is that there is a clear and understandable link between the quality of surface water in China and infant mortality levels. Counterintuitively, at a certain point reducing water quality then ceases to relate to mortality. The proposed reason for this is that eventually water quality is evidently poor and then substitution begins. It was shocking to learn that '56 per cent of the 436 major polluters fined in 2018 for excessive discharges were waste water treatment plants'.[72]

China has wide regional pools of excessive infant mortality which are associated with lack of breast-feeding and high levels of

69   https://www.who.int/bulletin/volumes/91/5/12-111310/en/
70   https://data.worldbank.org/indicator/SP.DYN.IMRT.IN?locations=CN-US-IN-DE-RU
71   https://www.who.int/bulletin/volumes/91/5/12-111310/en/
72   https://www.scmp.com/news/china/politics/article/3011820/why-chinas-waste-water-plants-are-some-its-biggest-polluters

pollution. Reduced infant mortality would, of course, stabilize, if not increase, the birth rate.

A Political Conclusion

One group of Chinese academics put forward a socio-political rationale for falling birthrates. They argue that this phenomenon is caused by globalization generating inequality and stress; education is in greater demand in the workplace; reduced public services and social security create uncertainty and decrease desires and behaviours; job migration is damaging marriage and fertility; and globalization generates materialism and individualism which distract from the satisfaction of raising a family. Overall, they argue that 'globalization has shaped a political and economic environment that bears huge uncertainty and hostility towards population reproduction.'[73]

Why are People Choosing to Have Fewer Children?

The fact that countries without stringent birth control legislation have equalled or exceeded China's fall in fertility over the last 40 years indicates that other more important forces are at work. Many of the most powerful are voluntary, including: rising divorce, later marriage, later childbearing, increased tertiary education and rising education and housing costs. Often the reasons overlap. Most of these factors are present worldwide. However, almost specific to Asia is the flight from traditional patriarchal marriage by highly educated women. All these drivers of lower birthrates involve a specific decision being taken.

Women's Education and Employment

It is socially and economically desirable that women as well as men should maximize their intellectual abilities through higher education and joining the workforce. However, we should note other factors which enter the equation. In some countries more women than men are now graduating from university. This has been the case in China since 2014. This is also true in the US where it has been estimated that at marriageable age the ratio of female to male graduates is now 4:3. We might link this with the fact that women

---

73   Guo Zhigang *et al*, *op. cit.*, pp. 241-3.

practise hypergamy - that is to say they characteristically 'marry up'. A woman will normally seek a richer, better-educated and better-looking man. Once there is a surplus of female graduates this intention becomes harder to achieve. Female graduates do not generally marry non-graduate men. The result is that a rising proportion of better-educated women are choosing not to marry.

The same applies to women in senior and well-paid jobs. They are reluctant to marry men who are junior or earn less. These may not be socially attractive facts, but they are nonetheless facts. They now meet the consequences of gender equality policy. There is nothing particularly wrong with gender equality except perhaps for its association with the notion of enforced quotas. Indeed, women probably win a majority of college places on merit. I am here only concerned with the associated effects of female graduate surpluses.

The benefits of maximizing female educational and work opportunity, which sound self-evidently beneficial, have met negative results in rendering marriage less likely. Associated with this is the increasing chance of divorce where women have succeeded in their careers and are no longer willing to tolerate marriage to an under- or average-performing husband.[74] It does, of course, also often apply to non-graduate women as well.

In East Asia these trends are quite evident. This may be because of a sharper distinction between, for example, an Asian female investment banker, with a Princeton doctorate, considering a patriarchal marriage with an Asian male and his conservative parents. China fully reflects these trends. Potential wives want to know in advance what is the husband's income, who will manage the couple's income, can he provide an apartment, will they live with her in-laws, are children expected and how many? That some of the answers are unsatisfactory explains why so many young Chinese women have not married. It may also partially explain the recent sharp rise in divorces.

Later Marriage

Female tertiary education and career planning tend to lead to late marriage, which is recognized globally as a prophylactic. Another reason for late marriage is that people may save to be in a position

---

74   https://www.asanet.org/sites/default/files/attach/journals/aug16asrfeature.pdf

to pay for housing, childcare and education costs. The average Chinese woman in 2018 was marrying at the age of 27.4, up from 23 in 2011. The number of men between 20 and 29 will have fallen by 20 per cent from 2010 to 2020, but the number of young women will have fallen by 25 per cent. Ninety per cent of births are to women between 20 and 29 years old.[75] This will cut birthrates in the future.

An internet survey revealed that 50 per cent of all single Chinese men believe that unmarried women over 25 are 'leftovers'.[76] This is despite the shortage of women and suggests that women may have almost as difficult a time as men. The combination of there being fewer women in their twenties and their marrying later in the critical childbearing years will compound the effect on the country's fertility rate. Thomas Sobotka has said that the European trend towards later parenthood is crucial to understanding low TFRs. Many emerging economies will experience this over the next 30 years 'with a depression of their TFRs to very low levels'.[77] China is already seeing a delay in marriage age. The choice of later marriage is effectively voluntary and has serious consequences.

Yet there are some discrepancies in this picture. We look later at a random sample of early and late first marriages for women by country and the accompanying average TFR. It seems that - usually - later marriages produce lower TFRs but China has rising but lower first marriages, but still lower TFRs.

Abortion without Cohabitation

Marriage in China is becoming less popular, cohabitation and procreation outside marriage are rare and there are more abortions than births. Compare this to the US, where there are about five births to one abortion, and England which has a ratio of 3.5 to one. This suggests that sexual activity with no intent to raise children is widespread. In many cases abortion is seen as little more than a

---

75   http://www.scmp.com/news/china/policies-politics/article/1903721/
      beijing-unfazed-drop-births-despite-ending-one-child

76   https://www.whatsonweibo.com/why-arent-you-getting-married-chinas-
      marriage-rates-keep-dropping/

77   https://www.cambridge.org/core/journals/journal-of-biosocial-
      science/article/posttransitional-fertility-the-role-of-childbearing-
      postponement-in-fuelling-the-shift-to-low-and-unstable-fertility-
      levels/87A525209AC856A1C279BDCDD310622E

method of contraception. There may be cultural prejudices against birth out of wedlock but abortion represents a clear personal choice to prevent life which has arguably begun. The numbers are sufficiently large that they are seemingly not restricted to cases of severe medical risk.

Weaker Marriage

While accepting that there are well-known special circumstances in China, such as fiscal incentives for couples to divorce in order to save tax on owning two apartments, there are nonetheless fundamental trends in place. In China from 1990-2017, the number of divorces grew steadily, at almost 6 per cent per annum on a per capita basis. In the US, the number of divorces from 2000-2017 steadily fell on a per capita basis. The most recent position is that divorces in China have become 8 per cent more common per capita than they are in the US. The two countries have long been moving in profoundly different directions. Trust between married couples in China seems especially weak and infidelity especially high.

In 2003, divorce in China was eased. It could be executed in a single day for about $1.60. In 2016, the process was slowed to allow an interview to take place. The combination of more procedure and the ever-rising numbers has meant the current system is struggling to cope.

Professor Pan Suiming of Renmin University in Beijing says that infidelity has been growing since 2010 and has reached a very high level. Among women, 13 per cent are reportedly having one or more affairs. For men, the figure is 33 per cent. These are apparently the highest rates in the world for infidelity.[78] However, a poll by the technology firm Tencent suggests the figure is 60 per cent for men. Both of these surveys only count those who admit to infidelity. It would be reasonable to assume that such extramarital activity weakens the urge to bear children in many couples.[79] Indeed, it seems unlikely that the purpose of infidelity is to have extra children.

Marriage in China seems to have become much shakier. Adultery certainly weakens marriages and is a voluntary decision by those who participate.

---

78   http://www.globaltimes.cn/content/1120254.shtml
79   http://www.globaltimes.cn/content/1120254.shtml

Cost of Education

There has been a decline in the number of university applicants, as we might expect with lower birthrates, and at the same time an understandable increase in places offered due to the explosive growth in new universities. This suggests that it has become much easier to enter a university. Nonetheless, there has been a steady increase in external coaching to help children with their examinations. In 2018 parents spent an average of US$17,400 and up to $43,500 per year on tutoring. The latter figure is similar to the cost of a full boarding school education in Britain. As one education expert in Shanghai has said, 'tutoring fees have become a heavy and unavoidable cost for many households.'[80] In fact, state media in China report that private spending on education in 2017 ran at an annual rate of $570 billion, or 2.48 per cent of GDP.[81] With this kind of expense one can understand the inclination to limit the number of children.

We might wonder why there is so much emphasis on tutoring for exams if it is becoming easier to go to university. There are two answers. The coaching is not in order to go to a university but to be accepted by one of the few very good ones. Second, the coaching is often aimed at accessing an overseas school or university. Fees are also required by kindergartens and creches. Observers claimed that the high cost of education deterred couples from having children.

A case can certainly be made that state education in China is weak and needs supplementing with external private investment. However, it can also be argued that there is a degree of hysteria and the sums are unnecessarily large. This suggests that the very large amount of money spent on tutoring is excessive and represents a voluntary pressure against marriage.

Remaining Single

The rapid rise in the proportion of the young remaining single has been an important factor in low fertility. *People's Daily* conducted a survey in 2019 of why singles do not wish to marry.

---

80   https://www.scmp.com/news/china/society/article/2176377/chinese-parents-spend-us43500-year-after-school-classes-their
81   http://en.people.cn/n3/2019/0402/c90000-9563197.html

Why Young Chinese Are not Marrying

Per Cent	Reason
29.5	Haven't met the right person
23.4	Have no ability to raise a family
16.5	Enjoy being Single
12.3	Don't have a stable life
8.8	Work pressure too much to think about it
5.1	Don't plan to marry before graduation

Source: *People's Daily*[82]

There are many reasons why people of marriageable age remain single. For women this can include giving priority to career over starting a family, finding young 'only child' men rather spoilt and not to their taste, being homosexual and 'not finding Mr Right'. These conditions may each endure and eventually become permanent, even if it is not inevitable that being single until 30 means remaining as such forever. For men, much the same conditions can apply. Hence quasi-voluntary bachelorhood can persist. In 2013, there were 170 million single people and later the Ministry of Civil Affairs stated that 'there were more than 200 million single adults in China in 2015, and the number was still rising'. Such status may be a temporary phase in life or it may become permanent. While the population is scarcely increasing, the number of singles grew by almost 10 per cent a year.[83]

In the 2010 census, 25 per cent of men and 19 per cent of women above 15 were unmarried. (This is a curious age profile to select as 15 is below the permissible marriage age.[84]) By 2017 *People's Daily* said there were 222 million single adults - 15 per cent of the population. Nearly half were between 20 and 29, 'with many citing it was their personal choice to remain single'. The Communist Party newspaper also observed that 'faced with high housing prices, high marriage costs, and extended costs of raising a family, many

82   https://www.theepochtimes.com/chinas-marriage-rate-drops-again-fueled-by-social-problems-plaguing-youth-2846088.html
83   http://www.globaltimes.cn/content/1026885.shtml
84   https://www.nytimes.com/2017/02/14/world/asia/china-men-marriage-gender-gap.html

young people shy away from the responsibilities associated with settling down, preferring to stay single.'[85]

According to the US Census Bureau, the number of people of 20 and over in China in 2015 was 1.045 million. The Ministry of Civil Affairs statement implies that almost 20 per cent of all adults were unmarried at that time. The percentage is not necessarily high. It is, for example, lower than that in Japan. However, it should be said that it is rare in China to raise children out of wedlock and so those wishing to raise a family would normally marry first.[86]

In 2017 Wang Guangzhou from the Institute of Population and Labour Economics at the Chinese Academy of Social Sciences said that 'about 4 percent of men aged between 35 and 59 are unmarried, while only 0.4 percent of women in the same age range are single'. This is interesting and amounts to a ratio of 10.7 million men to 1 million women. However, the key point here is that all those included were born before 1982 when the sex ratio at birth went stratospheric. A second point is that an age threshold of 35 misses all the young women today who are uninterested in marrying at all.[87]

The 2018 National Bureau of Statistics (NBS) Yearbook reported in 2017 that there was a surplus of 32.2 million males over the age of 15 who had never been married (105 million males and 72 million females). The surplus was particularly pronounced in Shanxi, Zhejiang, Anhui, Hubei, Hunan, Guangxi and Yunnan.[88] One wonders how the NBS and *People's Daily* can respectively calculate over-15 never marrieds at 177 million and single adults at 222 million. (Apart from the age discrepancy, the numbers are 20 per cent apart.)

Young people are spurring a new market for small-sized consumer items like mini-microwaves and washing machines owing to their proclivity not just for being single but for chatting online, having domestic animals for company and even talking to AI robots. Chinese young people are rapidly adopting some of the introverted habits of young Japanese. *People's Daily* warns here of

---

85   http://en.people.cn/n3/2019/0314/c90000-9556084.html
86   https://www.census.gov/data-tools/demo/idb/region.php?N=%20
      Results%20&T=10&A=separate&RT=0&Y=2015&R=-1&C=CH
87   http://www.chinadaily.com.cn/china/2017-02/13/content_28183839.htm
88   http://www.stats.gov.cn/tjsj/ndsj/2018/indexeh.htm

the 'challenges in interpersonal relationships' from adopting this virtual lifestyle. It will also affect the ability to engage in business or cooperate in combat situations.[89]

We should note that not all singles are so by choice. A key point is that the overwhelming majority are males. Many of them have little choice but to be single. If there is a 1:1.2 gender divide at birth, instead of 11 marriages with 1.1:1.1 births, there would only be 10 marriages, which is a minimum of 10 per cent fewer marriages. However, some women and men are clearly choosing to be single. It appears that remaining single or having very late marriages are becoming increasingly popular options. This specific choice is voluntary and a growing threat. Professor Guo Zhigang understandably says that 'rapid social changes in China, such as the rise in the proportion of the unmarried in the younger generation, also have their impact on the low fertility rates'.[90]

Consumer Mentality and Single Children

Another intangible influence is a growing consumer mentality among those who are themselves single children, frequently criticized for being spoilt and becoming selfish. Many prefer a BMW to a baby. We should note also a growing consumer culture with an increasingly different conception of the family unit. Hence a mutually reinforcing condition seems to be that single children are often pampered and selfish and grow up uninterested in having children and even unwilling to make the compromises which accompany marriage. Reduced childbearing becomes increasingly entrenched. Modern society, suffused with consumerist longings, seems to be creating a one-child model making single child families normative. This is the result of multiple individual voluntary choices.

Domestic Animals

Ownership of domestic animals, especially dogs and cats, is exploding. In Japan, there are believed to be more cats and dogs than children under 15.[91] In China, I would estimate there are probably still about 1.3 children to every cat or dog. This may

---

89   http://en.people.cn/n3/2019/0314/c90000-9556084.html
90   Guo Zhigang *et al, op. cit.*, p. 6.
91   https://www.ft.com/content/e425060c-61c4-11e9-b285-3acd5d43599e

reflect the fact that dog ownership only became legal in 1993 or that Japan is more affluent. Certainly, the gap is closing fast. The pet industry was reportedly the fastest growing in China between 2000 and 2016, compounding at 49 per cent annually. The owners are young, highly educated and 88 per cent female. Selecting food for the animals and dressing them has become an industry. As has been noted on social media, it may not be too whimsical to see domestic animals as a cheaper and easier alternative to children - or even husbands. This is perhaps a bizarre turn in individual choice.

A Key to Future Births is the Number of Women

The UN Family Planning Association has stated since at least 2012 that the intensity and duration of current birth imbalances will shape the future of both China and India and it is 'the growing scarcity of young women, which is going to affect family-building processes'.

It adds that 'the demographic weight of China and India and their skewed sex distribution explain why the world population should remain masculine for the next 70 years.'[92]

Given a distorted sex ratio at birth, we are not concerned with the number of births but the number of female births. Projections here are most discouraging. The fertile age for women is usually deemed to be between 15 and 49. Chinese demographers, however, focus heavily on the age range of 20-29 as being dominant.

Change in Numbers of 15-49-year-old Women in the Next 15 Years

Source	2018	2033	Change
UN	349m	302.5m	-13%
USCB	346.7m	294.3m	-15%
Global Demographics	346m	291m	-16%

As we have discovered, these estimates are only as good as their assumptions. Multilateral organizations have often overestimated demographic trends, even after birth. We could well see results worse than those shown above.

---

92   https://www.unfpa.org/sites/default/files/pub-pdf/Sex%20Imbalances%20
     at%20Birth.%20PDF%20UNFPA%20APRO%20publication%202012.pdf

The reduction in women of childbearing age over the next 15 years is a serious concern. However, we should note - as Professor Yuan Xin at Nankai University has stated - that in China 90 per cent of births are to women aged 20 to 29. Thus, it behoves us to observe what is happening to this demographic. The situation is much worse, indeed alarming.

Change in Numbers of 20-29-year-old Women in the Next 15 Years

Source	2018	2033	Change
UN	95.7m	75.7m	-21%
USCB	100.7m	69.8m	-31%

To be 20 in 2033, you have already been born. The data are known. By any forecast, the fall in 20-29-year-old females is much steeper than the fall in under-50-year-old women in general. The forecast from the US Census Bureau is particularly striking. Even if the interest in bearing children undergoes a sudden sharp increase, there will not be enough women to get births back to the levels China has seen in the past. This is now one of the biggest drivers of the future population outlook in China.

Renunciation of Birth is Voluntary

We should be clear about what has *not* taken place. Chinese citizens are not being told to have as many children as they wish. There are some - still limited - exceptions, such as Heilongjiang, where three children are permitted, and ethnic minorities. However, for almost everyone there is a maximum limit of two children. And yet Chinese people are not even taking advantage of the partial liberalization they have been offered.

There are several reasons for this situation. Some are beyond the control of families: they cannot afford childcare, education costs, a larger apartment or they are infertile. It appears that there are serious and rising issues of male fertility, which may well be connected to environmental or lifestyle conditions. They are not limited to China but are echoed in several regions of the world. The trend towards later marriage and conception increases the risk of inflicted infertility. These developments undermine the government's hopes of averting steep population decline.

Moreover, Chinese people are actively choosing to have small or no families. Even as early as 2007, researchers from the Max Planck Institute observed that 'young Chinese women today are more likely to consider child-bearing not as a necessity, but as a choice'.[93] The main decisions affecting childbirth in China are voluntary. Girls want tertiary education. Individuals choose to marry late, if at all. Abortions are widespread and can reduce child-rearing potential. Couples prefer a small family of one child, or none. Some feel it is less trouble to have a domestic animal than a child.

China Daily conducted a survey in 2016 which showed that nearly 60 per cent of working mothers did not want a second child. The reasons included cost, time and energy and 'other concerns included career risks, the pain of childbirth and little faith in their marriages'.[94] In fact, a surprisingly large number do not even want a first child. In 2017, the employment firm Zhaopin discovered from a survey of working mothers that only 22.5 per cent wanted a second child. 'Nearly three times that number said they did not want more than one.'[95] By 2020, it was reported that fewer than 25 per cent of women in Shanghai wished to have a second child.[96]

This will lead inexorably to a population collapse during the balance of this century. The state is still damaging its own overdue initiatives with retrogressive 'family planning' strategies. However, changes in China's habits are rendering the family planning officials redundant. There is no regulatory reason why Shanghai's fertility rate recently stood not at 0.99, constrained by the one-child policy, but at 0.7. I would suggest the reasons are not policy measures but predominantly social factors. Now the biggest driver in low birth is not the state but popular preference.

Emigration

There are two reasons for discussing emigration here. First, any population forecast takes account of births, deaths and migration flows in and out. It is not only a weak birthrate which is affecting the

---

93 https://pdfs.semanticscholar.org/dd2a/
     e38afae9bac8947d6fd4cdb5dec769d08c2c.pdf
94 http://www.chinadaily.com.cn/china/2016-05/09/content_25144103.htm
95 https://www.washingtonpost.com/world/asia_pacific/beijings-one-
     child-policy-is-gone-but-many-chinese-are-still-reluctant-to-have-
     more/2019/05/02/c722e568-604f-11e9-bf24-db4b9fb62aa2_story.html
96 https://www.ft.com/content/a245eef4-3a5e-11ea-a01a-bae547046735

population outlook. Many Chinese are also emigrating and taking citizenship in other countries. However, there are few foreigners applying to become Chinese citizens. As a result, there is net emigration. Second, the actual net emigration figure could be large enough to distort the published population data.

A report, citing OECD data, asserts that the level of emigration is presently low by world standards but is highly concentrated amongst the richest and most educated (five times that of the average person) and rising fast.[97] The total number of emigrants increased from 1990 to 2013 by 130 per cent. One survey of 'super high-net value individuals' discovered that 60 per cent had considered emigrating. Four reasons given for emigrating are low quality education, low food safety, political, economic and social conditions and weak rule of law. The United Nations estimates the accumulated total in 2017 at 10 million. As no-one really knows, and emigration is not encouraged, it might be appropriate to assume the numbers are larger than evidence shows, rather than smaller.

A 2013 OECD report calculated there were 3.9 million Chinese immigrants in the OECD countries.[98] In 2010/11, 1.7 million of them had tertiary education. Indeed, the report seems to indicate a 1.8 per cent annual rate of graduate emigration from China. The Centre for China and Globalisation, a Beijing-based think tank, stated in 2013 that China was the world's largest source of immigrants.[99] In 2018 it believed that it was merely the fourth largest source. The number of emigrants cited by the World Bank and the UN might be down around 20 per cent in the period.

Demographer Yi Fuxian adjusted his estimate for China's population on several grounds. One was the need to recognize emigration. He increased his estimate of the incorrectness of the national population estimate by 10 million to 100 million owing to his factoring-in emigration. Yi refers to UN data estimating 8 million emigrants.[100]

---

97   https://www.un.org/en/development/desa/population/migration/data/
      estimates2/estimates17.asp
98   http://www.oecd.org/els/mig/World-Migration-in-Figures.pdf
99   http://en.ccg.org.cn/archives/3080
100 ttps://www.scmp.com/comment/opinion/article/3018829/chinas-
      population-numbers-are-almost-certainly-inflated-hide

The Communist Party's *Global Times* newspaper stated in 2014 that a third of all Chinese billionaires had emigrated by the end of 2013.[101] It also pointed out that China is one of the top sources of immigrants into Australia, Canada and the US. One 2016 report said that 'between 2005 and 2015, China saw an average of 400,000 people emigrate to other countries every year'.[102] The World Bank estimates the number as an average 382,000 annually from 1997 to 2017. In 2019 the Hurun Research institute surveyed 224 rich Chinese and one-third said they planned to emigrate.[103]

A peculiarity of emigration in China is that surveys of the rich will often itemize the proportion who plan to emigrate and where, but the text will often mention that later they plan to 'retire back to China' which is not, of course, the normal definition of emigration. In 2018, Hurun said, 'It is also interesting to note that 90% of those considering immigration intend to live in China after retirement.' This might be thought to invalidate the survey. However, in the context of a rather repressive government, we should probably ascribe little significance to the 'later return'. We should assume that many Chinese find it inconvenient to announce to anyone that they are emigrating for good.

This does not mean that we should assume that few who leave will ever return. If food safety and air quality are improved, overseas education is completed and - one might add - property rights and political climate are improved, everything may change. We should not overlook the natural desire of Chinese people to speak in Chinese, eat Chinese food and live with other Chinese people.

It is clear that migration is a continuing feature in China, but, as we have seen, there are few figures. It would not be wise for a departing citizen to check out before he moved permanently from the country. It is possible Beijing is unaware of the number of permanent emigrants. They may retain homes in China. Thus, the scale is not adequately reflected in the censuses. Yi is probably right with his estimate of 10 million Chinese citizens having emigrated overseas. It is quite likely they are still being counted as Chinese

---

101 http://english.ckgsb.edu.cn/sites/default/files/files/CKGSB201609-Low.pdf

102 https://fred.stlouisfed.org/series/SMPOPNETMCHN

103 https://www.asiaglobalinstitute.hku.hk/news-post/china-has-chance-kick-start-its-economic-reforms-will-xi-jinping-push-ahead-key-meeting

residents in the domestic data. On this basis Yi may be justified in adding them to the figure he is deducting from the published total to estimate the actual population.

Bleak Future

We need to understand and accept what the UN Family Planning Association described in 2012 as 'the rootedness of … the small-family norm'. This has become what most Chinese people want if they want children at all, or indeed if they want marriage.[104] With a longstanding below-replacement TFR, China will need to prepare for population contraction that will be steep and should exceed that of any other major country this century, even Russia or Japan. The population of Japan is forecast to fall by 60 per cent to 50 million by 2120, in the next century.[105] China should experience a similar decline but faster- by the end of this century. This means that China's population collapse will be happening at a 20 per cent faster rate than Japan's and to a much larger country, with much less wealth or institutional capacity.

Beijing would like population growth, or at least stabilization, but the reality is that China needs to brace for extensive steep falls in coming decades, with the attendant social and economic impact. This is not an environment where Beijing can get what it wants. China's current minor birth 'hiccoughs' are irrelevant to the impending major trend of population decline.

The overall conclusion to be drawn is that Beijing does not know what is happening to its population after the partial liberalization of birth policy but is becoming aware that the desired results are not materializing. It finds it very difficult to address the fact that the population will peak well before 2025 and is then likely to suffer a sharp, long-term and unstoppable decline of well over one half.

The Outlook

Professor Guo Zhigang said in 2018 that 'the mainstream belief differs considerably from the actual low fertility levels revealed repeatedly in various survey data findings. This poses a serious

---

104 https://www.unfpa.org/sites/default/files/pub-pdf/Sex%20Imbalances%20 at%20Birth.%20PDF%20UNFPA%20APRO%20publication%202012.pdf
105 https://www.ft.com/content/29d594fa-5cf2-11e9-9dde-7aedca0a081a

problem in that a very low fertility rate is being ignored.'[106] Even more important for China is that it is most unlikely that it will regain replacement rates of birth and once the population has peaked in the 2020s, it should steadily erode for a prolonged period. In 2019, the Chinese Academy of Social Sciences called the decline 'unstoppable'.[107] This is already clear in the closure of primary schools and falling applications to university.

There are no quick policy fixes for low fertility except immigration. Given that most Chinese already live in China, any material demographic impact on a country of maybe 1.4 billion can only come from non-Han immigration. Chinese societies overseas are not only small but - to the embarrassment of Beijing - almost entirely more affluent than is China. We should note here also that fertility rates are even lower in Taiwan, Hong Kong and Singapore than in China. However, China exhibits considerable caution in its interaction with other races. It is not a natural candidate for mass foreign immigration and a multiracial destiny.

The administration in Beijing, confronted with an unappetizing demographic outlook, had until recently consoled itself with the perceived necessity of its harsh and intrusive one-child policy and the theoretical success of claiming to have avoided 400 million further births. Now that it has partly abjured the birth control policy, it has to claim that its partial liberalization will be sufficient to boost birthrates.

The inevitable result of collapsing births is that the population will eventually shrink. Longer life has delayed the impact but does not prevent it. The only debate is when China's population will start to fall and how steep and deep that decline will be. Pronatalist policies can have some effect on boosting the birthrate, but China is not taking them seriously. Between lack of money, infertility, rampant abortion, pollution, consumption bias and lack of interest we should not be very optimistic about China's ability this century to avoid large-scale population decline.

Reduced birthrates were not the result of the 'one-child policy', and the end of very tight birth control regulations has not resuscitated the birthrate. National fertility rates, while confusing, are evidently amongst the world's lowest. The number of women

---

106 Guo Zhigang *et al*, *op. cit.*, chapter.1.
107 http://time.com/5523805/china-aging-population-working-age/

of prime child-bearing age (20-29) will fall by a quarter by 2033. We know this because they have already been born. This will outweigh any increased interest in procreation.

We could try a simple calculation about that generation of women in 2033. If a mere 10 per cent do not marry and 10 per cent are infertile, then 80 per cent could marry and breed but may choose not to. Let us say that they all choose to do so. If 2.1 is replacement rate for a normal woman, then in this situation the required TFR for fertile married women is 2.63. That means the reduced female population in 2033 would stay unchanged.

This hypothesis rests on various subsidiary assumptions: the ending of excess female infant mortality; the excess male sex ratio at birth falls to around 1; no more than 10 per cent of couples have a partner who is infertile; and 90 per cent of women will get married during child-bearing years.

We could go further. If we would like to see the reduced female population of 2033 reproduce at a rate which would bring the female population back to where it was in say 2018, it would need to increase female births by 33 per cent. This implies a TFR of 3.5. We are not talking of the national TFR but the TFR of women who are married and fertile. Yet given that some couples do not want more than one child and other couples want no children at all, it seems most unlikely that the average can reach anywhere near 3.5.

The renunciation of children has already happened. The results will be seen in coming decades.

5

THE MIXED GIFTS OF URBANIZATION

It may at first seem strange but will, I hope, become clear later, why I devote an entire chapter of a book on demography to urbanization. It is because of the effects, direct and indirect, that urbanization has on population.

The Impact of Urbanization on Fertility

Urbanization is seen globally as a prophylactic or birthrate inhibitor. This is as true in Africa as it is in China. As people move from the villages to the cities birthrates tend to drop. The same applies to Muslims moving from rural North Africa to urban Europe. In China, the effect is the result of higher property prices, less need for farms to be maintained, more pollution and associated environmental issues, consumer culture, high stress and work demands, delayed or no marriage for career reasons, lengthy commutes, sedentary lifestyles and even saunas, hot springs and maybe sleep deprivation.

One classic study of the impact on fertility from migration to urban communities in 2008 in Ghana summarized the literature on the topic:

> Urbanization reduces fertility because urban residence would likely increase the costs of raising children. Urban housing is more expensive, and children are probably less valuable in household production in urban (vs. rural) areas. Furthermore, urbanization (or urbanism) may be associated with ideational change, that is, beliefs and attitudes surrounding large families. In addition, urban residents may have better access to modern birth control, allowing urban residents to more effectively act on any desire to reduce childbearing.[1]

---

1   https://www.ncbi.nlm.nih.gov/pmc/articles/PMC2834382/

Data from China further suggests that now around one-eighth of Chinese couples of child-bearing age are (involuntarily) infertile. In China and overseas, this is strongly associated with urbanization and the environment.

Numerous studies indicate that in almost every country surveyed rural fertility is higher than urban fertility, on average by around 1.5 children per family. Of course, there was a time when governments wanted lower birthrates and many - rightly or wrongly - still do. However, now that half the world is living in countries with birthrates below population replacement rate and other countries are moving to join them, the issue for many governments is no longer depressing birthrates but worrying about how to raise them.

Modern China and Urbanization

In the last 75 years, China has been one of the fastest urbanizing countries in the world. There are several ways to measure this process. At the 1949 communist victory there were 69 cities. By 2017 there were 627. In 2015 there were 106 cities with populations over 1 million, compared with 55 in all of Europe. From 1980 the urban population more than trebled from almost 200 million to an estimated 800 million by the end of 2017. In recent years, China's urban population grew faster than that of Pakistan, Indonesia and India, but more slowly than those in Bangladesh and certain African countries.

The extraordinary rate of growth over a long period has given rise to some arresting statistics. The *Financial Times* gives three such examples: 'In just two years, from 2011 to 2012, China produced more cement than the US did in the entire 20th century.'[2] In 2013, the building, selling and decorating of homes in China represented about a quarter of the total national economy. This is more than Spain, Ireland or the US combined during the height of their housing booms.

China has a lengthy urban record. In fact, in the two thousand years to 1800 AD it has been asserted that one-third to a half of all citizens of cities have been located in China.[3] And yet China does not

---

2   http://www.ft.com/intl/cms/s/0/4f74c94a-da77-11e3-8273-00144feabdc0.
      html?siteedition=intl#axzz31e69ANMo

3   Eric Jones, *The European Miracle: Environments, Economies and Geopolitics in the History of Europe and Asia*, Cambridge University Press, 2003, p. 165.

have a city in the world's projected ten fastest growing major urban areas. These cities - Lagos, Karachi, Cairo, Manila and Dhaka; Bangalore, Lima, Ho Chi Minh (Saigon), Istanbul and Chennai (Madras) - will grow by between 15 and 35 per cent between 2017 and 2030. The largest will approach 50 million residents. China already has several very populous cities, where the authorities are now attempting to limit the numbers and urbanization is being steered more towards towns and smaller cities.

Why is China urbanizing so fast? Prime Minister Li Keqiang has regularly urged China to accelerate its drive to urbanization. He wants a further 400 million citizens to pour into the cities and says urbanization is a 'huge engine' of China's future economic growth. It is anticipated that 15-20 million Chinese people a year will continue to move to cities. The anticipated growth effects are particularly appealing as China faces secular decline in its economic growth rate. In the face of pandemic and its impact on world trade, China is banking on increasing the consumerism of its own very large population. Urbanism is part of that strategy.

There is a global establishment pushing for urbanization as the solution to many ills. I suspect that much of this is reductionist thinking - or an inability to distinguish between causes and coincidences - along the lines of: urban income is higher than rural income; health care and state education are often better in the cities. Therefore, let's push people from the rural areas to the cities. There are clearly many advantages to urban life which are frequently expounded. These include the educational advantage, access to facilities such as sanitation and greater efficiencies. Less frequently mentioned is the draw to the cities of a wide range of skills which can power future innovation. However, there are also negative consequences from rapid and extensive urbanization. China is officially on this precise course. I will therefore now devote some time to examining the other - negative - side of urbanization.

Impact on Health

Many of our contemporary maladies seem inextricably bound to urban life. Whereas noise, for example, from aircraft or traffic has no clear impact, extensive international research links urban living with higher rates of schizophrenia, psychosis and other mental disorders. Such disorders are almost twice as prevalent in urban areas as in rural ones. Dutch research in 2009 suggests that 'living in a city roughly doubles the risk of schizophrenia - around the same level of danger that is added by smoking a lot of cannabis as a teenager'. The same study suggests that 'urban living was found to raise the risk of anxiety disorders and mood disorders by 21% and 39% respectively'.[4]

Official medical provision tends to be clinic-centred and this provides barriers for the chronically ill. External advice is for China to concentrate less on hospital-centric elderly care and more on 'ageing in place'. This is more financially sustainable for the state in the long term. However, it is undermined by the government's obsession with rapid urbanization. A prime example concerns those with dementia. This group is expected to treble in China between 2001 and 2040. There are an estimated 173 million Chinese with a mental disorder but 92 per cent have never had any treatment. Taking the young from the countryside will not improve the provision of medical care to the rural elderly, who are 'ageing in place'.

Physical health is also deeply affected by profound social change. According to an article in the *International Journal of Public Health*, 'Rural-to-urban migration will likely be a major demographic driver of the cardiovascular disease epidemic in China.'[5] In 2015, researchers noted: 'The health problems associated with rapid urbanization are profound, most notably the chronic non-communicable diseases (NCDs)—e.g., mental health disorders, and obesity and its correlates of type II diabetes, metabolic syndrome, and cardiovascular disease.'[6] These are certainly well represented among the leading illnesses of contemporary China.

Other research makes a similar point. An age-related increase in conditions such as cancer and heart disease is being accelerated by the mass migration from countryside to cities - a trend accompanied by more sedentary lifestyles and unhealthier diets. One analysis by Raymond Chung states that 'the increasing trend of deaths of NCD in China was due to rapid urbanization and industrialization'; Chung also noted the increase in toxins and poisons in foods produced in highly industrialized regions of China.[7] Elsewhere in

---

4   https://www.gwern.net/docs/nature/2010-peen.pdf
5   https://www.ncbi.nlm.nih.gov/pmc/articles/PMC3465962/
6   https://www.ncbi.nlm.nih.gov/pmc/articles/PMC4318214/
7   https://slideheaven.com/detoxification-effects-of-phytonutrients-against-environmental-toxicants-and-sha.html

the world, similar observations have been made. Studies have shown that in sub-Saharan Africa those moving from rural areas to cities have a 2-5 times increased risk of developing type 2 diabetes, while in Mexico City, one of the world's largest cities, diabetes is considered the main health challenge. Diabetes is clearly linked to obesity in increasingly affluent countries. Both have also been closely linked to high susceptibility to Covid-19, or coronavirus.

Urbanization correlates closely with dengue fever, which has seen a 30-fold growth globally over the last half century. A rising proportion of victims acquire the more virulent strains. Severe dengue fever can be fatal, is now a leading cause of death among children and has no effective medication. China is not only urbanizing rapidly but unfortunately its changing climate patterns are also unfavourable. Concreting the land restricts water run-off and creates pools in which dengue mosquitoes thrive. In many of China's southern neighbours, dengue fever is hyper-endemic. In 2016 Guangdong province was subject to a serious dengue epidemic almost three times the definition threshold. This is unsurprising given that it is half-tropical, but it has urbanized fast: its population has grown over the last 50 years at almost twice the national rate and it is 67 per cent urban, far above average. Even the 2014 plague of 'killer hornets' in northern China, which caused over 40 deaths and hospitalized almost 1,700 others, was blamed on rapid urbanization disturbing the habitat.

There seems to be a clear relationship between rapid urbanization and decreased years of healthy body and mind, maybe even reduced longevity. Any such trends will affect the proportion of the population available for the workforce. On the other hand, several research projects have shown that exposure to nature seems to offer a variety of beneficial effects to city dwellers, from improving mood and memory to even alleviating ADHD [attention-deficit/hyperactivity disorder] in children.[8]

Environmental Impact

Associated with the direct impact on health is the fact that creating mega-cities such as Beijing and Tianjin has built population concentrations so large that they have completely outgrown their

---

8   See, for example, https://academic.oup.com/bioscience/
     article/68/2/134/4791430

original water resources and supply planning. This has had the perverse consequences of aquifer depletion, subsidence, large-scale water diversions nationally and even internationally and engineering projects of gargantuan, if not grotesque, proportions, with unforecastable consequences. It also underlines the fact that few societies are as under-planned as a planned economy. Furthermore, the concentrations of construction and population in the coastal cities, often on uncompacted soil, at a time when China is facing further climate change, puts those cities at risk from rising sea levels. Threatened communities include some of China's largest cities, such as Guangzhou, Tianjin and, of course, Shanghai.

Much of China's urbanization has taken people straight from the countryside to the big cities and ignored the towns. This is also a global phenomenon, which can lead to skewed property development. Qiao Runling, a deputy director of the China Center for Urban Development, said in 2013 that 'China now has an oversupply of cities, given the number of new urban districts that we have.'[9] While global research is ambiguous on the subject, research from the Chinese Institute of Urban Meteorology suggests that rainfall reduction from 1980-2003 is 'statistically correlated with rapid urban development in Beijing since 1980'.[10] Research from Princeton echoes this. Beijing has certainly suffered drought for over 25 years, together with increasingly frequent sandstorms.

When populations flee country for town, energy use doubles and carbon emissions rise about 150 per cent. In 2008 the World Bank noted that China uses seven times the energy of Japan and 3.5 times that of the US for each unit of GDP. Moreover, urban residents use 3.6 times the energy per capita of rural residents. For example, in rural China there are only 16 air conditioners for every 100 households; in urban areas, that ratio is 112 per 100. Of course, some of this difference is attributable to relative income but other factors play a part.

Urbanization also seems to increase energy intensity (the quantity of energy to produce a unit of GDP) in developing countries. The concept of 'urban heat islands' is relevant here.

---

9   http://www.chinadaily.com.cn/business/2013-08/10/content_16885182.htm
10   https://www.researchgate.net/publication/265980973_Influences_of_ urbanization_on_precipitation_and_water_resources_in_the_metropolitan_ Beijing_area

Research in the Yangtze Delta and other parts of the world suggests strongly that urbanization and the creation of urban heat islands has a measurable effect on the observed climate warming which is increasingly proving a threat to highly populated areas along China's coastline, such as Shanghai.

The farmland compulsorily taken for urbanization must be replaced by local authorities, but this is often done through purchase in remote and precipitous areas where only excessive use of fertilizer can engender acceptable yields. These in turn run off in rivers, which are flooded with large amounts of nutrients that poison rivers and create potential 'dead zones' in the offshore seas. The flow of animal antibiotics into the groundwater system, particularly from industrial pig farms, contributes to rising antibiotic resistance in humans, which is plaguing global medical defences.[11]

The demands of Chinese megacities risk creating a resource depletion like that linked with the demise of the Mayan civilization in Central America in the ninth century AD. These urban areas may in the interim become difficult to live in and ultimately unsustainable.

Impact on Culture, Human Rights and Social Stability

Urban development is often facilitated through municipalities appropriating villagers' farmland cheaply and selling on more expensively to developers to generate much needed local finance. Indeed, Tsinghua University estimates that 16 per cent of all Chinese families - maybe 70 million - have had their land appropriated, a fifth of whom received no compensation.[12] Put another way, almost half of all villages - over 400,000 - have had this experience.[13] Such compulsory land acquisitions contribute to numerous violent mass protests which pervade rural China. In 2010 Tsinghua estimated these to average 500 per day. In the Tibetan areas of provinces such as Sichuan there have been successive government drives to push nomadic families into urban living. This is not just a communist

---

11   The 12-storey pig farm at Yaji Mountain in Guigang, southern China, has been designed to process 850,000 pigs a year. See https://www.theguardian.com/environment/2020/sep/18/a-12-storey-pig-farm-has-china-found-a-way-to-stop-future-pandemics-

12   http://usa.chinadaily.com.cn/china/2013-10/29/content_17067582.htm

13   https://cdn.landesa.org/wp-content/uploads/17-Province-Survey-Comprehensive-Report-eng_Final.pdf

trait; it was also a feature of dynastic China. It echoed the Manchu treatment of the Miao in 1872.[14]

There has been disdain for rural life in China since long before the communist state.

Evidence suggests that urbanizing experiments have often had harmful results. Adjustment from a pastoral life to menial urban labour has been difficult for the Tibetans; often there have simply been no appropriate jobs. Alcoholism and depression have ensued. There are suggestions that transmission of Tibetan language and culture are being impaired. Nonetheless, the government is pressing ahead with plans to make Tibet 30 per cent urban by 2020, up from 25 per cent in 2014.

Xinjiang, similarly, is experiencing the impact of a comprehensive urbanization drive. It has gone from a sleepy backwater in the 1940s to the frontline of China's Belt and Road Initiative (BRI). There is a 20-year plan to raise urbanization to 68 per cent. At least seven entirely new cities have been created. Twenty special industrial zones are being set up. The destruction of traditional architecture accompanies mandatory eviction and relocation. The fact that rural Uighur families can now usually have three children and urban ones two, suggests that urbanization may reduce Uighur child births. When the communists invaded Xinjiang in 1949, the Han minority constituted 7 per cent of the population. It is now over 40 per cent - around 9.5 million. Such a shift was not accidental.

The historic central government focus on developing cities can have the effect of marginalizing life in smaller towns. Targets for further growth are arresting. Between 2014 and 2020, 100 million people will have been moved by government plan from rural to urban life as their land is taken over and they are given apartments. As noted, municipalities often replace the naturally located farmland with precarious and over-fertilized farming in remote and unsuitable areas. It can contribute to the evisceration of smaller rural cultures. While many citizens may exult in a modern apartment, for others their human concerns - over family home or livelihood - are often a rounding error in the five-year plans. Large-scale, state-sponsored - utopian - projects usually carry the real risk of crushing human sentiment.

---

14   Max Weber, *The Religion of China: Confucianism and Taoism*, Free Press, 1951, p. 3.

Weaker countries with low levels of rule of law, high levels of inter-group grievance and high levels of income inequality are associated with higher violence in urbanized environments. Indeed, in 2016 two UK-based academics arrived at the conclusion that 'violence is increasingly a defining characteristic of urban living'.[15] This does not bode well for China. A prominent German researcher has compared the negative transformative impact of urbanization with that of climate change. The history of contemporary urban construction has been built on a well of unhappiness and thus creates a legacy of mixed memories.

Impact on Social Welfare

The under-provided-for elderly have traditionally relied on informal and non-institutional care from their families. However, China's drive for internal migration to the cities is undermining the capacity of traditional social protection by families for millions of elderly in the rural areas. Mass migration of the young working-age rural population to urban areas leaves children and the elderly without suitable care. It also weakens the economics of pension funds in the rural areas. International research also suggests that urban life substantially increases the risk of mental problems, an under-resourced area in China.

Foreigners frequently remark favourably on the absence of slums in cities such as Beijing, but rarely note that living conditions can nonetheless be harsh in China's modern cities. The OECD refers to 100 million urban residents in China living in 'shanty-town housing'. This definition is scarcely different from that of slum housing. Owing to central Beijing's high property costs, approximately 1.25 million people there live underground in basements, former bomb shelters and even sewers. This may be why foreign visitors do not notice them. There are simply too many people working in Beijing for the affordable accommodation available.[16] By 2025, more than 200 cities will have at least 1 million inhabitants, and 15 'supercities' could each have 25 million, or 11 massive urban conurbations could have 60 million apiece. If the mega-cities grow even larger, little suggests that they will be environmentally or otherwise better managed. There

15   http://www.ids.ac.uk/publication/the-dialectics-of-urban-form-and-violence
16   http://www.oecd.org/eco/surveys/China-2015-overview.pdf

are already openly expressed views, even in China, that this trend has gone too far.[17]

Alienation

Sociologists are engaged in a debate as to how far cities cause alienation amongst those who arrive from small towns and rural areas. Is the social interaction and community sense that is to be found in small communities lost when a person moves to a city? Looking at contemporary China, we can note symptoms such as physical violence against doctors and school children and the pervasive absence of trust even within families. Clearly alienation exists, but the issue is the cause. We might consider as factors the deracination stemming from the Cultural Revolution, an absence of moral and spiritual values, the Communist Party's war against religion and families and, finally, urbanization. It is hard to conclude that we should leave urbanization off the list of causes.

It is interesting that the authorities have begun to challenge urban gated communities and insist on public access at least for through traffic. This is a direct attack on property rights and segregated urban living or the 'tale of two cities'. Sociologists may say that cities do have less sense of community but in return offer more creativity and greater tolerance of non-traditional behaviour. Unfortunately, this is unlikely to be a trade of great interest to many of the rural migrants from Hunan. Alienation creates a class of citizens who find it hard to relate to others and are sub-optimal candidates for marriage.

An End to Fast Urbanization?

Urbanization was first a by-product of China's growth and then later seen by officials as essential to it. Several merits were attributed to urbanization both hard and soft. It was seen as efficient but also as positive for education, culture and civilization. It would mould consumers and thus mobilize consumer spending. Efficiencies would cut public spending. Urbanization was seen as an important driver of growth. As we have seen, it has expanded at a rapid rate in recent decades.

---

17   https://www.mckinsey.com/featured-insights/urbanization/preparing-for-chinas-urban-billion

In 2012 when China's state think tank, the Development Research Centre (DRC), and the World Bank produced the paper *China 2030: Building a Modern, Harmonious and Creative Society*, it was said that 'China's next phase of development will need to build on its considerable strengths - high savings, plentiful and increasingly skilled labor, and the potential for further urbanization...'[18] However, labour has ceased to be plentiful. It has peaked and started to decline. This makes urbanization sound even more important.

Of course, we could say that urbanization is not, strictly speaking, what is happening. Every year for almost 40 years, a net 17 million rural migrants have moved to the cities but have only rural citizenship documents, which means they have only partial or no access to social services in the cities. They generally leave the cities some years later and go home or to small towns. They do not change from being rural residents to urban residents on a permanent basis. They lend themselves to the cities. They are second-class citizens while there, in the same way that a tenant might be seen in relation to a freeholder. Then they leave. It is not surprising that in 2015 the number of migrants in the cities fell by almost 6 million, the first fall in 30 years.

Recent urban planning has shown markedly contrasting thinking. It was noted earlier that Li Keqiang, the prime minister, has been a strong advocate of urbanization since at least 2012 and has urged faster progress. However, there has been surprisingly little public debate about the case for urbanization. Cautious critiques have emerged since at least 2005 but independent and academic work rarely influences policy makers in China. In 2014, Guangzhou announced colossal plans to double its urban area. Meanwhile, the National Plan of New Urbanization 2014-2020 was quite novel, reflecting wide thinking with sensitive objectives. The plan was a reaction to environmental pressures, rising inequality, weakening economy and a high level of large-scale violent incidents. Sustainability was well emphasized. As Professor Jun Yang of Tsinghua University observed in 2016, everything depends on the implementation. He suggested that urbanization must slow down owing to changing international factors, social problems and environmental challenges. Yet in the same year, it

---

18   https://www.worldbank.org/content/dam/Worldbank/document/China-2030-complete.pdf

was officially reasserted that the plan remained for urbanization to reach 60 per cent by 2020, which would require a further 50 million to head to the cities.

From 2015 it began to appear as if there was some support for a slowing down of urbanization. Early that year Xi Jinping pushed for removing administrative functions from Beijing. In a series of remarks he and the official news agency Xinhua discussed not concreting over the countryside, not tearing down traditional housing to erect high rises and not homogenizing town and country. It is an irony to see Xi Jinping in flat contradiction to Point 9 of Karl Marx's *Communist Manifesto*, which called for the 'gradual abolition of the distinction between town and country'. That year the Communist Party's Central Committee agreed that China should promote human-centred new urbanization. In 2016, the DRC wrote that 'the new approach to urbanization differs from the traditional approach in that it demands more in terms of the quality of urban development and management.' It emphasized a 'human' element and stressed that the market, not government intervention, is the factor which drives urbanization. This is largely aspirational at this point but there are hints that since 2012 there has been a small but growing desire to break with the way urbanization worked in the past.

To make urban development human-centred it was clear to the leadership that the distinction between rural and urban citizenship - based on the *hukou*, household registration of each person - would need to change. In 2014, the State Council made this a clear goal. However, change has been minor. There have been adjustments in the smaller cities but not really in the larger ones. Of course, *hukou* reform is not a popular cause amongst urban residents concerned about access to kindergartens, schools and hospitals. Similarly, land rights - fair compensation for farmers when their property is needed for urban construction - are a necessary condition for peaceful and equitable development. Regrettably not much has happened here either.

Also, the 2014 New Urbanisation guidelines made it clear that rural migrants would be steered as much as possible to large towns and small cities, then - in an ascending order - larger cities would be made more difficult to settle in. Cities with populations above 5 million would be strictly controlled. This partly explains why *hukou* reform has made little progress in the main cities.

To allow the market to determine resource allocation for urban development, it was decided to follow the route of public-private partnerships. However, there is an admission that those projects which have got off the ground have been almost entirely funded by state-owned enterprises. A leading reason, says the DRC, is that 'private investors are doubtful of the government's credibility'. It is remarked that many cities have tried to create innovative development through building knowledge cities or 'eco-cities'. Yet these are not new ideas, they go back decades and have often been complete failures.

For those not already cautious about urbanization, a real wake-up call appeared in the Communist Party's *People's Daily* newspaper in 2016 when it was revealed that local governments in aggregate were planning to construct 3,500 new areas for a total of 3.4 billion people. As the president of the South China Association of City Planning said, this is 2.5 times China's total population and half of the world's total. For a country heading for population collapse it is particularly pointless.[19]

Beijing, Shanghai and some other cities have begun acting to limit their populations. Beijing has announced its intention to cap its long-term population at 23 million 'and keep it at that level for the long term'. Xi Jinping has stressed the need for 'suitable people' to migrate to the urban areas. By way of some explanation, Beijing declared its intention to combat 'urban diseases'. This fits with the plans to move SOEs, universities, government offices and particularly polluting factories out to surrounding Hebei province. In 2016, Beijing knocked down 300 million square feet of small shops, stalls, bars and restaurants. It was followed by a plan to destroy another 400 million square feet of similar properties. This will constitute 5 per cent of Beijing's entire built area. Much of this space will be used for parks and gardens.

Another factor is the seeming reduced enthusiasm of today's rural young to repeat the journeys of their parents to take up urban work. Thus there have been contrasting views in Beijing about the nature and benefits of urbanization. We should in any case assume that with a theoretical 56 per cent urbanization, the process should now be slower. The form of urban growth sponsored back in 2012

---

19   https://www.scmp.com/news/china/policies-politics/article/2076346/why-chinas-rush-urbanise-created-slew-ghost-towns

by Premier Li Keqiang, perhaps more broad brush, appears to have been derailed in favour of a new approach championed by Xi Jinping which is slower, more selective and not expecting growth in the major cities.

Shrinking Cities of the World

It looks as if Chinese policy makers are exhibiting a weakening passion for fast urban growth, and other countries have for some time experienced outright contraction in many cities' sizes. The phenomenon of cities which have lost their purpose and are visibly shrivelling has been apparent for some time. Prominent examples are Detroit in the US and Halle in Germany, but others can be found in Latin America, in the Baltic and the Balkans, Korea, Japan as well as China. Causes cited by researchers include weak economy, de-industrialization leading to unemployment and emigration, suburbanization, longevity, rising crime and falling fertility rates.

There are many troubled cities in the US. In the case of Detroit, it went into a death spiral of decay and rising crime until it eventually declared bankruptcy in 2013. The lack of diversification from the auto industry combined with municipal mismanagement meant there were falling revenues at the same time as rising pension and social costs. Forty per cent of European cities with over 200,000 citizens have lost population. Germany has suffered markedly since unification. East Germany is estimated to have lost 10-20 per cent of its inhabitants in the first decade after unification. It was stated in 2000 that over 1 million apartments were vacant in East Germany and the number was expected to increase. In the early 2000s research indicates that 75 per cent of the larger cities in Eastern Europe had falling populations. There are also reductions in several West German cities.[20] China is also following. Recently - between 2010 and 2017 - 90, or 14 per cent of China's 661 cities, were reported to have shrunk.[21]

Yichun city, in China's north-east province of Heilongjiang, was built on logging. From 1948, it produced 10 billion cubic feet of timber until the logging ban in 2013. Its forest area has been noted

---

20   http://www.policy.hu/mykhnenko/a46269-proof.pdf
21   https://www.scmp.com/economy/china-economy/article/3004152/
      growing-pains-chinas-shrinking-cities-are-addicted-building

as one where the development is fast and the scale is large. Gradually the wild and remote outskirts have been stripped of forest. By 2006 there had been a 98 per cent decline in mature forest reserves. It is now an environmental disaster, subject to destructive floods owing to the loss of woodland. The population has reportedly fallen by over a quarter since the peak in 1990 and it is now where it was in 1973. It is one of China's many 'resource-depleted cities'. It has been the scene of labour protests, which is not unusual in the depressed north-east. By 2015, it is estimated that a fifth of all families had lost their jobs through the logging ban. Yichun has become something of a case study and yet it is not alone.

A study by Tsinghua University of 3,300 Chinese cities and towns measured the change in the intensity of light emitted from these conurbations between 2013 and 2016. The conclusion was that in 28 per cent of cities the light had reduced over this period. This reflects the fact that 938 of the country's cities and towns have falling population and reduced economic activity. In an earlier study from 2000 to 2012, China had fewer shrinking cities than the US, the UK, Germany and France. So the relative rate of shrinkage appears to be rising. For towns, the situation is worse. Between the censuses of 2000 and 2010, 51 per cent of all townships suffered falling population. The team leader, Long Ying, described the situation as 'underrepresented, understudied, and underreported'. Long has noted that ironically town planners are still operating on the assumption of continuing growth, often on orders from local leaders. Of the 90 cities reporting falling population by 2017, 70 of them had nonetheless expanded their city area during the period.

We might ask whether urbanization has got out of hand, is perhaps often driven by local self-aggrandisement and needs to be restrained. The key for most of such cities is to realize that the objective is generally not a resumption of growth but to create stabilization and survival or to calmly manage decline.

The Future

We have seen that many different aspects of urbanization have negative consequences, sometimes indirect, for the country's society and demography. But for us the most important impact of urbanization is that rural to urban migration is driving (optionally) falling fertility rates worldwide: from Africa to Asia. It is linked with such factors as more expensive property, less need for farm labour and high family education and childcare costs. In 1980 falling birthrates were seen positively but with China facing a population collapse in coming decades this needs to be reassessed. Academics have assigned urbanization a major (22 per cent) share of the causes of low fertility in China. There is a technical term - demographic transition theory - that holds that part of the reason for fertility reduction is the result of modernization and socioeconomic development.

One particular reason for the extreme nature of urbanization in China is that since at least the nineteenth century there has been disdain by officials for rural life. Whereas a Western statesman might retire to the countryside, this would not happen in China. Urbanization is accordingly seen as natural. YC Wang made the points: 'In a sense the men of 1911 were the last generation of the old elite who lived close to the land and had intimate connections with the peasantry... The absence of educated men from the rural areas rendered good government impossible.'[22] Professor Zhou Zhonghe, one of China's most respected and experienced palaeontologists, has gone further and noted, 'the general lack of interest in nature has been a characteristic of the Chinese educated classes for thousands of years.'[23] This goes some way to explain the disregard for rural life, and we might even say rural people, in elite discourse.

Recently there has been a large number of migrant labourers returning to their villages for good and a reduction in the number of first-time migrants. As a result, the overall number of migrants seems to have peaked between 2012 and 2014 and since then has been falling each year. The numbers are opaque as they include those moving to nearby towns and those making a major migration to a distant city.

There are signs that urbanization is slowing. This will affect future economic growth rates. It is only to be anticipated as the more urbanized society is, the more slowly we might expect future

---

22 YC Wang, *Chinese Intellectuals and the West, 1872-1949*, University of North Carolina Press, 1966.
23 http://www.scmp.com/news/china/article/1630310/fossil-champion-fights-chinese-ignorance-darwinian-theory

urbanization to proceed. Arguably China now has an oversupply of cities and urban life and may in future seek an alternative and more viable long-term strategy by generating policies to invest in a more balanced society through improving rural life as well as city life. One possibility is to invest heavily in making rural life more attractive, and one of the plans in the 2008 stimulus initiative was to link all villages by formal roads. This could be followed through and amplified into other fields. Better transport links, job opportunities, more equal education together with the already superior environment could make rural life become much more popular.

The state needs to change its priorities and give more investment - and respect - to rural life. It needs to create a balance in the country. A nation needs a heart, lungs and a reproductive system as well as a brain. It may take a considerable time to diminish the damaging impact of urbanization on fertility. Yet we may already have seen a turning point which can at least put a brake on the headlong trend.

5

ASSESSING THE KEY FORECASTS

All data from everywhere can be contested and weak. As I indicated in the Introduction, as indicated elsewhere in this book, however, the data for China are particularly frail, even those provided to the senior leadership of the CCP. Here we try to describe the challenges faced in putting the picture in numbers - to create reliable forecasts of what could happen and by when. Before doing that, we need to examine the sources of information and look into the debate about accuracy.

Deep Debate in Demography

The team that produced the respected worldwide research on national TFRs ('total fertility rates') and population sizes for the Global Burden of Disease (GBD) programme in 2018 discussed methodology at the beginning of their report.[1] They noted that most international demographic studies draw from data provided by the UN Population Division (UNPOP). However, they stated that UNPOP, the US Census Bureau and other organizations use mutually similar approaches in which 'estimates are not based on standardized, transparent, or replicable statistical methods'. While not itself perfect, the GBD research appears to offer some fresh approaches to demography.

Clues to the weakness of Chinese statistics are not hard to find. As long ago as 2007 scholars from the highly respected International Institute for Applied Systems Analysis (IIASA) in Vienna, who collaborated with demographers from Peking University in a paper aptly entitled 'China's uncertain demographic present and future', summarized the difficulties in forming a clear view of present circumstances:

---

1   https://www.thelancet.com/journals/lancet/article/PIIS0140-6736(18)32278-5/fulltext

Recently published figures of China's total fertility rate around 2000 range from 1.22 to 2.3 - a remarkable difference, especially seen on a relative scale (a factor of 1.89). There are probably few countries in the world where estimates about current fertility rates differ by such a factor.'[2] They added: 'If fertility in China were currently below 1.5, as many authors estimate and the UN publishes in its 2004 fertility data sheet, instead of the 1.85 assumed by the UN in its recent long-range projections, this would influence the assumed fertility level over the coming decades and result in markedly lower projected rates of population growth (shrinking later in the century) both in China and the world... Fertility is not the only uncertain demographic condition in China today. Estimates for the sex ratio at birth range from 113 to 123. This is a remarkable difference that will significantly influence the future proportion of men to women in the adult population and hence population dynamics.[3]

Both the GBD team and IIASA use different approaches from UNPOP and come to conclusions which look more credible.

In 2011 a research paper (Alkema, Raftery and five other noted academics) questioned the then UN TFRs for China noting that they were at the time unchanged over a 15-year period from the late 1990s and stating that 'there is controversy about whether the sudden halt to the decline over the past 15 years is real. The UN estimate of 1.77 for China's TFR in 2005-2010 was based on official estimates.'[4] Again, there is the suggestion that the UN is influenced by member governments, and here China specifically. Independent academic research suggests that the TFR may have been around 1.5. Guo Zhigang wrote a similar critique in 2016 in *Contemporary Demographic Transformations in China, India and Indonesia*.[5]

The UN Population Division seems to have an institutionalized bias towards assuming a regression to the mean in its projections. High fertility countries are assumed to see their TFR come rapidly

2   http://www.austriaca.at/0xc1aa500d_0x0017f0d7
3   http://www.austriaca.at/0xc1aa500d_0x0017f0d7
4   https://link.springer.com/article/10.1007/s13524-011-0040-5
5   See CZ Guilmoto and GW Jones (eds.), Contemporary Demographic Transformations in China, India and Indonesia, Springer, 2016, pp. 97-111.

close to the replacement rate of 2.1. Similarly, low fertility countries are assumed to be going through some short-term aberration and the core assumption is an eventual return to replacement rate. This bias seems to be built in part on a disregard of cultural and social drivers and a view that everyone is the same and also, in one particular respect, in response to Chinese persuasion.

In 2016 Patrizio Vanilla of Leibniz University in Hanover commented on the UN's German projections, saying that 'since the UN approach is based on quite strong assumptions regarding the three phase-structure whereas it uses relatively little country-specific data on Germany itself and instead simply assumes convergence towards 2.1, the author believes that these projections might be highly error prone.'[6] Joseph Chamie is also sceptical about the UN's fundamental assumptions:

> Other than the demographic expediency and political acceptability of population stabilization, there appears to be little, if any, empirical or theoretical rationale for the widely cited UN projections to assume convergence to replacement level fertility. Resting on the dubious assumption of convergence to replacement fertility, the weighty message to scholars, government officials and the general public that world population is expected to approach stabilization at 10 billion by the end of the century appears tenuous.[7]

Worse than disagreement over data is the deliberate distortion of data for policy and career reasons. Beijing officials have admitted that there has been conscious falsification of data in the economic area as well as on the environment. After a spate of such incidents a regulation was issued in early 2017 to prevent data falsification. It was officially stated that 'penalties raised by the newly enacted regulation will be an effective deterrent'.[8]

Not everyone would be so optimistic. It has been a regular source of mirth to economists that the total of China's provincial economic results often exceeds the national economic output.

---

6   http://diskussionspapiere.wiwi.uni-hannover.de/pdf_bib/dp-579.pdf
7   https://yaleglobal.yale.edu/content/global-population-10-billion-2100-not-so-fast
8   http://www.xinhuanet.com//english/2017-08/01/c_136491451.htm

Individual Chinese provinces have been caught out in scandals in recent years where they have overstated their economic growth rates in order to enhance the careers of local officials. When it was announced that national officials would become involved in the compilation of provincial data, we saw that in 2020 more than two-thirds of provinces reduced their forecasts.

In early 2019 the statistics regulator, Ning Jizhe, stated that the government 'will step up efforts to prevent and punish data falsification and other fraudulent practices, in an effort to ensure data authenticity ... and improve statistics quality'.[9] In mid-2019, Ministry of Environment inspectors complained about a spate of such incidents which usually involved corrupt ministry officials seeking to distort or misreport pollution data.[10] Perhaps we will later see something similar happen with population data. If the state frequently admits to the existence of widespread distortion of official statistics in fields as varied as economics and the environment, it would not be surprising if ambitious family planning officials did the same.

Chinese demographers point out that there has also been bias and falsification in population data. Independent scholars have suggested that before the party's policy reversal, China's state family planning commission distorted its own statistics in order to give a misleading view of its success in birth control. One academic research team has comprehensively criticized official statisticians, saying,

> it was not rare for subjects in surveys to hide or cheat on the information they reported for various social motives. Neither was it rare to manipulate the post-survey data or statistical analyses... Unfortunately, the demographic statistics and forecasting in China have long been misled, with unfounded statistics in birth, death, urbanization and population aging... Together with the problematic method used, the quality of population forecast was thus compromised... The huge deviation in the population projections for only a few years did not arise from a faulty

9   http://www.xinhuanet.com/english/2019-01/10/c_137734144.htm
10   https://www.scmp.com/news/china/politics/article/3010679/chinas-green-efforts-hit-fake-data-and-corruption-among-grass

method used in the projections, but from the baseline population and demographic parameters that deviated greatly from the reality.[11]

In fact Yi Fuxian, who is an indefatigable analyst of official population data, is critical of reported statistics on items such as annual birth levels and population totals up to at least 2020.

In summary, much of the data on the ground in China is false. The demographic community is divided on many issues. The UN is the most widely cited authority and yet is frequently criticized. This does not mean that we should not attempt to forecast, but we need to go into the process aware of the obstacles.

Making Forecasts

Any forecasts of future developments are naturally fraught with risk. Fortunately, there are certain facts we know about demography and there is a field of learned specialists, even if they hold diverse views. This makes demographic forecasting somewhat less uncertain than economic forecasting.

It is my intention here to review available - and contrasting - literature, use reasonably widely accepted guidelines, construct some simple tables and suggest some conclusions about the direction of China's demographic development. It will need repeating in this section that we cannot aim for mathematically precise truths but must rely on estimates broadly illustrative of what is likely. There are several estimates of population at different dates. We might like to have had more but nothing known has been suppressed. The future picture is reasonably clear. What I am providing in this narrative is what we might rather grandly call a meta-analysis in different areas of population change.

Demographers sometimes give their estimates without the calculations and sometimes the calculations without the estimates. It is possible to take the consensual base data for the period and apply the suggested calculations to reach a series of estimates. We know that they cannot all be correct and possibly none of them will be. However, they are produced by recognized authorities in the field using methods which appear accepted and logical. Some

---

11   Guo Zhigang, Wang Feng and Cai Yong, *China's Low Birth Rate and the Development of Population*, Routledge, 2018, pp. 160-61 and p. 184.

emphasize certain factors over others. No attempt has been made to reproduce their calculations. The models are each taken to be accurate, merely using different assumptions.

Critical Factors for Making Estimates

Certain data are needed to construct estimates, including estimates of the recent past situation (not always easy), assumptions about sex ratios at birth and assumptions about TFRs. There is controversy surrounding all of these areas. This shows why making demographic projections cannot be an exact science. One generally accepted critical factor is that demographic trends change only very slowly. For the purposes of this discussion, TFR is one of the most important of these. Therefore - ironically - it is probably more important to decide what it has been than to calculate what it will be. This seeming paradox can be explained by the fact that there is considerable dispute about what it has been and wide acceptance that it will not change much in the short to medium term.

When it comes to the forecasting, one research team gives the example that - all other things being equal - if TFR is maintained at 1.8 then a population would halve every 117 years. Similarly, if it maintains at 1.5, then a population would halve every 54 years. A particularly striking point here is how a difference in TFR of 0.3 can make such a massive difference.[12]

There are disagreements among academics regarding the immediate past data - whether recent fertility rates, sex ratios at birth or even the total population. Without clarity on the starting points, we must recognize that we are on shaky ground when constructing models to project the future.

Sex ratios at birth are an important element for forecasting future population. Since the early 1980s China has had an abnormally high male surplus of babies at birth. Research in 2002 indicated that the difference between persisting in the abnormality rather than not having had it at all would lead to a total population by 2100 that would be 14 per cent lower. That was before 2004 when Chinese data showed an increase in the distortion to a rate of births of six boys for every five girls.

---

12   *Ibid*, pp. 201-2

For our purposes here, the most important effect of such an unbalanced birth pattern in the recent past is that there are increasingly fewer fertile women in a given population for the purposes of calculating reproduction potential. This abnormality arose in 1982, increased, fell, but has persisted since then. After well over 30 years, forecasters accordingly need to form a broad view as to the future size and duration of this 'abnormality'.

Fertility rates are hotly disputed. This is not just the case between the Chinese government and independent academic research, but even between sources within the Chinese government, principally the NHFPC and the National Bureau of Statistics. As we have previously explained, in a worldwide context demographers tend to use 2.1 as the average number of children each woman should have in her lifetime if a country is to replace each generation with a successor of similar size. If the country is to grow its population, it needs the TFR to be higher than 2.1. If the TFR is below 2.1, the country will eventually experience a shrinking population. The reason a couple need to be replaced by 2.1 children is to allow for infant mortality.

This is the theory. However, the rate of infant mortality, and indeed child mortality, worldwide, fell by almost a half between 1970 and the early 2000s. Yet the magic 2.1 necessary replacement rate is regularly repeated.

On the other hand, as is so often the case, China is different. Two key factors affect China in this regard. First, as noted earlier, it produces an abnormal surplus of male babies. In recent years, the view has been advanced by several Chinese demographers that the high level of sex imbalance at birth in China requires the marginally higher rate of 2.2, or even 2.3 to create full replacement of the population. Needless to say, there is some disagreement about the level of gender distortion in China and so even the notion of a 2.2 replacement rate is not universally accepted.[13]

On top of the excess male surplus at birth, which is around 7 per cent, China has a further male surplus which arises from significant excess female infant and under-5 mortality. Most of the rest of the world has an overall male child mortality surplus. This suggests that it might require a TFR of 2.3-2.4 to replicate the parental generation's total population in the future.

---

13   https://www.un.org/en/development/desa/population/publications/pdf/
      mortality/SexDifferentialsChildhoodMortality.pdf

Slowly, educational levels are being seen as important to population forecasting on the assumption that more educated women tend to have fewer children. This is principally due to a greater inclination to use contraception but increasingly important because female education tends to delay marriage and thus childbearing. Higher levels of education also discourage female acceptance of patriarchal, or traditional-style, marriage relationships, so prevalent in Asia. Given that prevalence, it impedes marriage as a whole.

These brief notes illustrate some of the issues with which our brave demographers are required to wrestle. Fortunately - taking the approach I outline above - we can sit back, conscious that the experts are well-versed in the literature and will make their own decisions on these contentious questions and see what models and estimates they create. My role is simply to ensure as much as possible that all approaches are captured in the summaries here and no alternative perspectives are excluded.

What to Estimate?

There are several major issues to examine regarding China's future. We should ask where the size of the workforce will go. Will it decrease faster than jobs? We should be interested in the size of the elderly community as a proportion of the country, the size of the workforce and the accumulated future size of the male surplus. Most important of all is to form a view of the overall size of the total population in the decades to come. Each of these issues represents a serious social challenge. In this section we address the development of the total population. All else follows from that.

Total Population

The central government published a target in 2000 projecting that 'by the mid-21st century, the total population would reach its peak number of 1.6 billion to be followed by a gradual decrease'.[14] Now, the experts appear (with the sole exception of the ever-optimistic UN) to agree on certain facts. The population will continue rising for now, albeit very slightly. It will come to a peak between 2025 and 2030 and then it will decline in the subsequent decades. I have not encountered any recent forecast which disagrees with this narrative.

---

14   http://www.fmprc.gov.cn/ce/celt/eng/zt/zfbps/t125259.htm

Given this, there are probably two critical junctures in the future evolution of the total population.

There has been no shortage of forecasts of when China's total population will peak. I have identified well over 20 since 2005. Needless to say, there is much greater homogeneity of opinion about the timing and the size of the peak than there is about developments much further out. To put matters in perspective, China's population is estimated in 2017 to have been:

1.41bn	UN Population Division
1.38bn	US Census Bureau

We should first note that there are academic estimates of recent population which calculate it to be below 1.38 billion. This is principally based on arguments that the data are incorrect. Two sources, but not the only, are Yi Fuxian and Liang Zhongtang.

Table of Estimates of When and at What Level Population Will Peak

Peak Dates, Estimates in Billions, Year of Forecast, Source

Year	Number	Year	Source	
2040	1.5	2005	CPS, CFPA[15]	
2033	1.5	2007	PRC	https://www.demographic-research.org/volumes/vol25/26/25-26.pdf
2020-25	1.5	2007	IIASA	http://www.iiasa.ac.at/web/home/research/researchPrograms/WorldPopulation/Reaging/The-growing-divergence-in-population-trends-and-concerns.pdf
2025	1.38	2007	IIASA	https://core.ac.uk/download/pdf/6459392.pdf
2026	1.395-4	2009	USCB	http://www.census.gov/newsroom/releases/archives/international_population/cb09-191.html

15 http://www.asianews.it/news-en/One-child-policy-and-the-fear-of-zero-growth-2748.html

2030	1.443	2009	Chen, Liu	https://www.copsmodels.com/ftp/workpapr/g-191.pdf
2025-30	1,374+	2010	Lutz, Samir	http://rstb.royalsocietypublishing.org/content/365/1554/2779.figures-only
2026	1.395-1.4	2010	UN	https://www.demographic-research.org/volumes/vol25/26/25-26.pdf
2024-	1.4-	2010	Wang Feng	https://www.brookings.edu/articles/chinas-population-destiny-the-looming-crisis/
2040	1.47	2010	CPDRC	http://www.chinadaily.com.cn/china/2010-05/20/content_9870078.htm
2025	1.38-39?	2011	Jiang, Li	http://www.ncbi.nlm.nih.gov/pmc/articles/PMC3867633/#!po=59.0909
2026	1.358+	2011	Zhao, Chen	https://www.demographic-research.org/volumes/vol25/26/25-26.pdf
2030	1.453	2012	UN	http://esa.un.org/unpd/wpp/unpp/p2k0data.asp
2025	1.41	2015	CASS	http://news.xinhuanet.com/english/china/2015-10/07/c_134688757.htm
2022-30s	1.4	2015	UN	https://esa.un.org/unpd/wpp/publications/files/key_findings_wpp_2015.pdf
2029	1.45	2015	NHFPC	http://www.scmp.com/news/china/policies-politics/article/1877679/chinas-population-peak-2029-under-two-child-policy
2025		2016	Fujian PBS	http://www.globaltimes.cn/content/964569.shtml
2030	1.45	2016	NHFPC	http://europe.chinadaily.com.cn/china/2016-01/15/content_23110395.htm
2026	1.408	2017	USCB	www.census.gov/data-tools/demo/idb/informationGateway.php

2030	1.45	2017	NHFPC	http://www.scmp.com/news/china/policies-politics/article/2078071/china-will-never-suffer-labour-shortage-says-family
2028	1.41	2017	WB	http://datatopics.worldbank.org/health/
2026-34	1.441+	2017	UN	https://esa.un.org/unpd/wpp/Download/Probabilistic/Population/
2026	1.408	2018	USCB	https://www.census.gov/data-tools/demo/idb/region.php?N=%20Results%20&T=6&A=separate&RT=0&Y=2025,2026,2027,2028&R=-1&C=CH
2029	1.44	2019	CASS	https://www.bbc.com/news/world-asia-china-46772503
2031	1.464	2019	UN	https://population.un.org/wpp/DataQuery/ World Population Prospects 2019
2023	1.41	2020	CI, GD	https://www.globaldemographics.com/

For comparison we should note that the official NHFPC forecast for 2020 is 1.42 billion, although this is not the forecast for the peak.[16] The forecasts for peak population range from 1.35-1.5 billion and this is expected between 2023 and 2040. The development in official forecasts has been that 1.5 billion seems to have been recently dropped. There is one unchanged high forecast of 1.45 billion from the NHFPC and at the lower end several academic forecasts in the range of 1.35-1.39 billion. In between these lie the US Census Bureau, the World Bank and the UN with 1.4-1.45 billion.

It is worth mentioning that CASS added a rider to its forecast of 1.44 billion by 2029, by saying that if the TFR did not rise above 1.6, the population should peak in 2027 at a lower level.[17] Being an official research institute of the state, CASS may not be comfortable highlighting what might be seen as 'negative' forecasts.

---

16 http://china.org.cn/china/2017-02/20/content_40322126.htm
17 https://www.express.co.uk/news/world/1067686/china-news-economy-trade-population-decline

In 2015, the UN expected the peak to come between 2022 and the 2030s. By 2017 they had narrowed this down to 2026-34. The earliest projection now is from two East Asian consultancies - Global Demographics and Complete Intelligence - which estimate the peak arriving in 2023. Overall, the expected population peak, if we weight official and academic estimates, seems to be around 1.4 billion in the mid-2020s. Certainly the estimates are now not very far apart. A reasonable summary might be that China's population is likely to peak at about 1.4 billion in around or before 2025. It will then start a process of decline.

Size of Total Population by 2100

Until recently, there were only a few estimates of population out to 2100. However, gradually more have emerged. I have identified below ten forecasts from public and private sources, inside China and overseas, which have been produced in the ten years 2007-17.

Table of Estimates and Implied Estimates for Total 2100 Population in Millions

Best Guess	Estimate	Date	Source	
1,021	1,021	2017	UN	Official Estimates
1,100+	1,100+	2017	NHFPC	
850	850	2007	IIASA	Academic Estimates
690	633-750	Late 2007	IIASA	
595	525-700	2008	Ebenstein, Jennings	
637	637	2010	Wang Feng	
670	638-703	2011	Jiang, Li, Feldman	
595	700by2080	2016	Yi Fuxian	
471	471	2016	Huang+Liang	
383	198-472	2016	Yu Ning	
577	average of latest 7 academic forecasts			

The estimates to 2100 fall into two clearly different groups. Two are official forecasts: from the United Nations Population Division and China's National Health and Family Planning Commission (NHFPC). The other eight are derived from non-official academic sources inside China and overseas. We should take the later of the two IIASA forecasts. There is a very clear distinction between the estimates of the two groups. The non-official academics' views reflect to varying extents the analysis summarized here by Gu Baochang and Cai Yong, the Chinese academics who were able to state for the UNPD in 2011 that 'China's population's growth potential has reversed itself from doubling every 30 years to halving itself every 30 years'.[18]

The International Institute for Applied Systems Analysis (IIASA) is an international research organization located in Austria. It conducts frequent research on population subjects. Avraham Ebenstein is an academic who has written for the World Bank. Dr Yi Fuxian is a demographer based at the University of Wisconsin-Madison who regularly speaks in China on national population issues.

Huang Wenzheng is a demographer who was an assistant professor at Harvard and is now associated with the Center for China and Globalization (CCG), an independent think tank in Beijing collaborating with Liang Jianzhang, a professor at Peking University. The work by Jiang, Li and Feldman was a collaboration between two demographers from Xian Jiaotong University in Xian, China, and Marcus Feldman from Stanford. Yu Ning is a demographer contributing to the Shanghai Academy of Social Sciences. Wang Feng was at the Brookings Institution in Washington before becoming professor at Fudan University in Shanghai and at University of California, Irvine.

I should first say that few of the non-official sources mentioned above have been particularly focused on giving an estimate of the population in 2100. Therefore, the estimates derived are frequently drawn from the context the researchers have given and which I have reproduced below. Nonetheless the context can be quite eloquent for the purpose. I have applied broadly accepted starting data and - where necessary - to the best of my ability applied their models or arithmetic to calculate an end estimate. Given the weight necessarily placed on these sources, I discuss the origins individually below and cite and quote what seem to be the relevant available texts:

---

18   http://citeseerx.ist.psu.edu/viewdoc/download;jsessionid=B5B133A3EE B36A72191337FC9FC1663C?doi=10.1.1.640.964&rep=rep1&type=pdf

The United Nations Population Division

This is both the principal data source for most writing about international demography and yet - among many demographers – is a controversial provider. Its work is regular, updated every two years, and comprehensive. There is, however, a feeling by some that the assumptions are sometimes flawed by an excessively positive view about the direction of TFRs and a tendency occasionally to allow its judgement to be swayed by strong governments. The figures in the table come from the 2017 Revisions.[19] The forecast given here is a clear and deliberate part of a global exercise. However, there are later figures in the 2019 Revisions.[20] These show an estimate of 684 million, based on low fertility figures remaining the same.

The National Health and Family Planning Commission

This Chinese state organization acts as policy arm, executor and statistician. This by-no-means-unusual situation in China creates a conflict of interest in measuring the results of policy actions. Combined with the well-known issues surrounding statistics in China, any data need to be treated with caution. We should note, for example, the quite different data given by the NHFPC and China's National Bureau of Statistics (NBS) for births and TFR over several years.

In this case Wang Peian, Vice-Minister of the National Health and Family Planning Commission, is quoted in March 2017 'speaking at a briefing on the sidelines of the National People's Congress on Saturday' as saying that the population would be 'more than 1.1 billion by the end of the century'.[21] As government policy has changed from 2013 to promote more births and NHFPC is responsible for execution, they will be very aware of the academic discussion about the poor performance of the policy in the last four years. We should not expect the NHFPC to make totally disinterested estimates.

---

19 https://esa.un.org/unpd/wpp/Publications/Files/WPP2017_KeyFindings. pdf
20 These can be found here: https://population.un.org/wpp/Download/ Standard/Population/
21 http://www.scmp.com/news/china/policies-politics/article/2078071/china-will-never-suffer-labour-shortage-says-family

IIASA

IIASA tends to write frequently and incisively, but often generically, about population issues. Their experts may say that - and explain at length why - China's TFR will stay lower for longer than the conventional view, but seldom provide end estimates. Only in rare instances can a country population estimate be glimpsed. It is interesting to trace the evolution of their thinking. In 2002 they wrote research on *The End of Population Growth in Asia*.[22]

Despite the title, the implied projections for China (given that the chart provided an aggregate of China and some smaller neighbours) showed a modest parabola from a base of about 1.4 billion in 2000 rising to around 2035 and declining to about 1.3 billion by 2100. By 2007 they were projecting 850 million in 2100.[23] This was interesting for suggesting a possible area for 2100 population for China alone but also being one of the earlier demographic sources to suggest a marked fall. Their Winter 2007 piece by Lutz, Sanderson and Scherbov on world population projections moved the thinking further forward.[24]

Clearly the expression was somewhat lacking in precision: 'The new outlook for China shows more rapid population aging and shrinkage than just a few years ago, again under the same long-term assumptions, after an initial increase China's population is likely to be back down to its 2000 level during the 2040s and then, by the end of the century, possibly almost down to half the 2000 level.'

There are several estimates for the population in 2000:

1,268m	US Census Bureau[25];
1,267m	National Bureau of Statistics (China)[26];
1,263m	World Bank.[27]

---

22 https://www.researchgate.net/profile/Warren_Sanderson/
    publication/225698057_The_end_of_population_growth_in_Asia/
    links/5893b1be92851c545748ceb1/The-end-of-population-growth-in-Asia.pdf
23 https://core.ac.uk/download/pdf/6459392.pdf
24 http://www.iiasa.ac.at/web/home/research/researchPrograms/
    WorldPopulation/Reaging/The-growing-divergence-in-population-trends-
    and-concerns.pdf
25 https://www.census.gov/data-tools/demo/idb/region.php?N=%20
    Results%20&T=6&A=separate&RT=0&Y=2000&R=-1&C=CH
26 http://www.stats.gov.cn/tjsj/ndsj/2016/indexeh.htm
27 https://data.worldbank.org/indicator/SP.POP.TOTL?locations=CN

If we just select three fairly uncontroversial sources and average the result, it is 1,266 million. Thus in 2007, IIASA was estimating that the 2100 China population would be 'possibly almost down to' 633 million. Not wishing to ignore their previous research, shall we call that 633-750 million, with an average of 690 million?

Ebenstein and Jennings

This paper discusses the issues of excess males, prostitution and sexual disease and the resultant policy options. In the course of the exercise, population projections were made based on three variants. Figure 4 in the paper shows the results. Although published in 2008, it starts with a surprisingly high base of around 1,350 million in 2000. The first scenario 'assumes that the TFR remains stable at 1.45 for the duration of the century, which leads to a massive population decline'. This appears to suggest an estimate of 500-550 million. The second scenario 'assumes a phased-in increase in the TFR, reaching the replacement rate of 2.1 in 2030'. This leads to a population estimate of 700 million. The third scenario 'assumes that the One Child Policy is immediately abandoned and the TFR increases to the replacement rate in 2010'. No estimates are given in the text. We are required to calculate them by reading the chart in the Figure. This leads to a population of 900-950 million in 2100.[28]

Clearly the third scenario did not happen, although the One-Child Policy has been substantially relaxed, and the TFR appears little changed over a decade later. The second scenario appears endangered as half of the period to 2030 allocated to the 'phased-in increase in the TFR' has elapsed with little evident change. The first scenario is based on a constant TFR of 1.45. In the decade since this research was published, the average TFR has probably been well below this figure and forecasts suggest that it is unlikely to average above it for a long time. On this basis, the best estimate from the Ebenstein model is between variants one and two and weighted towards variant one, in other words about 595 million. Any lack of improvement in the coming years would point to a downgrade.

---

28   http://citeseerx.ist.psu.edu/viewdoc/
      download?doi=10.1.1.452.408&rep=rep1&type=pdf

Wang Feng

While at the Brookings Institution in 2010 Wang wrote a paper that stated that 'China's current TFR of 1.5 implies that, in the long run, each future generation will be 25 percent smaller than the one preceding it'.[29] The USCB estimates that the total population in 2018 was 1,385 million. If we assume that a generation is 30 years, then 2100 represents the elapse of 2.73 generations since 2018. That would bring the population to 637 million. This is based on the TFR running at 1.5 throughout the period. Above it is noted that 'the average TFR has probably been well below this figure and forecasts suggest that it is unlikely to rise above it for a long time'. Therefore, it hardly seems feasible to average 1.5 for a very long time.

Jiang, Li and Feldman

Their 2011 paper focuses on the variables of whether sex ratio at birth can normalize and whether female infant mortality can reduce to the male level.[30] There are four scenarios for total population in 2100 based on variations in these two variables. What is particularly striking is that the four variations they have chosen all produce markedly similar results in 90 years. The difference between highest and lowest are 703 and 639 million - only 10 per cent. This is well reflected in Figure 3. All four results are: 639, 650, 680 and 703 million. Whether we split the difference between high and low or average the four makes little difference. The result is a population of 670 million by 2100.

Yi Fuxian

In 2016 Dr Yi returned to China from America to address a government-sponsored forum. He had been away for 17 years having fled after helping his sister-in-law escape a forced abortion at seven months. His cousin's wife also had her pregnancy terminated just a week before delivery. In his speech to the Boao Forum for Asia, which promotes economic development in the region, he said China could never overtake America economically because of its falling

---

29 http://www.brookings.edu/research/articles/2010/09/china-population-wang

30 https://www.ncbi.nlm.nih.gov/pmc/articles/PMC3867633/#!po=59.0909

population. 'People say we can be two to three times the size of America's economy,' Dr Yi said. 'I say it's totally impossible. It will never overtake America's, because of the decrease in the labor force and the aging of the population.' He added that 'by 2060 there will be one billion Chinese. By 2080 there will be 700 million.'[31] His forecast to 2080 represents a fall of 49 per cent in 65 years. If pro-rated to 2100, it would bring the population to 595 million.

Huang and Liang

In a 2016 commentary in *Caixin* magazine, Huang and Liang refer to the National Bureau of Statistics and Yang Wenzhuang of the NHFPC and conclude: 'If China's TFR stays at an optimistic 2015 reading of 1.4 (roughly halfway between the NBS's 1.05 figure and Yang's estimate of a 1.6 TFR), the country would still see 36.4% fewer people being born in each successive generation. The total population would shrink by 50% every 50 years. Even if Yang's calculations do prove to be accurate, a constant 1.6 TFR would still result in a 40% population decrease every 50 years.' 'More importantly,' they added, 'even if China's government simply allows people to have as many children as they want, the TFR could still fail to return to the replacement fertility rate. Put simply, for various reasons Chinese people today just don't want to have more children.'[32]

If we take the USCB estimate of 1,385 billion for the 2018 population as the starting point, a reduction of 50 per cent every 50 years over 82 years would be a fall of the population to 471 million. A reduction of 40 per cent every 50 years over 82 years would bring the population to 615 million. Huang and Liang clearly favour the first calculation, that of 471 million.

Yu Ning

Yu Ning wrote a study for the Shanghai Academy of Social Sciences in the *Journal of SASS Studies* in 2016 where he outlined how he calculated the evolution of the population.[33] He provides three scenarios:

---

31 https://www.nytimes.com/2016/03/24/world/asia/china-yi-fuxian-boao-family-planning.html?_r=0
32 http://archive.fo/yXyEM
33 http://english.sass.org.cn:8001/u/cms/www/201610/081007066foa.pdf (check ref)

If the average childbearing age is 30 and the total fertility rate is 1.3, the future population will decrease at 1.5% per year, and total population size will decrease by 50% within the next 45 years. If total fertility rate remains at 1.5, the future population growth rate will rise to 1.1%, which means that total population size will decrease by 50% within the next 65 years. If fertility rate drops to 1.0, the annual growth rate of stable population will reach 2.4%, and the total population size will decrease by 50% within the next 30 years.

Again, taking the USCB estimate of 1.367 billion in 2015 and using these three variants we find: a TFR of 1.3 leads to a 50 per cent fall in 45 years and if pro rata would be 383 million by 2100. A TFR of 1.5 leads to a 50 per cent fall in 65 years and if pro rata would be 472 million by 2100. A TFR of 1.0 leads to a 50 per cent fall in 30 years and if pro rata would be 198 million by 2100. This analysis shows such steep falls that it seems prudent to choose the middle variant of a 1.3 TFR which produces a slightly above average result for the three scenarios of 382 million.

Given the controversy over the UN and NHFPC estimates, it is unfortunate that the US Census Bureau has not yet advanced its estimates for foreign populations to 2100.

Statement of Belief

I would like to state clearly that I have undertaken no demographic research and make no claim to being a demographer. I have brought to the forefront the work of others. I should say that from my research in this field in recent years, it is possible that there are individual forecasts which I have overlooked but it is difficult to believe that there is an entire school of markedly different views which I have missed out. No forecast has been excluded by design. There are many other estimates available which are not original work but simply derivative of the UN data. Everything which resembles an original estimate or can be without deformation worked into an estimate has been used. It is striking how similar is most of the academic work.

This means that the figures in the estimates are often my own calculations but are simply deduced from and based on the arithmetic models published by the researchers concerned. Any mistakes should of course be presumed to be my own rather than the fault of the original researchers.

Summary

If we take the view that the projections from the Health and Family Planning Commission and the UN lack credibility through repeatedly being wrong and using criteria which appear flawed, then we should recognize the independent academic researchers as being more likely to be correct. This might be particularly so as their results - although reached by different methods - are surprisingly close. Yu Ning is an exception here, but we should accept that he is using quite low TFRs as examples which may not be wrong, but which will produce lower results.

Where scenarios are employed in reaching forecasts, the variants are generally based on different TFR assumptions. In one case the assumptions are largely based on sex ratios at birth. I would not distinguish between the different academic results but accept that they all come from credible sources. An effective approach is simply averaging all seven (the last IIASA projection and the six subsequent ones). This produces an average estimate of 577 million population in 2100. This suggests there would be a fall of about 60 per cent in China's population from an estimated peak of 1.4 billion.

6

LABOUR LOSSES AND ECONOMIC PROSPECTS

One of the side effects of a shrinking population is a falling workforce. The timetables for the two are different but both will rock China. Weakening economic growth is under threat from a number of directions, as evidenced by China's Dual Circulation Policy, introduced post-COVID, to transition away from an export and investment-driven growth model and towards one more driven by domestic consumer spending.[1] This makes the falling workforce a significant trend. We might argue that the workforce reduction is an involuntary hit on the economy and that other adverse factors such as protectionism are voluntary. However, state policy could improve many of these trends.

The Past Workforce

After China began opening up to the world in 1979, its youthful, abundant, and growing population enabled it to compete effectively with traditional manufacturing countries. By welcoming foreign manufacturers into joint ventures and slowly permitting domestic entrepreneurs to develop private enterprise - often prudently under the disguise of collective or township enterprises - young people, mostly from the rural provinces, were increasingly drawn into the rapidly growing industrial economy. Huge numbers of working-

---

1   Chinese policymakers first used the 'dual circulation' term at a Politburo meeting in May 2020, but it was not until late July 2020 that the CCP journal *Qiushi* offered a more detailed explanation. It stated that the main idea of 'dual circulation' is to strengthen China's vast domestic market ('internal circulation'), while shifting its foreign trade ('external circulation') to suit the needs of Chinese customers more closely, rather than those of overseas buyers, as is typical for an export-led growth model. For the Center for Strategic and International Studies take on the policy, see https://www.csis.org/analysis/dual-circulation-and-chinas-new-hedged-integration-strategy

age youth living in rural farming regions were under-employed and willing to move to the cities for work. The chance of full-time employment and higher wages, albeit far from home, appealed to generations of rural young from the 1970s onwards.

From the 1980s, there was an irruption of agricultural labourers migrating to the urban areas of their own provinces and to the big cities. At one stage there were 278 million such migrants, or a third of the nation's workforce. They tended to stay for an average of eight years and 80 per cent came without their families. In the latter years, salaries rose fast. A maid in Beijing would have seen her wages quadruple in the five years 2009-2014. Beijing grew 87 per cent in population between 1990 and 2011 to over 20 million; migrants made up 80 per cent of the increase. This was described as the largest internal migration in world history. But, as has been observed, 12.30 in China is the world's largest lunchtime.

This mass movement from the countryside to the cities obscured a growing crisis as, nationwide, births peaked in the mid-1960s at 27.1 million a year and have declined ever since. In the decade from 2009-2018 they averaged below 16.5 million, a decline of 40 per cent. With this background, it has been obvious for many years that the country's workforce will cease growing and begin to decline. The years of surplus labour supply would end and eventually be replaced by labour shortages.

This labour decline began to be reflected in industrial areas such as the Pearl River Delta, where after 12 years of zero wage growth from the 1980s to 1990s, demand outstripped supply and wages began to rise. Provincial governments have consistently pushed up minimum wages, but market forces were already pushing in that direction. For example, from 2005-2013 wages in Japan, Germany and the US rose by under 3 per cent annually compared to over 15 per cent in China. Manufacturers complained of rising costs, particularly labour, and many either moved from China to other locations or decamped further into the interior in search of cheaper labour and land, despite potentially longer and costlier supply lines.

The Future Workforce

Eventually in 2013 the National Bureau of Statistics declared that the working age population had finally declined in the previous year. While, as always accepting the weakness of domestic statistics

- and noting a change in the statistical base from 15-59-year-olds originally to 16-59-year-olds later - from 2011 until 2015 the working age population reduced by around 14 million. In 2017 the reduction increased to over 5 million in one year. Given the falling rate of births from the 1970s onwards, we are likely to see a continuing and steeper fall in entrants to the workforce.

We should also note recent sociological changes. The World Bank is not the only institution now questioning the static definition of the working-age population as people aged from 15 to 64. Many people now work on well after 64. At the same time, the government is trying to drive university and college enrolment up to 50 per cent of the post-school age group, despite the lack of success in providing jobs for graduates.

The number of migrant labourers across the country has also begun to fall and was estimated by the end of 2015 to be 247 million, a fall of maybe 30 million, or over 10 per cent, from the peak. China's urban residency rules have been strict, sharply dividing the population between those described as urban and those deemed to be rural. This has excluded many domestic migrants in the cities from the benefits of social services and education. As a result, families have often been split, reducing the birthrate, or couples have left their (single) child behind, creating mental stress and a disturbingly high number of rural child suicides.[2]

Another feature to note is Chinese women's steady exit from employment. Historically, China has had high rates of female labour participation. In 1990, it stood at 73 per cent but by 2020 it had fallen to just 60 per cent.[3] Despite this, 70 per cent of all mothers work.[4] Compare this to the situation in the UK where the percentage of mothers working between 1996 and 2019 rose from 62 to 75 per cent.[5] This seems to suggest that in China women without children choose not to work. However, the global norm is that when women have fewer children they work more.[6] In China - paradoxically - women are having fewer children and working less. Maybe more arresting is the fact that four-fifths of all female self-

2   See https://www.scmp.com/news/china/society/article/2145372/child-
       suicide-covered-china-says-think-tank-it-calls-authorities (Paywall)
3   https://data.worldbank.org/indicator/SL.TLF.CACT.FE.ZS
4   http://time.com/5523805/china-aging-population-working-age/
5   https://www.ft.com/content/360de9aa-f650-11e9-9ef3-eca8fc8f2d65
6   https://ourworldindata.org/female-labour-force-participation-key-facts

made billionaires in the world are Chinese.[7]

Hence, the pool of work-aged adults, as traditionally defined, is shrinking and within that pool women are falling out and young people are seeing a growing number of college places offered to a diminishing number of schoolchildren.

Accepting the inconsistencies and inaccuracies of the data, it is reasonable to estimate that between 2011 and 2018 more than 26 million Chinese working-aged people have been taken out of the world workforce, or roughly the equivalent of half of Germany's working population. And this trend still has a long way to go.[8]

The Ministry of Human Resources has predicted that from 2011 to 2030 China would lose labour at an average rate of 5.4 million a year, leading to a cumulative loss of around 100 million potential workers. After that there would be a steeper fall averaging 7.6 million a year.[9] Faced with this phenomenon, China has some tough issues to confront. The fall in births has been exacerbated by the fall in the number of migrant workers, which reached a peak in 2014, and the exit of female labour. Workers are still moving within their home provinces but are increasingly reluctant to live and work far away. This introduces an unwelcome new rigidity into the hitherto relatively flexible national labour market. We have already been made aware of the widespread reluctance of graduates to seek jobs nationwide. The localization of migrant labour movement, the provincialism of graduate work horizons and the collapse in new labour supply could make the labour market arthritic. Each of these trends undermines efficiency.

The Educated Young

When weighing the effect of a declining birthrate on the size and competitiveness of the workforce, we should also see the impact on education. There has been a rolling impact beginning among the primary schools. Primary-school enrolment declined by 30 per cent from 1995 to 2017. The number of schools fell from 950,000 in 1978 to 160,000 in 2019, a fall of over 80 per cent.

---

7   http://time.com/5523805/china-aging-population-working-age/
8   https://www.caixinglobal.com/2019-01-29/chart-of-the-day-chinas-
     shrinking-workforce-101375782.html
9   http://www.chinadaily.com.cn/business/chinadata/2016-07/22/
     content_26187716.htm

Junior secondary school pupils peaked at 23 million in 2000 and by 2017 were down by 33 per cent. Indeed, some new schools were closed within two years of opening.[10] This was partly a result of migration to the cities or the uneconomic situation of very small schools. However, the trend is not surprising when we consider that there were 322 million children aged 0-14 in 2000, but by 2017 this figure had dropped to an estimated 237 million, a fall of over 26 per cent in just 17 years.

Two other factors are relevant. First, with migrant worker parents moving to the cities, children have often either followed even if they cannot get school places, or they have stayed at home and dropped out of school. Second, there has been an increasing interest among middle-class parents in taking children out of state schools and sending them to foreign or private schools in China or overseas - although access to foreign schools in China is now subject to tighter state restrictions.

Universities are somewhat different. They face challenges similar to those confronting other countries, with the addition of what might be described as Chinese characteristics. Tertiary education has been encouraged; from 2000 to 2013 a new university was built on average every 78 hours. Applications peaked in 2008, then fell, have never recovered since then and are currently (2020) over 10 per cent down. Against a background of falling population, greater interest in overseas education and rising numbers of domestic universities, colleges are competing for a reducing quality of student.

It is estimated that the number of college-age young fell by at least 20 per cent between 2010 and 2020. The authorities want to increase university participation to 50 per cent of all young people. In 2017 it had already reached 42 per cent. (The World Bank thinks by then it had already reached 51 per cent from 5 per cent in 1997.) This suggests that perhaps 40 per cent of those going to college in 2020 would not have been accepted in 2010.

The acceptance rate of those sitting the university entrance exam in 2006 was 56 per cent but by 2013 had reached 76 per cent and in 2017 it was 81 per cent. The ratio between candidates for the university entrance exam - the *gaokao* - in a given year and those

---

10   Guo Zhigang, Wang Feng and Cai Yong, *China's Low Birth Rate and the Development of Population*, Routledge, 2018, p. 3.

who graduated from undergraduate courses four years later seems to have gone from 65 per cent for *gaokao* applicants in 2009 to 80 per cent in 2012. The indications are that the rate has continued to rise. This suggests that almost everyone who applies to university gets into one and graduates from it. This may explain why the fall in the number of applicants for university has been less severe than the fall in the birth rate. At some point the falling population will mean that the target for university participation will either have to be further increased to three-quarters of the young or else those gleaming new colleges will follow the primary schools and gradually close down.

These points probably contribute to the sceptical attitude of Chinese employers to students, the low graduate salaries and the high levels of graduate unemployment. In 2018, over a quarter of graduates failed to secure employment within six months of graduation.[11] And when we look at this percentage, we should also bear in mind the widespread use of fictitious research contracts from universities to bolster the jobs on offer after graduation.

It is ironic that there can be severe graduate unemployment at a time when the labour supply is reducing. It is also politically important now that up to two-thirds of all workers joining the labour force are likely to be university graduates.[12] However, without radical reform of education, the dire graduate unemployment numbers will inevitably rise further. This will provide a less numerous and less competent boost to the economy than hoped.

Is China a Market Economy?

There has been plenty of debate over whether China is a fair and open market for domestic and foreign companies, state and private. In other words: is it a market economy? This is not only an issue for governments and trade bodies but also for the foreign firms in China which are continually reassessing their analysis.

Many have noted that despite promises by Premier Li Keqiang in 2013 to cut or decentralize control over 1,700 approval and certification procedures within five years, little happened.[13]

---

11   https://www.economist.com/china/2019/08/01/the-growing-ranks-of-unemployed-graduates-worry-chinas-government
12   *Ibid.*
13   https://www.ft.com/content/c1bf8224-6edb-11e6-a0c9-1365ce54b926

The much-heralded withdrawal of state enterprises from 'non-strategic' areas seems to have been replaced by a consolidation and strengthening of state enterprises to be more profitable and dominant and to place them firmly under party control.

In 2016, the European Union Chamber of Commerce in China stated, rather simplistically, that any agreement to confer market economy status on China would require ending the overcapacity, or 'dumping', of steel. In 2017 the same body also commented that China's attempts to create advanced technology were not based on releasing market forces but on government efforts to steer development and pick the winners. The EU Chamber also asserted that 'foreign carmakers with electric models were being pressed to turn over their battery technology to Chinese partners in exchange for being able to produce and sell in China'.[14]

Perhaps the EU chamber should also note India's wish to buy jet fighters from companies willing to manufacture there. However, the strategy in China seems more comprehensive. The EU chamber said it was particularly concerned that China's national manufacturing plan 'specified precise targets for market share, both domestic and foreign'. The same year, the EU chamber said its 'companies are increasingly pessimistic and perceive China's reform progress to have stalled'. It called on Beijing to cease delaying and honour promises over many years to create a level playing field.[15]

In a well-received speech to the World Economic Forum in Davos in January 2017 President Xi exhorted the audience to 'remain committed to developing global free trade and investment, promote trade and investment liberalization and facilitation through opening-up and say no to protectionism'. He vigorously championed reform, opening up and free trade, adding that China had introduced more than 1,200 reform measures over the previous four years. The very next day the US Chamber of Commerce in Beijing published its annual survey of members' opinions.[16] Those believing foreign companies were less welcome than before had risen from 77 per cent in the previous year to 81 per cent. Among

---

14 https://www.ft.com/content/a7215292-02e4-11e7-ace0-1ce02ef0def9
15 https://www.eurobiz.com.cn/still-keeping-faith-european-business-china-business-confidence-survey-2016/
16 https://media.bain.com/Images/China_Business_Climate_Survey_Report_2017.pdf

the five most important challenges facing foreign companies in China were 'inconsistent regulatory interpretation and unclear laws', 'increasing Chinese protectionism' and 'difficulty in acquiring required licenses'. Over 60 per cent of the chamber's members had 'little or no confidence that the government is committed to opening China's markets further in the next three years'.

In early March 2017 Industry Minister Miao Wei, speaking in defence of the 'Made in China 2025' white paper and in response to the European report, said, 'I want to reiterate once again, there is no discriminative policy against foreign firms.'[17] During a telephone call later the same month between President Xi and Germany's Chancellor Angela Merkel, both leaders vowed to 'support free trade and open markets'. That was on the Thursday. On the Sunday, the same Miao Wei said that 'restricting market access is important for domestic growth... In some areas, we determine that a certain percentage of the market share must be controlled by domestic players.'[18]

In 2019, one-fifth of European and British companies in China admitted they had been victims of forced technology transfer - double the proportion of the previous year. Little seems to be changing.[19] For several years, both the US and the EU have been stuck in unrewarding discussions surrounding potential investment agreements, but both are concerned about Beijing's demands to continue blocking many industries. US trade initiatives have been aimed at encouraging a more open marketplace in China.

Rising labour costs are a severe pressure, leading to China's desire to upgrade its manufacturing quality and increase innovation. Unlike Singapore in the 1980s, this is not a clearly thought-out Beijing strategy to move industry up-market. It is more a reaction to rising wages and the keenness of provincial governments to raise social charges to quell worker dissatisfaction and avoid riots.

Professor Christopher Balding has said that not only are China's average tariffs higher than those in the US or even Europe

17 https://www.scmp.com/news/china/economy/article/2078056/beijing-industry-minister-says-no-discrimination-against-foreign

18 https://www.reuters.com/article/us-china-forum-miit/head-of-chinas-industry-ministry-says-country-right-to-limit-market-access-idUSKBN16Q05O

19 https://www.scmp.com/news/china/diplomacy/article/3010914/china-needs-change-european-firms-say-many-doubt-it-will

but 'China is nothing if not creative in protecting its local industries. Although it has liberalized its economy in recent years, it has also erected a sophisticated set of barriers to safeguard companies it views as national champions.'[20] In 2018 Professor Balding's contract at Peking University's HSBC School of Business in Shenzhen, where he had taught for nine years, was not renewed.[21]

The combination of tariffs, non-tariff barriers and subsidies is pervasive and effective in hurting both foreign companies and the Chinese domestic consumer. Beijing officials appear to be muddled about whether to reform and pursue free trade, although there is little clarity on what free trade is. Foreign companies in 2017 employed 6 per cent of the workforce but paid 20 per cent of tax revenues. They are very important to China's economy. Those companies which have to operate in China are very clear about the barriers to business.

Rising wages are a major contributor to the deteriorating competitiveness of substantial areas of the Chinese economy and are a factor in foreign companies deciding to switch manufacturing to cheaper countries. In this sense the link between demographic challenge and lack of open markets is direct. They jointly prejudice China's future GDP growth. Labour availability or serious reform are probably the minimum expectations for foreign firms.

Offshoring of Manufacturing

Labour costs are especially important but not the dominating factor in China's commercial competitiveness. Even so, the impact of a decreasing (thus more expensive) workforce and other rising costs has resulted in foreign manufacturers in China 'reshoring' or 'offshoring', that is the tendency to move manufacturing to cheaper regions. Even before President Trump assumed power in 2017, Boston Consulting said in a 2014 survey that 54 per cent of over US$1 billion revenue companies were considering reshoring from China to the US. Many of these companies have become increasingly concerned about the hostile business environment, typified by intellectual property theft, unsympathetic courts, attempts to introduce Communist Party branches and the well-known attempts to capture private commercial data in government servers.

---

20   http://www.koreaherald.com/view.php?ud=20170326000017&kr=1
21   https://www.newsweek.com/us-professor-fired-chinese-university-1030284

The US government's position on import origin and fair trade fits in very closely with a widespread reassessment by American - and other - companies of the cost/benefit of manufacturing in China. This issue stems partly from the workforce contraction and will have an effect on global trade patterns, global consumer prices and the health of the Chinese economy. These trends will only be strengthened as a result of the Covid-19 pandemic, where shorter supply lines and increased emphasis on national solutions will speed up reshoring or near-shoring operations.[22]

Job Losses amid Labour Shortage Create a Conundrum

While the working-age population decreases, there is also a reduction in the number of jobs in many areas. The China Institute for Employment Research says that job offers in western Chinese cities from late 2017 to late 2018 fell by 77 per cent. In the east coast region the fall was 36 per cent. Furthermore, it is likely that small private-sector service companies' efforts to recruit fell below the radar screen of such a survey.[23] Employment in state companies, or SOEs, has been falling for a long time, both through low recruitment and lay-offs. In the most recent 20 years (1997-2017), it has fallen from 110 to 61 million, a reduction of almost a half.[24] In late 2018 into 2019, according to a survey using data from Baidu, the most searched terms on the Chinese internet were 'lay-offs' and 'job-seeking'.[25]

Small private companies create 90 per cent of new jobs but in a difficult economic environment they have been struggling to pay the heavy social costs of 19 per cent of employee wages towards pensions and 10 per cent towards health costs. Many are on the verge of bankruptcy, made worse by the Covid-19 crisis. On the other hand, the state cannot afford to pay the pensions of the growing number of retired people and is seeking bigger corporate contributions. Beijing is acutely aware that if it is too exigent towards small companies it will tip them over the edge, resulting in fewer new jobs or the loss of existing ones. The government will

---

22   https://link.springer.com/article/10.1007/s12063-020-00160-1
23   https://www.scmp.com/economy/china-economy/article/2185176/
      chongqing-battling-rising-unemployment-chinas-traditional
24   http://www.stats.gov.cn/english/statisticaldata/annualdata/
25   https://www.scmp.com/business/banking-finance/article/2186381/chinas-
      job-market-has-worsened-amid-trade-war-sharper

then have to support even more people. It has already told local authorities not to demand unpaid past contributions. This dilemma is disciplining the state into treading very softly.

There are several reasons for the unemployment crisis, including manufacturing companies failing in a weaker economy and foreign companies shifting manufacturing to other countries. Factory closures can result from margin pressure in a good export economy or slow demand in a weakening domestic economy. Planned reduction or termination of inefficient state enterprises is an occasional factor. In aggregate, we are looking at millions of job losses each year.

This fall in employment opportunity has been masked by increasing employment in the service sector. Thus, we are seeing rotation of job opportunities. Yet not all workers can make the change from manufacturing to service. Service sector jobs do not necessarily pay as well or carry the same benefits. They are often in the informal sector and thus do not offer many of the normal benefits. However, many young people accept the disadvantages over the grind of employment in factories. Thus labour shortages coexist with significant unemployment.

The Economic Impact

Despite optimistic imagery overseas, the Chinese economy has struggled with serious problems for many years, due to unresolved political conundrums. For example, there are effectively two, if not more, capital markets in China. State-linked businesses borrow more cheaply than private companies, which are often forced to rely on the much-maligned 'shadow banking market'. However, as the lenders to the shadow banking market have little protection or security, the lending rates are penal. This is a serious cost to the economy. Equity markets are accessible at the whim of officials and often not to private companies. This raises costs to the private sector and slows domestic investment. Furthermore, academics note that throughout history, private credit rates are higher where there is corruption or the risk of seizure. Traditionally, arm's length lending rates have been higher in China than in Western Europe.

Chinese agriculture is particularly inefficient largely because small farmers are not allowed to own their land and thus have no assets to pledge for bank borrowing for machinery or other capital requirements. This means farming tends to remain labour-intensive. The party's thinking revolves around the fear of financial default by millions of peasants through incompetent practices. This is probably more relevant than distaste for private land ownership.

Barriers to entry in many sectors of the economy keep private-sector competition at bay. In whole sectors of the economy this preserves inefficient state companies at the cost of efficient production. Similarly, the lack of openings for overseas companies and the failure to ensure a level-playing field prevents domestic companies from learning how to function in a competitive environment.

The rising demand for party branches in businesses and party officials in decision-making committees - as directed by the Party leadership - has introduced non-economic actors into decision-making, which will not benefit business practice or strategy. Subsidies and tax breaks may help domestic state companies to compete but not to be competitive. In the long run in a competitive world, these practices will harm domestic companies.

A critical weakness of the economy is that after 20 years of incessant reform up to 2000, the party has settled into reform inertia. Not much happened after 2000 and even that seems to have been snuffed out after 2012. Without reform the economy is hobbled. The factors which allowed China to continue to prosper after reform ended have quietly subsided. Domestic migrants are less mobile and accommodating. A higher-grade economy wants brighter workers rather than physical labourers, but the education system is failing to provide them. That 17 of China's wealthiest citizens in 2019 were in prison or under investigation does not encourage entrepreneurs.[26]

A less noted issue for the economy is that there is little clarity regarding its size or growth rate, either nationally or by province. By the time the raw data have survived a residual socialist accounting system, tampering by local officials to boost their promotion prospects and political adjustments from the central leadership, we have a set of figures which tells us little and pleases few. This helps neither business nor the central leadership to plan for the future.

---

26   https://www.hurun.net/EN/Article/Details?num=CE08472BB47D

Those few independent forecasts for China's economy from semi-official sources are mostly cautious, if not pessimistic. The *China 2030* report in 2010 looked forward 20 years and estimated 5 per cent growth by 2025-30. The National Institution for Finance and Development (NIFD) in 2019 predicted one year ahead that China's economic growth rate would slow to 5.8 per cent in 2020. Both were brave calls at the time. And, from the West, in 2019 JP Morgan estimated that China's GDP would fall to 4.5 per cent by 2030. Looking at these estimates, only the most optimistic can believe the Chinese economy will overtake that of the US - although the pandemic may have had an impact.

All of China's population challenges have an economic impact. Given the scale of demographic change facing the country, we need to consider what it means for the economy that since October 2020 has been ranked as the largest in the world.[27] A shrinking workforce endangers total economic output. An ageing society creates intense budgetary pressure, reducing the capability for productive investment, reducing the prospects for innovation and potentially making a society more closed-minded. It can create budgetary antagonism between age groups. Through the difficulty of finding a wife, gross gender disparity distorts the balance between saving and spending and the associated potential for rising crime generates nugatory public and private security spending. It also reduces the prospect for marriages and children. A contracting society makes a relatively less attractive target for foreign investment, a smaller market for domestic business, a smaller budget for research and development and public infrastructure, reduced capability to tackle education reform and - it is widely believed - a narrower base for innovation. It also harms the capacity for national debt repayment.

When faced with the long, steady collapse of births, the stasis among policymakers has been quite remarkable. However, it is habitual in China's one-party state, and more so under what seems to have become since 2015 a climate of caution. There is a tendency in Beijing to defer difficult decisions. The failure of a strategy as dramatic as the birth management policy in China is a very good example of why the party loathes admitting that it was wrong and changing course. Putting state pressure on the already collapsing

---

27   https://nationalinterest.org/feature/china-now-world%E2%80%99s-largest-economy-we-shouldn%E2%80%99t-be-shocked-170719

birthrate in 1979 was irresponsible. The perpetuation of a state-sponsored culture of small families will leave a dark psychological and cultural legacy. This has contributed to the country today suffering an unnecessary, unsatisfactory and lengthy period of low births.

All the factors which drove fast economic growth from 1978-2008 have recently been weakening. The country's economic prospects are becoming fragile for unrelated reasons. However, the demographic shocks will compound the risks. The country is unlikely to collapse, but it will be profoundly affected by these developments, both practically and psychologically. Indeed, if we consider the party's three great campaigns of the past 70 years - the Great Famine, the Cultural Revolution and the birth control campaigns - China has probably had more of a self-inflicted collective psychological battering than any other major country. China now believes that stimulus is more important than reform. Copying the mistakes of Japan and the Eurozone region is understandable for a developing state but it comes with consequences more painful than for the advanced economies. As China's economy is weakening, it is now also threatened by demographic headwinds and yet the authorities have no clear solution in mind.

Ageing: The Demographic Dividend Reverses

There has been considerable debate about how an ageing society plays out. Does an ageing population mean less growth, more spending, less saving, higher interest rates and lower asset values? Or do the old adjust and work beyond retirement age? A third option is that a falling population reduces corporate investment and leads to 'secular stagnation'.

There is sharp controversy about the effect of demography on the direction of interest rates. Charles Goodhart, a former member of the Bank of England's Monetary Policy Committee, who has researched this topic, argues that the last 40 years of global labour increase was directly linked to the eventually decreasing interest rates. Now, in an era of a declining global workforce, savings flows are likely to fall below investment flows and thus push up real interest rates.[28]

---

28   https://www.bis.org/publ/work656.pdf

Considering the future decreasing workforce, a research team led subsequently by Goodhart concluded that the swelling numbers of pensioners is inflationary. 'Both the young and the old are inflationary for the economy,' the team said. 'It is only the working age population that is deflationary.'[29] The looming shortage of workers is therefore inflationary as it will increase the cost of labour. 'That will raise the return on labour relative to capital. That will turn into a redistributive mechanism within society.' Longer life has a negative aspect in that people often live to a point at which they need help and need to spend more on care and health. This is, of course, inflationary. With current high actual lending rates to the private sector, China does not need substantial upward pressure from an ageing society.

China is ageing as a poorer country than, say, Western Europe or Japan, which means worker productivity is much lower. Even at these lower levels, China's productivity growth appears to be faltering. Professor Wang Feng at University of California Irvine has noted that aged societies are associated with slow growth economies, as in Japan or Western Europe. He projects that such demographic change on its own will cut half a point off China's growth rate. This will become more serious 'when the growth rate drops to 3 per cent'. It also implies that 'a greater portion of economic activity will be devoted to elderly care compared with productivity-enhancing investment'.[30]

As societies age, it affects how they think and act. Consider the comparison between Japan and the US. In 1950, their median ages were respectively 22 and 30. By 1967, Japan's median age advanced beyond that of the US and in 1992 the proportion of over 65s exceeded that of the US. The message is that this was reflected in relative economic performance. Japan initially outperformed, then faltered and later under-performed when compared to the US.

In 1980, the median age of the US was 30 and China 22. This is the same difference as between the US and Japan in 1950. China has well outperformed the US economically since 1980. China and the US both had a median age of 36.[31] Some estimates have China already older. The oldest country in the world is estimated

29   https://www.ft.com/content/df61dc42-99fa-11e6-8f9b-70e3cabccfae
30   https://www.ft.com/content/f34bb0b0-2f8b-11e9-8744-e7016697f225
31   *The CIA World Factbook 2017.*

to be Japan, with a median age of 48. By 2030 the US will be three years younger than China and in 2050 six years younger. There are projections of a 12-year gap in 2050, with China already then at a median age of 56. Increased longevity and improved healthcare will take some of the edge off China's relative deterioration, but it remains a stark fact.

The proportion of over-65s will change as well. To date, the US has had the higher proportion. The UN forecasts that China will become the more aged after 2035. There are other estimates that this will happen earlier. Even CASS, the Chinese research institute, expects China to overtake Japan by 2030 in proportion of elderly - and Japan has a much higher proportion of elderly than the US.

As China becomes a much more aged society, its economy is likely to be less vigorous. The most vocal commentator on this subject has been Yi Fuxian who proposes that a more aged China will have less economic vitality, less innovation and be more closed-minded.[32] Professor James Liang of Peking University also argues rather similarly that ageing will create 'a sort of degradation in the vitality of the human population'. He says that a 30-year-old is more productive than a 50-year-old in taking risk and starting a new business. In an ageing society vitality is diminished. In his view ageing, population size and geographical concentration have a direct effect on innovation. Hence a society which is ageing and contracting will likely be less innovative.[33]

The rising ratio of China's economy to that of the US could reflect Japan's trajectory. As China's median age overtakes that of the US and then its proportion of elderly, the Chinese economy will slow down. The 2030s could see US growth rates surpass Chinese rates. Yi Fuxian has - rather bravely - even put a year on this: 2033. Indeed, some forecasts suggest a closer date.[34]

Demographic trends indicate that in the twenty-first century the US will probably exemplify youth, vigour, agility and innovation. History indicates these are powerful weapons in an economic armoury. America may have spluttering population growth now,

---

32 https://www.scmp.com/comment/insight-opinion/asia/article/2180421/worse-japan-how-chinas-looming-demographic-crisis-will

33 James Liang, *The Demographics of Innovation: Why Demographics is a Key to the Innovation Race*, Wiley, 2018, p. xv.

34 https://www.msn.com/zh-hk/news/other/why-ageing-china-wont-overtake-the-us-economy-as-the-worlds-biggest-now-or-in-the-future/ar-BBVmiH7

but it is in a different league to Europe and East Asia. If the US in 2010 with a modest 13 per cent proportion of over-65s began paying out more to the elderly than it was taking in from current workers, then we should feel very worried for the societies facing ballooning elderly populations. In 2040 this figure will be over 25 per cent in China and over 35 per cent in Japan.

By February 2020, healthcare was by far the largest sector in the US, way above manufacturing or retail, with 16.5 million employees (against 15.7 million in retail and 12.9 million in manufacturing) and estimated by the Bureau of Labor Statistics to be the fastest growing employer.[35] Over a quarter of workers will be above 55 by 2025. One report suggested that America's ageing could lead to more demand for healthcare and 'declining productivity and electoral showdowns between a young, diverse workforce and an older, whiter retirement bloc'.[36] If this is the employment situation in the US, what will it be later for countries in continental Europe and Asia with greater ageing problems and of course reducing workforces?

Furthermore, it has been argued that it is no longer a nation's debt that indicates its creditworthiness but the proportion of elderly. In the past most of a country's debt was usually held by its older citizens. Now that is less likely to be true. Older citizens now have such a huge and competing call on the nation's budget - namely social security entitlements - that it has changed them from being the champions to potentially the enemies of the national credit. The old are unlikely to vote for pension reform and see their income reduced. However, they make up an increasing proportion of voters. It is also relevant here to say that even in countries with no formal voting systems, older citizens can make their feelings known.

Here, we might note the case of China. The trend of post-revolutionary communist leaders coming to power at ever younger ages (75 falling to 59) may well have run its course. The Chinese *nomenklatura* is likely to become replete with 50- and 60-year-old cadres. Their relatively distinct interests in an ageing society are likely to be very clear. They are unlikely to take the risk of choosing a 40-year-old leader.

---

35   https://fred.stlouisfed.org/series/CES6562000101
36   https://www.theatlantic.com/business/archive/2018/01/health-care-america-jobs/550079/

The argument over the financial and political risk of having a large elderly population was developed during the global financial crisis when tough questions were being asked. However, it is a valid point. While elderly welfare benefits grow as a proportion of the national budget, they are increasingly threatened by, or a threat to, other financial 'obligations' or options. Just as the elderly are becoming a substantial voting bloc, they are ceasing to have congruent interests with the bond markets. Fast ageing and a likely substantial associated rise in welfare burden can weaken economic growth, yet it can also have the effect of curbing military expenditure and thus the prospect of adventurist confrontations.

Falling Workforce

Research from the US Federal Reserve in 2016 proposed that its economic model was 'consistent with demographics having lowered real GDP growth 1¼ percentage points since 1980, primarily through lower growth in the labor supply; this decline is in line with changes in estimates of the trend of GDP growth over that period.'[37] This suggests that lower labour supply caused all the decline in GDP growth in the period between 1980 and 2016. If a lower new labour supply can wreak such impact on US economic growth, the sharp and continuing contraction of the Chinese workforce is likely to damage China's future GDP growth more.

In the falling workforce, the front line is young workers. In 2019 the UN said that the total China workforce in 2050 will still be higher than it was in 1990. However, the number of 20-24-year-olds available for work or study in 1990 was 130 million and in 2050 this number will have broadly halved to 70 million. According to the Brookings Institution in Washington, this will have 'profound consequences for labor productivity, since the youngest workers are the most recently educated and the most innovative'.[38] Given the UN tendency to optimism, the fall may be yet more severe. Possibly the worst aspect of this is the Brookings point about the impact on innovation. *The Economist* makes the same point but more broadly

---

37 https://www.federalreserve.gov/econresdata/feds/2016/files/2016080pap. pdf
38 http://www.brookings.edu/research/articles/2010/09/china-population-wang

that the steep fall in the number of young joining the workforce represents that 'segment of the population that is best educated, most technologically astute and most open to new ideas'.[39]

A shrinking workforce is likely to increase labour costs. It is widely believed in China that the tough birth control regulations accelerated the arrival of the crucial moment where an under-employed rural workforce is largely exhausted and can no longer swell the urban workforce. This is generally known as the 'Lewisian turning point' after St Lucia-born Sir William Arthur Lewis, the James Madison Professor of Political Economy at Princeton University, who noted the resulting rising wages. After 2000, his work attracted considerable attention in China. This was particularly true during 2007 to 2010 among academics such as Cai Fang.[40]

Whether it was birth regulations or, more likely, the changing social norms, we know that lower supply usually increases labour costs, which was even obvious during the Black Death in the fourteenth century. A smaller workforce can have other effects on the economy. Mainland economist Li Xunlei has stressed that a shrinking workforce undermines rising consumption in the economy, which it is one of the government's goals. The working age population forms the majority of consumers. Moreover, younger workers have a greater propensity to spend than older workers, so the current squeeze is particularly hard.

Effect of Anthropogenic Disasters

Disasters, regrettably, are a continuing feature of human existence. Some, like epidemics, can be moderated by human agency. Other, natural, disasters are relatively immune. The geographical incidence of different kinds of disaster can naturally have differing impacts on economies. Historically, Europe had more epidemics and Asia more earthquakes and typhoons. First, epidemics tend to destroy labour, while earthquakes cause greater destruction to capital. Historically, as societies have had growing populations, while often capital-short, this has been a disadvantage to Asia. Second, epidemics have become more manageable, whereas there

---

39   http://www.economist.com/news/asia/21661805-europe-shows-how-asias-demographic-crisis-might-correct-itself-asias-new-family-values
40   https://www.tandfonline.com/doi/abs/10.1080/17538963.2010.511899

has been no noticeable change in the twentieth century in the average 15 major earthquakes each year with a magnitude of 7 or more. This again has been an advantage to Europe.

It is still too early to decide whether or not COVID-19 has affected China's economy more or less than others. For countries with well below replacement birth rates and thus in clear danger of population contraction - essentially East Asia - there is now the heightened risk of epidemic mortality enhancing the impact, while at the same time for East Asia there is the continuing added danger of natural disasters. The relative economic risk has risen in East Asia.

How does Demography Affect the Economy?

Several experts have understandably linked population factors to the economy. The OECD warned in 2019 that the US economy would be slowed by demographic trends.[41] Zhou Tianyong, deputy dean of the International Strategic Research Institute of the Communist Party School in Beijing, said in 2016 that demographic developments 'may result in a wave of downward movement in the national economy'.[42] In 2018 he admitted that China's adverse population trends had severely hurt demand, wages and economic growth and this will worsen if Beijing takes no serious action. This is at a time when the economy was under stress for other reasons.

The National Bureau of Economic Research in Washington DC published research in 2018 proposing that fertility falls before a recession. The conclusion was that 'the growth rate for conceptions begins to fall several quarters prior to economic decline. Our findings suggest that fertility behaviour is more forward-looking and sensitive to changes in short-run expectations about the economy than previously thought.' This has startling implications for China. It suggests that the long-term falling birthrate indicates a serious future secular fall in the economy.[43]

Yao Meixiong, deputy head of the Fujian province census centre, has predicted that population changes are likely to lead to labour shortages, lower consumption, less innovation and

---

41   https://www.oecd-ilibrary.org/sites/9b89401b-en/index.html?itemId=/
      content/publication/9b89401b-en

42   http://www.china.org.cn/china/2016-07/01/content_38789736.htm

43   https://www.nber.org/papers/w24355

'inadequate propulsion' for the economy, with profound effects on demand, wages and economic growth rates.[44] There is a paradox in the commercial world. It is frequently noted that business in China has relied heavily on family and trust. However, this is a society with two clear problems: the predominance of single-child families in recent decades has almost eliminated siblings. This means few people have an uncle or cousin. The potential business network today is much smaller than it was. Second, there is very little trust. This seems, similarly, a result of the diminution of family and perhaps the personality of the single child.

The reduction in marriages is also likely to have an impact. Researchers suggest that married men tend to earn salary premiums over unmarried men in the same roles. Unmarried men are likely to have less drive to perform without families to support.[45] It is clearly undesirable in demographic terms that many women see education and/or career as an alternative to raising a family, at least simultaneously. If it only causes a delay, there is still a distinct demographic cost. Whichever choice many feel obliged to make is hurting either the present economy or birth rates and the future economy. Cambridge professor Dr Diana Coyle has said that economies are either in a virtuous circle or a vicious spiral. A country which has so little faith in the future as to have no children will have a bleak economic outlook. She says that the ageing and shrinking we are seeing is so novel that no one knows if growth will be possible either overall or even on a per capita basis.[46]

Fear of Japanification

There is a real concern in Beijing that China could change trajectory and start to reflect the recent economic history of Japan, where everything looked splendid and then there was collapse. The Tokyo stock market had been booming and suddenly in 1989 crashed from a high on the Nikkei Dow index of 39,000, finally bottoming at 7,000 in 2009 and then over the following decade crawling back over 20,000. The economy reflected this in having 'lost 30 years'.

---

44   http://www.china.org.cn/china/2016-07/01/content_38789736.htm
45   http://sustaindemographicdividend.org/wp-content/uploads/2012/07/SDD-2011-Final.pdf
46   http://www.ft.com/intl/cms/s/0/afbfab86-515d-11e5-b029-b9d50a74fd14.html#axzz3kadXZ7ez

There is a significant literature on this subject. In late 2019, the *Harvard Business Review* published research indicating that China was on the same road as Japan in the recent past.[47] The authors make the well-used point, for example, that China's world-size companies are mostly the largest companies inside a large country and show little global culture to support continuing growth. The fate of Japan really worries many Chinese policymakers, who see China in some respects following Japan after its successful 'breaking out' and becoming a first world economic and financial power. They are driven by anger and fear. There is partly an anger that the West is trying to stifle China's rise and partly a fear that destiny may turn against it. The Japanese economy has been stagnant since the 1989 market collapse although - owing to falling population - GDP per capita has been quite strong. This is not the future China wants. It does not want the high GDP per capita of a Luxembourg but rather a large population and a large and growing economy.

Economists have often blamed Japanese policymakers for the persistent low growth after the market collapse. However, Masaaki Shirakawa, a recent Governor of the Bank of Japan, stated his view very clearly in 2019 that 'low GDP growth since the early 2000s has actually been mainly the consequence of unfavourable demographics'.[48] He noted - referring to his country - that 'no country has ever lost workers on this scale for reasons not related to war or illness'. A clear example is that some areas are having problems keeping up basic infrastructure as there are not enough taxpayers. Shirakawa says that prolonged monetary easing is no solution. What is really needed to address demographic challenge is economic and fiscal reforms. By implication, where China is troubled by population dilemma, the solution is effective and thorough reforms.

Little Benefit from Low Birthrates

It has been argued that the collapse in East Asian birthrates from a TFR of 6 to under 2 has been a principal driver - over 25 per cent - towards per capita regional growth. However, by its nature, we cannot expect this to be sustainable. Over several centuries in

---

47 https://hbr.org/2019/09/can-china-avoid-a-growth-crisis
48 https://asia.nikkei.com/Opinion/Emerging-Asia-should-learn-from-Japan-s-demographic-experience

Europe marriage participation was lower and marriage age was higher west of a line from St Petersburg to Trieste. According to Professor Eric Jones of La Trobe University, writing in his influential book *The European Miracle*, 'Profound consequences for capital accumulation and living standards may have flowed from this.'[49] It is suggested that this may be one of the reasons why Europe developed more rapidly than Asia. However, in that case we are discussing the long-range impact of different habits which affected births at a time when global birth rates were much higher. Today, global birthrates are much lower. All actions taken in this generation which reduce birth are compounding an already fragile population level. Overall, there is little positive message in low fertility in the twenty-first century.

Productivity and Growth

'*Productivity isn't everything, but, in the long run, it is almost everything.*' (Paul Krugman)[50]

An official report in 2018 from the Chinese People's Political Consultative Conference forecast that the working-age population of China would fall by 2050 to almost half its present level.[51] This likelihood has serious implications for the economy. Normally a smaller workforce means less output, smaller GDP. However, the report protests that this need not be so: 'There are also factors contributing to the efficiency of science and technology. At present, China's new industries, new formats, and new economic development characterized by intelligent manufacturing and sharing of the economy are very active. The technological revolution characterized by new energy, new materials, information technology, biotechnology, and artificial intelligence is underway.' Do we believe China can substitute its missing workforce with sufficient new technology and efficiencies to create compensating productivity? This is certainly a contested topic.

---

49 Eric Jones, *The European Miracle: Environments, Economies and Geopolitics in the History of Europe and Asia*, Cambridge, 2012, p. xxxiii.
50 https://asia.nikkei.com/Opinion/Emerging-Asia-should-learn-from-Japan-s-demographic-experience
51 https://asia.nikkei.com/Opinion/Emerging-Asia-should-learn-from-Japan-s-demographic-experience

Michael Brown, innovations director of the US Department of Defense, said in 2019 that China was gaining on the United States in a whole series of critical technologies. However, observers in both the US and China have commented that he has a financial motive to promote China's technology rise, in order to increase funding for his department.[52] Independent academics are more concerned than the Chinese government. For example, in a 2019 paper, Su Jian, an economist at Peking University, and Yi Fuxian, the demographer, argued that 'China may have started to see a long-lasting fall in its population … and economic vitality has weakened.'[53] So, a falling workforce is weakening economic vitality.

Professor Wang Feng has forecast that 'population trends will reduce Chinese GDP growth by 0.5 per cent annually over the next few decades … A half percentage point off a 6 per cent growth rate is a lot more benign than a half percentage off when the growth rate drops to 3 per cent.'[54] Depending on the extent of the reduction, this would make China a less important country. Of course, we might also mention again here that China's economic data are inaccurate and inflated, there is no clarity about where the economy is and what the growth rate has been. It seems that, rather than the reported recent 6 per cent, growth was much smaller in recent years and possibly more like 4 per cent.[55] What is clear, though, is that if the workforce is steadily reducing, it is difficult to grow the economy.

The concerns could theoretically be mitigated by greater automation, efficiency or new techniques. There has, for example, been a huge increase in robot installation in recent years. The factors which are generally measured are the flow of workers into the economy, the rate of participation in the economy by those of working age and the increase in productivity by the workforce. The influences which slow down the economy and maybe in future will stall it are lack of reform and gradual demographic change. If the workforce contraction continues over decades, then to have

---

52   https://www.scmp.com/news/china/diplomacy/article/3036053/us-still-out-front-tech-race-china-experts-say-response
53   https://www.scmp.com/economy/china-economy/article/2180339/china-birth-rate-expected-fall-lowest-level-2000-creating-new
54   https://www.ft.com/content/f34bb0b0-2f8b-11e9-8744-e7016697f225
55   https://www.brookings.edu/wp-content/uploads/2019/03/BPEA-2019-Forensic-Analysis-China.pdf

economic growth, labour productivity alone must outweigh the effect of reduced working numbers by a substantial margin. Even if this is possible, several important changes are needed. It will be much harder to sustain economic growth with a falling population without innovation. The need is for drive and innovation. As Professor Coyle has noted, it is unlikely for a society to demonstrate drive and create innovation if it does not even want children.

Global Experience

In a general sense innovation seems to be becoming more difficult. Peking University's Professor James Liang is a specialist in innovation. He makes the point that globally 'the average age of patent applicants is increasing' and 'the probability that an inventor will switch fields is decreasing'.[56] This is a worrying picture. He relates Japan's ageing to its current prolonged lack of growth. This has a clear implication for China as it becomes a rapidly ageing country.

If innovation is the mother of productivity, then we should be interested in Liang's view that the essential drivers of innovation are a youthful population, a large population and a concentrated population focused on metropolises. Clearly China's rapid ageing will soon be more marked than that of other countries and enhance the existing characteristic of dependence on seniority. Although a large population can still be guaranteed way into the future, Liang has a clear caveat that it must operate within a free market economy with clear respect for property rights, neither of which exist today. The only requirement for an innovative society that China can provide is a concentration of its population in cities.

The US enjoyed a golden half century up to 1970. Hong Kong University's Professor Richard Wong states that 'the fast growth of labor productivity from 1920 to 1970, at 2.8 percent per annum compared with periods before (of 1.50 percent per annum) and after (of 1.62 percent per annum), is due mainly to total factor productivity, which represents innovation and technical change.' In fact, we might say that the whole century from 1870 to 1970 was driven by electricity and the internal combustion engine.[57]

---

56   James Liang, *op. cit.*, p. 27.
57   http://wangyujian.hku.hk/?p=7462&lang=en

Recent research tells us that over the last 50 years the G20 countries have had 3.5 per cent annual GDP growth, half of which came from increases in the labour supply and half from productivity growth. However, recent US figures show that productivity growth has generated about 80 per cent of total GDP growth, compared with around 35 per cent in the 1970s, when the rest came from growth in labour supply. This has to be the case, as there is little growth now available in the US workforce. Indeed, it has been estimated by some researchers that fertility there has already fallen below replacement.[58]

Demography and Productivity Decline

Labour productivity and total factor productivity in the US in 2015-16 were both the lowest they have been in any period in the last 30 years. Total factor productivity grew in the period 1993-2004 by an average 2 per cent annually. In the period 2005-16, it declined by an average 0.3 per annum annually. There was some recovery in 2017 and 2018.[59] US Federal Reserve research in 2016 refers to 'demographics having lowered real GDP growth [1.25] percentage points since 1980, primarily through lower growth in the labor supply'.[60] The implication is that demography alone has caused almost all the weakness in GDP growth from 1980 until 2016. The demographically-driven model indicates that low economic growth is 'here to stay, suggesting that the U.S. economy has entered a new normal'.

So, in the US, according to the research, a mere reduction in the growth of the workforce was enough to produce woeful productivity numbers and weak GDP growth, lower than otherwise by 1.25 per cent annually for over 30 years. The challenge arising in Europe and China is far worse. In those regions, serial falls in the size of the workforce is much more dangerous.[61] One bank research

---

58   https://www.mckinsey.com/~/media/mckinsey/featured%20insights/
     employment%20and%20growth/new%20insights%20into%20the%20
     slowdown%20in%20us%20productivity%20growth/mgi-the-productivity-
     puzzle-discussion-paper.ashx

59   https://www.bls.gov/opub/mlr/2018/article/multifactor-productivity-
     slowdown-in-us-manufacturing.htm

60   https://www.federalreserve.gov/econresdata/feds/2016/files/2016080pap.
     pdf

61   Ibid.

team points to 'population ageing in advanced economies as one factor that may account for the drag on productivity seen since the recession beginning in 2007'.[62]

Having enjoyed 15.5 per cent productivity growth from 1995-2013, China in the years 2014-18 saw 5.7 per cent growth. Falling labour supply from 2010 has certainly had an effect.[63] A falling workforce will have another grim consequence - ageing. Twenty years ago, prescient independent Chinese demographers discussed the pending 'drastic decline' in numbers of incoming young workers and stressed that 'it will also have profound consequences for labour productivity, as these are the most recently educated and tend to be the most innovative'.[64]

Research from the Global Burden of Disease (GBD) programme indicates that even the US now has a TFR of 1.8 - below replacement - and the only factor which could increase labour supply is a rise in immigration, legal or not.[65] It indicates that over half of all countries - including the five most populous - now have a birthrate at or below replacement. On that basis, in the long term we can no longer expect more workers born every year to drive GDP growth. So, how can we generate more labour productivity? It can stem from more employees working, employees working more hours or productivity gains. The last would be the ideal.

Workforce Participation

We can get more women into the workforce, bring back some of the men who have ceased looking for work or make part-time or informal work more attractive to those who cannot or prefer not to enter the formal full-time workforce. However, in several countries these categories - especially women in work - are in practice close to full. In China, half of all urban workers are in the informal sector, meaning that they do not enjoy social benefits. Their employment is not registered with the authorities and possibly their employer is not

---

62   https://www.ft.com/content/eb35c06e-cae7-11e7-ab18-7a9fb7d6163e
63   https://hbr.org/2019/09/can-china-avoid-a-growth-crisis
64   http://citeseerx.ist.psu.edu/viewdoc/download;jsessionid=
     B5B133A3EEB36A72191337FC9FC1663C?doi=10.1.1.640.964&rep=rep1
     &type=pdf
65   https://www.thelancet.com/journals/lancet/article/PIIS0140-
     6736(18)32278-5/fulltext

registered. This is not necessarily a situation to be 'cracked down' on. In a labour market as fragile as China's - as the authorities know very well - these may be the only jobs available. Being practical it might be a case of informal jobs or no jobs. At least they (usually) get paid. This is not Sweden. But neither is it the Congo, although in some respects the Chinese labour market more closely resembles the latter.

The labour participation rate is the proportion of those of working age who are employed. In the US, it is 62 per cent and in China 68 per cent. The trend over the last 25 years has been declining in both countries. These participation figures suggest room to increase the workforce despite a static or reducing working-age population. However, there are several categories which are inapplicable: disabled people (a rising proportion in the US), sufferers from drug damage, those who do not wish to work and those who would find it difficult, such as ex-convicts. The US has the largest disclosed incarceration rate globally and China is believed to hold a high proportion of its citizens on various undisclosed terms. This limits the slack in the non-working population.

As noted, female participation in the Chinese workforce has collapsed over the last three decades from 73 to 60 per cent. It is not evident why this has happened. An increasing middle class may have opted for wives not to work. There are also certain barriers to female executive careers. On the other hand, 30 per cent of all working women are reported also to have a second job.[66] With the usual concern about Chinese data, we cannot be sure if China's low female labour participation might principally be due to under-registration.

Both the US and China have experienced the worldwide fall in female labour participation in recent years. However, Japan has bucked that trend. In 2014 it exceeded the world average for the first time and then saw an increase of two percentage points in 2015-17. More distinctive yet is the trend for prime-age women (25-54). There, since about 2012, Japan has overtaken the US and the OECD bloc. As the Brookings Institution has noted: 'If US prime-age women had gained as much ground from 2000 to 2016 as their Japanese counterparts, one simple calculation suggests that GDP in

---

66   https://data.worldbank.org/indicator/SL.TLF.CACT.FE.ZS?locations=CN-US-1W-JP

the United States would have been around $800 billion (over 4%) higher in 2016 than it actually was.'[67]

One of the structural supports for working mothers in China is that over 50 per cent of grandparents give active support to childcare compared with 16 per cent in the US. Research indicates that 'overall, females with grandparental support earn about 81% more than those without support; those with children aged 0-2 earn almost three times as much if they are supported by the grandparents.' This situation is now threatened by current plans to delay retirement. The result of such phased changes is likely to be further erosion of female labour participation or reduction in the birthrate.[68]

Given the steep fall in participation in China over the last 30 years, reversing this trend must be a key target for policymakers if productivity is the priority. If births are the priority, however, it may be that increased female labour participation cannot be encouraged. There is a dilemma between three desirable results: increased female work, delayed retirement age and more births. It is likely to be impossible to maximize all three.

Sectoral Rotation and Productivity

If measures to increase workforce participation have been unsuccessful, then other measures will be needed, such as technology or policy changes. The industrialization of the country and then the development of the services sector have been a policy priority. In China, according to the OECD in 2015, 'productivity gains resulting from the movement of labour from less to more productive sectors (the so-called "shift effect") explain about 2 percentage points of annual labour productivity growth in the past decade'. This incorporates such policy themes as urbanization, the moving away from agricultural work and transition from primary and secondary industrial sectors to services.[69]

Some of this will continue but there are signs that urbanization may become smarter: less fast and furious and more targeted on smaller cities and towns. The Covid-19 pandemic highlighted

---

67   https://www.brookings.edu/research/lessons-from-the-rise-of-womens-labor-force-participation-in-japan/
68   https://voxeu.org/article/labour-past-present-and-future-trilemma-china
69   OECD Economic Survey, China 2015, p. 37.

the ability of companies and government to function while staff remain at home. There is less interest among rural workers to go to the cities. Several large cities plan to cap their populations and actively discourage migrants. Agriculture is now less over-manned than it was. The primary workforce in agriculture and mining has decreased; manufacturing is becoming less competitive. There has already been a substantial move of labour into the service sector. We cannot rely on natural population growth to swell the cities.

Sectoral work shifts are an issue in the US and China. By 2030, according to one global investment firm, 'one-third of American workers may need to change occupations and acquire new skills', while 'nearly two-thirds of the 13 million new jobs created in the U.S. since 2010 required medium or advanced levels of digital skills'.[70] Education and training will be transformed from one-off events to lifetime processes. Unfortunately, the US spends a fifth of the sum European countries spend on retraining programmes to get the unemployed back to work. The COVID-19 crisis has undoubtedly speeded up these processes.

In China, some industries are in terminal decline. However, it will be a rare coal miner who can re-brand as an Uber driver. Most physical jobs a miner could do may be safer but pay much less than he was earning. Food delivery couriers can earn an average 7,800 yuan a month but this usually means moving to larger cities. There are government retraining budgets but the challenge to retrain laid-off workers is formidable. Age is often a severe impediment. A particular issue in China is the unwillingness of the unemployed to move province for jobs. Neither the US nor China is looking like a fully fungible labour market.

While there is undoubtedly more sectoral change to come, we should be careful about projecting these factors too far into the future. We will probably not see the 'shift effect' anywhere near 2 per cent productivity growth again.

Prospects of Productivity Growth Resuming

Productivity growth is weak globally. Europe, Britain, Japan and even China are seeing low and/or declining productivity growth. China has higher rates of productivity growth but lower actual

---

70   https://www.kkr.com/global-perspectives/publications/outlook-2019-game-has-changed

productivity and the growth rates are sinking. As noted, the US had its golden years until the early 1970s and then largely a series of reductions until 2015 since when we actually saw some negative, as well as positive, periods for productivity growth. There was negative multi-factor productivity for 2016 as a whole. The US then saw some productivity recovery in 2017 and 2018. The OECD reports that since around 2000 almost all member states have experienced mediocre labour productivity growth rates. Even Korea reported three bad years out of four. Countries such as Poland, Slovakia and Slovenia have seen productivity reduced to mundane levels.

Economists are divided as to why productivity has declined so markedly. One school suggests that there are technology-driven gains but our capacity to measure them is defective. Others suggest that we are not innovating in a meaningful way as we did in the late nineteenth and early twentieth centuries. Our innovation has been focused on information and entertainment. The implication is that this is entertaining or convenient but not world-changing. The reason is perhaps that these have been identified as areas where people will pay. The degree of innovation is not the determining factor. There is a link between reduced capital investment and reduced productivity growth but confusion as to whether lower investment means lower growth or lower growth deters increased investment.

Optimists suggest either that the technology which has recently been and will be invented will have a greater impact productivity or that there are several important bottlenecks which can be addressed to release productivity enhancement, such as patent reform, deregulation or infrastructure investment. To give an example, one-third of US jobs now require a licence compared to 5 per cent in the 1950s. The Brookings Institution points out that 'the expansion of licensing seems designed to restrict entry into these professions rather than to protect consumers'.[71]

There are signs of improvement in productivity from strong increases in jobs and some success in the war against opioids. What would be helpful is a greater focus on reduction in the long-term increase in occupation licensing. There is a linked argument that

---

71   https://www.brookings.edu/blog/up-front/2015/01/27/nearly-30-percent-
of-workers-in-the-u-s-need-a-license-to-perform-their-job-it-is-time-to-
examine-occupational-licensing-practices/

GDP is higher than we calculate because our systems are not set up to measure the intangible results of contemporary technology. There is a certain circularity here in that if we are not set up to measure an activity, we may not be able to prove the argument is true.

As is usually the case, there is probably substance in each of the arguments about technology gains and the impact on productivity. Yet it is unlikely that that substance will be great enough to replace the missing productivity growth of recent decades and beyond that to compensate fully for a shrinking workforce. Although technologically behind the West, China does not show a broad-based improvement in its innovative capacity. There is some clear improvement in super-computing, space engineering and in a limited number of other areas. China might currently be ahead of the US in Exascale computing. However, advances are more apparent in the state domain and not in the commercial realm. We need an answer to the question: why are Chinese people creative and innovative in Silicon Valley but not in China?

This suggests that we may in future see productivity growth resume - as happened in the US - but not to the extent of compensating for falling total hours worked in China, and similarly in Europe; thus China's GDP growth should be lower than in the past, reduced by falls in employee numbers. In the eurozone, for example, the workforce started to decrease in 2009. It will continue to shrink despite immigration. Between 2015 and 2050, we may see 1.5 per cent productivity growth netted down by 0.5 per cent average annual falls in workforce, giving 1 per cent GDP growth, with the per capita figure little better owing to an increasing elderly population.[72] Although the population will stagnate, the working-age population will fall by over 20 per cent and the over 60s will grow by over 20 per cent.

There will be proposals to delay retirement age. We can speculate as to how many in their 60s will choose to continue working. In Japan, the weakening workforce has been bolstered by greater elderly participation in work. Half of those aged 65-70 and a quarter of those 70-75 are in work. [73] However, the overall trends are clear; fewer young will enter the workforce and the elderly will live somewhat longer. We should note, however, the sharp slowing

72   https://www.ft.com/content/1954c468-449a-11e9-b168-96a37d002cd3
73   *Ibid.*

down of life expectancy increase in the major economies. The Chinese and European workforces will shrink. It is not surprising that in 2018 for the fourth successive year, the Chinese private-sector employers' organization declared rising wages as the most serious threat.[74]

Outside the Chinese government, most opinion is quite cautious about China's prospects of out-pacing demographic decline with technological advance and thus producing further significant growth. The expectation for Asia's middle developing powers such as China, in the view of the World Bank, is that unlike the more developed ones such as Korea, 'even with sustained productivity growth … (they) will not reach the income levels of … (richer and older) East Asian and Pacific economies or OECD and middle-income countries … at similar points in the demographic transition'; and even if they undertake structural reforms 'these countries will become aged societies at much lower levels of income than the (more developed ones)'.[75]

While productivity is difficult to measure with confidence, according to one interpretation by The Conference Board it accounted for almost half of China's growth between 2001 and 2007 period – but it has since slowed to almost zero, or even begun to decline.[76] The report showed Chinese productivity falling from 2007 to at least 2013.

Masaaki Shirakawa cautions that it is not the development or access to technology which matters but how it is applied. He is gloomy about the resultant benefits. One of the principal reasons is that politicians have no incentive to wrestle with controversial challenges such as the implications of ageing, pension reform and roboticization. There has been considerable exaggeration around artificial intelligence, or AI. In 2019 research by London-based investment firm MMC Ventures concluded that 40 per cent of Europe's 2,830 'AI start-ups' had no AI content at all.[77] It should

---

74 https://www.scmp.com/economy/china-economy/article/2179666/how-us-trade-war-could-leave-chinese-private-firms-risk-being

75 http://www-wds.worldbank.org/external/default/WDSContentServer/WDSP/IB/2015/12/17/090224b083cb86bc/1_0/Rendered/PDF/Live0long0and00ast0Asia0and0Pacific.pdf

76 https://www.conference-board.org/retrievefile.cfm?filename=KBI-FY15---China-Slowdown---Final-Draftv2.pdf&type=subsite

77 https://www.ft.com/content/21b19010-3e9f-11e9-b896-fe36ec32aece

be expected that the ratio in China could be higher. AI companies generate higher funding rounds.

Impact of Demography and Productivity on China's GDP Growth

If productivity growth does not resume, we could imagine workforce declines in several regions of the world being greater than productivity growth, leading to GDP declines. According to the UN - which is conspicuously sympathetic in the forecasts it makes for China - China will see average working age population declines of 0.7 per cent annually from 2015 to 2050. This is 40 per cent more than the annual average decline in Europe and still significantly less than other forecasts. While China's labour productivity growth is still above that of the US, it is falling. There are suggestions that China's productivity is actually well below the official figures. Furthermore, one report estimates that Total Factor Productivity in China from 2008 to 2012 measured almost -1 per cent annually. It is possible we could see labour productivity in China less than the 0.7 per cent average annual fall in working age population, thus causing negative productivity growth. The Ministry of Human Resources in Beijing has forecast that from 2030 to 2050 the workforce will fall by 16 per cent or 0.8 per cent a year.[78]

James Liang has written extensively on the impact of ageing. He has said that 'the ever-aging population is a ticking time bomb that has the potential to stifle innovation and hamper economic growth... (There is a threat of) a decline of economic dynamism'.[79]

Barriers and Opportunities in Productivity Growth

As we have noted, the Chinese government puts great reliance on future innovation.[80] The CPPCC report paints a romantic picture of humans and machines working harmoniously together to increase productivity without a threat to jobs. Workers should treat redundancy that results from the introduction of machines as an opportunity to retrain.

---

78 https://www.weforum.org/agenda/2016/07/china-working-ageing-population/

79 https://www.amazon.com/Demographics-Innovation-Why-Key-Race/dp/111940892X

80 http://www.cppcc.gov.cn/zxww/2018/07/13/ARTI1531443023003519.shtml

Yike Guo, a professor at Imperial College London, has said that 'China has started to play a "leading" role in development in such areas as AI (artificial intelligence) and big data as the country is transforming from a labour-intensive economy to a greener and more innovative one.'[81] These are conceptually attractive ideas but there are practical problems, particularly in the Chinese context. The extent of Chinese innovation is controversial. Americans and Chinese can argue that China is making great strides in innovation, yet Chinese and Americans can flatly reject this thesis. There is an argument that China can eventually win the innovation war by redefining what innovation is.[82]

As growth is no longer going to come from population increase, it will need to come from innovation, labour market adjustment and policy reforms. The OECD estimates that the combination of innovation and policy reforms (and a rather positive view on births) 'can jointly add one to two percentage points to GDP growth over the next half century'. It could, but there is absolutely no guarantee that it will. There are reasons to be cautious about expectations for the input from either of these factors. Furthermore, given the negative outlook for births, the demographic input to growth can become negative.

Nor is productivity unproblematic. In recent years the advanced world has not shown significant productivity growth. Most large economies have failed to exceed 2.5 per cent productivity growth in over a decade, since 2001-6, except the US and Japan - and their peaks were in 2010. Since these peaks, growth has looked anaemic.

As noted, even China's productivity growth from a low base has been decreasing in recent years. Furthermore, China is constrained by inefficient capital allocation, barriers to entry in businesses and a profuse but inefficient graduate supply. Each of these harms productivity growth if not addressed. In the economy's value added, the share of manufacturing has now been overtaken by services. The OECD has pointed out that 'productivity in the service sector is held down by the fact that the playing field is not level for all firms'. It is ironic that 70 per cent of technological innovation is said to arise from the private sector but as we have

---

81   http://www.xinhuanet.com/english/2019-02/27/c_137853898.htm
82   file:///F:/Books/Population%20Book/Research/Productivity/2019-china-catching-up-innovation.pdf

noted earlier, the private sector is largely starved of capital.[83] China ranks 31st among countries for the ease of doing business but it ranks ever lower for ease of access to credit.[84]

McKinsey has suggested that China's current economic model is failing and that a new approach is required. China's service sector productivity is way lower than OECD countries. Its overall labour productivity is 70-90 per cent lower than advanced economies. A conscious and comprehensive assault on this disparity could be extremely rewarding. One example they cite is self-check-out at supermarkets. The same applies to manufacturing where raising the current level of robot usage from 63 per 10,000 workers compared to Korea's 631 and increasing energy efficiency can both have a strong impact on productivity. McKinsey quantified the impact on GDP of success in this as $5 trillion by 2030.[85]

One area where China is weak, in contrast to the US, is in basic research. Professor Xiang Songzuo at Renmin University is one of the rare outspoken voices urging China towards reform, noting that the country has failed to nurture original talent and to originate outstanding scientific research. Top-down, government-led research is not likely to produce creativity. The lack of scientific competition and flow of ideas is stifling. According to Professor Ouyang Liangyi of Peking University, many of China's technological innovations are application-oriented which requires the backing of foreign suppliers, in areas such as chips. This emphasizes the need for more basic research.

Among business leaders in the developed world there is a view that the rising cost of compliance and human resources is choking the funding which might otherwise have gone into research and development. It has been estimated that the cost of compliance alone will increase from 4 to 10 per cent of revenue by 2022. On this view, the West may need to become accustomed to low productivity growth.[86] China - to its advantage - has not yet moved decisively down this path. The US is an exception here. There has also been a deliberate drive to reduce the regulatory burden.

83 https://www.bloomberg.com/news/articles/2018-11-19/why-xi-leads-a-chorus-backing-china-s-private-sector-quicktake

84 https://www.doingbusiness.org/en/rankings?region=east-asia-and-pacific

85 https://ifr.org/ifr-press-releases/news/robot-density-rises-globally

86 https://www.scmp.com/business/companies/article/2182879/nearly-half-chinese-hong-kong-companies-have-gone-ahead-deals

There has been criticism that tax reductions have not led to capital investment but to share buybacks. Yet, on the other hand, there are signs of productivity improvement and a huge increase in jobs.

Globally, this environment needs a big boost to productivity and that means capital investment, deregulation, policy measures and other incentives to growth. This is true whether we consider the US, Britain, Japan, the Eurozone or China. In China specifically, priority focuses for reform to encourage productivity growth are improving capital allocation, education reform, strengthening intellectual property rights, improving general property rights (including land ownership reform), removing barriers to entry in sectors currently dominated by the state sector and encouraging higher levels of R&D spending by the private sector.

The Talent Gap

One area of the labour market which continues to grow is fresh graduates. But there is clearly a gap between the skills and qualities of the graduates produced by universities and those which employers prize. This has been labelled the 'Talent Gap'.

Despite the shrinking workforce, graduate salaries are surprisingly low. In 2016, over half of those graduating expected a monthly salary below 3,000 yuan. There was no cumulative rise between then and 2018. In 2019, there was an increase in wages but a reduction in job offers. Still 70 per cent of graduates accepted pay of under 6,000 yuan.[87] In comparison, the average food delivery courier's wage is 7,750 yuan. This is a polite way of saying that employers do not generally value the skills of new Chinese graduates. In 2019, the number of graduates rose by 2 per cent and yet total job offers to graduates fell by 13 per cent and within that 'blue collar' job offers rose by 25 per cent. As one recruitment firm said, it 'indicates that college graduates' capabilities are yet to be recognized by employers'.[88] In this environment, many graduates are either under-employed or even unemployed for prolonged periods.

This situation is a common feature of what has been described as 'the massification', or dramatic expansion, of tertiary education,

---

87 https://www.scmp.com/economy/china-economy/article/3012635/chinas-834-million-graduates-fighting-fewer-jobs-vacancies

88 http://www.chinadaily.com.cn/a/201901/22/WS5c46d08fa3106c65c34e5da0.html

which has been pursued in many countries. In 2013 in the US, for example, research indicates that 48 per cent of four-year college graduates were overqualified for their job. In New Zealand in 2011 a very high 55 per cent of young people graduated each year with normal university degrees as opposed to the OECD average of 39 per cent. The OECD average salary premium for a graduate over a secondary-educated worker was 57 per cent, whereas in New Zealand it was 18 per cent. While massification may not account for all the difference, it is hard to believe that it is not a major contributor.[89] In Britain by 2016 about half the college-age population was in tertiary education and the 'graduate premium' scarcely existed.

In the late 1990s, the Hong Kong government decided to increase the proportion of school leavers going to university from 20 to 60 per cent. That target has now been exceeded. The level in 2015-16 was 70 per cent. In the decade 2007-17, the number of skilled jobs rose by 18 per cent but the number of graduates in the workforce rose by 60 per cent. As a result, inflation-adjusted graduate salaries have actually fallen. In the 15 years from 1992 to 2017 they fell by 10 per cent. The proportion of graduate level employees doing non-graduate jobs has doubled in 20 years to over 16 per cent.[90]

The number of PhDs in China surpassed the number in the US in 2008 but the US economy is much larger. Not surprisingly, the quality of Chinese PhDs has been described, with remarkable understatement, as 'uneven'.[91] This situation has led certain elite secondary and primary schools in Beijing and Shanghai to demand PhDs from all would-be teachers. As Professor Wang Dan of Hong Kong University has observed, 'the expansion of higher education has resulted in more university graduates, and people with Master's and PhD degrees are becoming more and more common… The market simply cannot absorb so many people with high educational qualifications, so many of these people may be willing to teach in primary and middle schools.'[92]

89 http://www.oecd.org/education/New%20Zealand_EAG2013%20
    Country%20Note.pdf
90 https://www.scmp.com/news/hong-kong/education/article/3010178/
    university-graduates-face-tough-competition-and-low
91 https://www.scmp.com/comment/insight-opinion/united-states/
    article/2186957/actor-zhai-tianlins-plagiarism-scandal
92 https://www.scmp.com/news/china/society/article/2176920/exclusive-
    chinese-school-tells-would-be-primary-teachers-they

Why are policymakers in a wide variety of societies seduced by massification? There are two principal reasons. The first is that they genuinely believe that the more graduates there are, the more the economy will prosper. The second reason is that telling their public who have largely never been inside a university that their children can become university graduates scores a lot of political points.

In 2005, a McKinsey report on *China's Looming Talent Shortage* said that 'less than 10 per cent of Chinese job candidates, on average, would be suitable for work in a foreign company in the nine occupations we studied'.[93] In engineering, McKinsey found the education system's principal problem was the bias towards theory. Hence there was little practical project experience. In the other careers, poor English, communication style and cultural fit were the main issues.

Chinese graduates, say McKinsey, have a 'generally low suitability'. They are not very mobile and only a third move to other provinces to find a job. The combination of these factors creates a 'shortage of world-class graduates', which presents a serious problem. If the proportion of graduate engineers who could work in international companies reached the Indian level of 25 per cent, China would have the world's largest reserve of qualified young engineers. Per capita education spending must rise and English must improve. In agreement, the OECD has said that 'spending on education is comparable to that in some other BRICS economies, but lower than in OECD countries'. China should do more to ensure that when its overseas students return home to work, their enhanced international skills are better utilized. There is widespread distrust of overseas education. In 2015, the OECD observed that 'the difference between the self-reported acquired skills at the time of graduation and the skills needed in their job six months after graduation, based on a 2013 survey of 150 000 graduates, indicates the mismatch in the graduate labour market'.

Following the extensive critique by McKinsey in 2005, which was widely read at the time, and surveys such as the OECD mentioned in 2013, it is disturbing to note the publication - in 2016 - of a study by teams from Tsinghua and Fudan Universities,

---

93   https://www.mckinsey.com/~/media/McKinsey/Featured%20Insights/
      China/Addressing%20chinas%20looming%20talent%20shortage/MGL_
      Looming_talent_shortage_in_China_full_report.ashx.

entitled *Skills Shortages in the Chinese Labor Market*.[94] The report states that China 'faces an acute skills shortfall' and that 'with further globalization, shortages of workers with expertise in internationalized management, strategic planning, and capital management will become a major challenge for firms, impeding growth'. Not only did the two reports have almost the same title but - 11 years apart - the conclusions were essentially the same. While using different vocabulary, the 2016 report is almost identical to the one in 2005 in the nature of its analysis of the labour market. Beijing's inability to address the functioning and quality of its labour market will become more of a problem as labour shortages become commoner. The gap between supply and demand for highly skilled labour was bad and is growing worse.

Potential Impact from Improved Skills

The dire quality of national education in China has been discussed earlier. There are consequences from the massification of higher education. University courses, according to the Tsinghua-Fudan team, 'are determined by higher educational institutions without a proper consideration of market demand'. Most company managements believe that what graduates learn is of little use. Vocational schools are poorly funded, lack cooperation with business and have low application levels. Over 250 million migrant workers receive virtually no access to skills training. Proposals include permitting universities to work with business to establish effective programmes for students, getting more people into vocational training with state subsidies and reforming household registration, education and social security to ensure a more effective and mobile labour market.

One Chinese postgraduate from Yale and Columbia, noting widespread plagiarism in China, has asked the question: 'Why can't a degree-obsessed society develop more truly world-class universities?'[95] The OECD notes that 'the most acute deficits are in practical and soft skills and in knowledge areas needed for rapidly

94 https://www.jpmorganchase.com/corporate/Corporate-Responsibility/ document/skillsgap-in-chineselabor-market-exec-summary.pdf
95 https://www.scmp.com/comment/insight-opinion/united-states/ article/2186957/actor-zhai-tianlins-plagiarism-scandal

expanding industries such as services'.[96] Given the widespread research and reporting on this subject, it suggests that either there is no will by policymakers to address the subject or that there are strong barriers preventing reform.

It is important to reform education to close the wide skills gap which has long existed amongst young Chinese. The problems exist at the secondary as well as the university level. The problem of quality in secondary education is exemplified by the 2019 report of a 15-year-old schoolgirl buying a robot to handle her repetitive homework.[97] Copying passages hundreds of times is common in secondary schools. Rote learning has its part in education but is excessive in China. There needs to be a greater focus on critical thinking and a reduced reliance on rote learning at all levels. This may not be popular with middle-class Chinese families who are always on guard for methods whereby officials can give their children an advantage. They tend to see any departure from memorization as allowing subjective performance measurement. Ultimately, there needs to be more analysis and judgement encouraged in the system.

The Outlook

Births in China are on a downward path. Unless pronatalism succeeds or society takes a counter-intuitive path, the signs are pointing to lower birthrates for the long term. The current demographic balance of China almost automatically dictates that it will become an ultra-aged society in the coming decades. However, urbanization, which discourages fertility, appears to be slowing and this could eventually temper the plunging workforce numbers.

Innovation is a controversial subject but clearly not improving enough in all areas and arguably impeded by a poor education system and what the party feels are necessary constraints on information flow and critical thinking. In a remark meant for universal application, Diana Coyle has said that to compensate for population shrinkage, innovation will be needed and enough to raise productivity at an accelerating rate - a prospect she finds

---

96   http://www.oecd.org/eco/surveys/China-2015-overview.pdf p.41
97   https://www.dailymail.co.uk/news/article-6721537/Pupil-buys-90-copying-robot-homework-caught-assignment-quickly.html

implausible. In fact, she says that innovation and technology *cannot* make up for shrinking populations. Hers is one of the gloomiest views on this subject.[98]

A return to productivity growth in China through increasing the labour force is not going to happen. Making the existing, decreasing workforce gradually more productive through process and innovation looks like a long-term strategy. The ageing population combined with a contracting workforce will encourage a less energetic, less flexible and risk-averse culture to arise. China's current cultural emphasis on seniority will be further entrenched and promotion prospects for the young will become bleaker.

If innovation requires youthfulness, a large-scale free economy and population concentration, then there are problems. China can currently only look to one of these - the last. China's government refers frequently to reform but executes rarely. Market reforms could achieve much in improved productivity but seem to be viewed as a threat to party control. There appears to be little driving increased productivity in China.

Summary

The loss of long-distance migrant workers, of female workers and the diminishing overall workforce coincide with a *dirigiste* economy with unequal opportunity and high entry barriers and an education system that has not satisfied a huge skills shortage. Each of these issues are inter-connected and unless resolved will be highly damaging for China's economy in the coming years.

The solutions may include robots and AI applications. Work is being done in these fields, but the overall economic impact is not yet apparent. Although automation will not necessarily lead to job destruction it almost certainly requires job rotation. In China the problem can be that those who are being rotated often lack the ability to adjust to new employment opportunities.

The rising number of graduates and weak graduate starting salaries are a particular problem. It could be argued that there is a race between a falling working-age population and reducing jobs. However, the falling working-age population is a secular event. What is less clear is whether the current large-scale loss of jobs is a cyclical

---

98   http://www.ft.com/intl/cms/s/0/afbfab86-515d-11e5-b029-b9d50a74fd14.html#axzz3kadXZ7ez

or structural phenomenon. In the absence of serious market reforms, the likelihood is that economic growth will continue to be weak.

This suggests that there will be times when jobs are hard to get - when the economy is weaker than the fall in labour supply - and times when jobs are easier to get - when the economy is less weak than the fall in labour supply. Mixed in, there will be times when there is an uneasy equilibrium.

The economy faces a massive challenge from falling labour numbers. Economic weakness is the product of many factors and looks to be secular in nature. The labour effect could be mitigated by automation. Simultaneous unemployment presents a different problem. Overall, there is a clear need for reforming markets and education and, in particular, vocational education, to meet these challenges. The future of the workforce is at the centre of some critical policy debates. If labour contraction is seen to be inevitable it could force the government into reform. From problems can come opportunity. Unfortunately, in China reform is a word which is praised but a practice which is shunned.

It can be unhelpful to reduce every discussion to one of numerical GDP data. There are many other measures such as happiness and well-being indices. Sadly, however, every measure is in some way flawed. However imperfect, GDP seems to be a broadly effective measure of how a society is progressing. We should also appreciate that about a third of the Chinese population still lives in the countryside in a principally agricultural society which is marked by a careless, inefficient and unreformed economy. Thus any national economic data are an inaccurate residual of two different societies. Overlaying this is a statistical system that is neither efficient nor honest.

China's economic development from 1978 until around 2010 was quite astounding. While the data were of dubious quality, it was evident to any observer that the economy was charging ahead. The largest driver was the 'demographic dividend' - essentially the freshly released, under-employed youth from the countryside who flocked to fill the new factories. Young girls were the first choice. The high proportion of the population in the workforce and the low proportion of dependants was a magic formula. This has been credited with constituting 15-33 per cent of China's economic growth after 1978.

However, just as demography was a great aid in the recent past, so again it will be an important factor in future - but this time in a negative sense. A lower labour participation rate among the total population, thus a higher dependency rate, a shrinking overall workforce and a long-term lack of children create conditions conducive to economic slowdown or even contraction. We are probably almost half-way down the decline from 10+ per cent reported annual growth rates to no growth. It would be realistic to assume that all the keys on the piano may eventually be played.

I have not sought to quantify the scale of damage to the economy from the developing trends in the hope that policy measures will be taken which will substantially ameliorate the effects. Later I discuss what these measures could be.

China has found a way to prevent birth, but only to delay death. Beijing is likely to find it more difficult than it expected to prevent the looming population decline. From an investment perspective, cemetery management seems more of a growth industry than baby clinics. In the coming decades the demographic crisis will eventually dominate analysis of the Chinese economy - in both supply and demand.

7

THE MILITARY EFFECT

The severe demographic challenges facing China will have a significant impact on the country's military capacity. To assess the potential effect, we need to first consider the military - the People's Liberation Army (PLA) - as it is and how Beijing would like it to develop and then think how the impending developments will affect this key institution.

Observations on the Current State of the PLA

As ever, we must be cautious when discussing facts and figures in relation to China. According to the European Union in 2020, China's military expenditure totalled $228 billion (1.9 per cent of its GDP).[1] This compares to $610 billion (3.1 per cent of GDP) for the US. It has 2.3 million active personnel, reserves of 8 million and another 385 million individuals available for military service. It has substantially fewer armoured fighting vehicles than the US, but more tanks, artillery pieces, self-propelled artillery and rocket artillery. It has a third of America's military aircraft, but twice as many naval craft, although the US has ten times as many aircraft carriers. China has been a nuclear power since 1964 and is believed to have around 280 nuclear warheads.

China is spending substantial resources in upgrading its military forces, particularly its space forces and rocket technology. It has successfully launched numerous military satellites - especially the Yaogan 33 - and in 2020 retrieved samples from the moon's surface and brought them safely to earth. That year it launched 35 successful space missions. There were four failures. It has the Indo-Pacific's largest air force, the world's largest sub-strategic missile force and one of the world's largest and most sophisticated surface-to-air missile forces. The PLA is expanding its reach around the

---

1   https://armedforces.eu/compare/country_China_vs_USA

world and now has port facilities for the PLA Navy in both Asia and Africa. And it is not afraid of military tension on the border between India and Tibet, or of criticism over its regular threats to invade Taiwan. It has continued to build military bases on disputed islands and sandbanks in the South China Sea, despite criticism from neighbouring countries.

According to the US-China Economic and Security Review Commission's 2020 Report to Congress, 'The PLA's long-term strategy to gain advantage over the US military includes developing "informationised" capabilities and exploiting ostensibly civilian information systems, likely including those built overseas by Chinese companies. The PLA is complementing these efforts by developing cyberattack, space and counterspace, and long-range precision-strike capabilities and expanding its capacity to delay and threaten U.S. military forces at increasing distances from China's shores.'[2] Chinese leaders say they intend to have a fully modern military by no later than 2027, the centennial of the PLA.

Much of China's modernization has occurred under President Xi Jinping, who also inherited many changes initiated by his predecessors, including the indigenous aircraft carrier *Shandong*, the Type-055 guided missile destroyer, the J-20 stealth fighter, the Y-20 long-range transport aircraft, the DF-21D anti-ship ballistic missile and the DF-17 ballistic missile fitted with a hypersonic glide vehicle. Technical questions remain over some of these platforms, but the speed with which they have been brought into service has surprised some observers.

Where Xi has been successful is in his ability to push through innovative organizational changes in the PLA, in the process taking on both corrupt officers and political enemies. He has often visited units to give speeches on military affairs and intervened in promotions down to the level of corps commander, to put his backers into key positions. He targeted officials appointed by his predecessor Jiang Zemin, including former Central Military Commission vice-chairmen Xu Caihou and Guo Boxiong, and has been able to push through controversial changes.

These changes saw the top-heavy, Soviet-style, senior command replaced by a modern structure more like the US joint command

---

2   https://www.uscc.gov/sites/default/files/2020-12/2020_Annual_Report_to_
     Congress.pdf

system. As noted by Joel Wuthnow, a senior research fellow in the Center for the Study of Chinese Military Affairs at the National Defense University, Washington DC: 'A Joint Staff Department oversees five regional theatre commands, each having authority to plan, train for and conduct operations tailored to specific regional missions. The Eastern Theatre Command handles operations against Taiwan, for instance, while the Southern Theatre Command oversees the South China Sea. Signalling a deeper "joint" mentality, more naval and air force officers now occupy senior positions in the theatres.'[3] Wuthnow adds that the creation of two support forces complemented these new arrangements. The Strategic Support Force consolidated PLA capabilities in the space, cyber, electronic warfare and psychological warfare arenas. And a new Joint Logistic Support Force created a more centralized and efficient structure for operational commanders. Other changes included a shift from army and air force divisions to brigades, designed to increase the PLA's manoeuvrability and interoperability.

For all this, the PLA is a military force which has not fought a war for decades. The last was the Sino-Vietnamese war in the late 1970s. As a result, few serving officers have any combat experience. For those older officers remaining, we need to remember that the war was over 40 years ago, it only lasted 27 days - and China lost. It is not clear what lessons the military learned from that experience. Indeed, even the original military victory of the Red Army has to be put into context, with the nationalist government simultaneously having had to defend the country from the Japanese and the state from the communists. The PLA was able to pick its fights and be absent when it chose. The nationalist government had its hands full on a full-time basis.

We know that considerable sums have been spent on the military and weapon systems since the 1980s in rising amounts. However, this alone does not tell a clear story. It is very difficult for us to assess the PLA's current combat worthiness and it is equally difficult for China's leaders to make an evaluation. After 1979, the PLA became an enthusiastic participant in United Nations peacekeeping operations, alongside the militaries of countries such as Ethiopia, Bangladesh and Pakistan. The latter were certainly

---

3   https://www.eastasiaforum.org/2020/12/16/chinas-military-modernisation/

grateful for the funding for their military offered through their participation. For China, the appeal is to expose its military to the weather conditions and logistical issues involved in peacekeeping operations everywhere from the snows through the jungles to the deserts. In practice they found that instability tends to be an equatorial pursuit. While there may not always be direct fighting in these peacekeeping missions, there is much to learn which could be useful later.

Similarly, China learned much from participating in the joint anti-piracy patrols in the Gulf of Somalia before 2013. Since 2000, Beijing has also organized many complex evacuations of its citizens during civil strife, most notably from Libya, Kyrgyzstan and Vietnam. Given the lack of combat experience, probably the nearest comparable situation was responding to the Sichuan earthquake of May 2008 in which over 85,000 people died and 350,000 were injured following tremors recorded at 8.0 on the Richter scale. The military sent in 130,000 soldiers to carry out rescue activities. Unfortunately, both Western and Chinese analysts were unimpressed by the performance. The lack of training and of suitable equipment undermined the mission. There was widespread public criticism in China of the PLA's poor command structure, inadequate equipment, and slow response to the Sichuan crisis. According to the *South China Morning Post*: 'A lack of large cargo planes and helicopters and bad weather delayed the arrival of the first batch of 1,300 PLA soldiers in Wenchuan County, close to the epicenter of the earthquake, until 24 hours after the quake. Premier Wen Jiabao, who went to the disaster zone a few hours after that quake, at once made a tearful call to the army to send helicopters to save people, but there was no response because the army takes its orders only from the Central Military Commission, and Wen has no military rank. The PLA eventually directed helicopters to the disaster area, but only after President Hu Jintao, the CMC chairman, issued the order on May 14, two days afterwards.'[4]

According to one Indian military assessment of China's military response to the earthquake: 'The earthquake exposed the ill-preparedness of the PLA - the best equipped and organised force capable of dealing with such incidents - for effectively managing

---

4   *South China Morning Post*, 16 April 2010.

a disaster of this magnitude. The disaster areas presented a real battlefield-like scenario which required good coordination, communication and cooperation amongst different force components for delivering effective results. However, the forces were often found to be struggling with many tasks that would be considered standard and routine in modern warfare."[5]

A rare official survey of more than 1,100 soldiers who took part in the relief effort in Sichuan by medics at Beijing Military General Hospital found that just under half of those who responded reported mental health symptoms, including irritability, sleep disturbance, sadness and depression.[6]

Shortly after President Xi Jinping came to power in 2012, he called for the PLA to make itself combat-worthy. He bluntly stated that it was essential for the military to 'be able to fight and win battles'. This is a clear indication that at that point it was no such thing. The goal became a continuing theme in which Xi cajoled and admonished the military leadership on a regular basis for both corruption and ineffectiveness.

Since then, Xi Jinping has called for and implemented reforms in the structure of the military to achieve a series of aims such as greater loyalty to the party leadership, avoidance of corruption and achieving combat-worthiness. From the string of corruption cases and continuing exhortations it seems the aims have not yet been achieved. In fact, considering that one of the worst aspects of military corruption was the systematic sale of promotions for cash, we have no right to assume that high competence is dominant among the senior ranks. Short of sacking most of them, we might see the cleansing as a generational challenge. The battle continues.

After the collapse of the Soviet Union - which did challenge the world - China so far has only challenged little Vietnam - and been seen off. Xi Jinping would not like his epitaph to reflect Marx's dictum that history appears twice 'the first time as tragedy, the second time as farce'.

---

5   Kamlesh K. Agnihotri, '2008 Sichuan Earthquake and Role of the Chinese Defence Forces in Disaster Relief', *Journal of Defence Studies*, vol. 6, no. 1, January 2012, p. 37.

6   Wei Qiang Zhang *et al*, 'Physical and mental health status of soldiers responding to the 2018 Wenchuan earthquake', *Australian and New Zealand Journal of Public Health*, 2011; https://doi.org/10.1111/j.1753-6405.2011.00680.x

What Effects Are There on the Military?

An estimated halving in China's future population is certainly an existential threat to one of the largest armies in the world. However, the 4.5 million-strong PLA was cut after the early 1980s by 2.2 million and in 2015 a reduction of another 300,000 was announced. There is a strategy to reduce and streamline the military and produce a smart and 'lean' force. Hence there is in fact no direct relationship between the country's predicted population fall and the desire to develop a leading global fighting force. There is now and will be great emphasis on the latest modern equipment and operational strategies, including cyber warfare. There are, however, other effects of the demographic and social changes underway which will have more impact.

Fitness of Military Recruits

For several years there have been recurrent reports of the low suitability of potential military recruits. Observations include being physically unfit, watching too many video games, frequent masturbation, excessive alcohol consumption and a sedentary lifestyle.[7] In some areas of China over half the applicants are rejected on fitness grounds. The Beijing recruitment office found in 2013 that 60 per cent of applicants failed on these grounds alone. Generals have been found to be around 11 pounds overweight. Soldiers are two inches fatter than those of 20 years ago and as a result often finding it difficult to fit into the cockpit of a tank. When the World Military Games were held in Wuhan, China, in October 2019 in front of President Xi Jinping the entire PLA orienteering team was expelled for cheating. Selfishness has been proposed as a normal characteristic of single children. A quarter of serving soldiers have psychological problems - and that is without seeing a shot fired in anger. Eighty per cent of combat troops are single children and there is concern as to their fighting ability. There is a perception of a lack of comradeship under fire. In the wider society, men are fatter and weaker than in 2000 and have weaker grip strength and back strength. By 2015, the military had to reduce the standards for recruits for height, width and eyesight.

---

7   https://news.abs-cbn.com/overseas/08/24/17/chinese-military-links-fitness-test-failures-to-too-much-masturbation-video-games

A further expression of this issue emerged in January 2021, when China's Ministry of Education published a call to prevent the 'feminization' of boys by encouraging schools to employ more male gym teachers.[8] The call was mocked by many on Weibo, but the ministry's statement reflected officialdom's increasing unease with growing social acceptance of gender diversity. The official anxiety over a 'masculinity crisis' can also be seen in state media's condemnation of a group of young male movie stars, known as 'little fresh meat' by their millions of fans, who present themselves as outside traditionally gendered style guidelines.[9]

The Education's Ministry's call to cultivate masculinity in young men by balancing physical strength and mental health came after a delegate from the Chinese People's Political Consultative Conference suggested that Chinese schoolboys are 'weak, self-effacing and timid', and may be unduly influenced by the 'little fresh meats'. In September 2020 the country's top sports and education authorities announced that physical fitness would soon carry greater weight on the national high school entrance exam and that gym classes should be added to the national middle school core curriculum.

Many of these problems relate to the size, character and movement of the population, particularly urbanization. Young military recruits are less likely now to come from families engaged in agricultural work and more from those with sedentary lifestyles. Contemporary diets are less healthy than before. Most members of the military come from single-child homes and have characteristics which may reflect this.

The most important way in which demographic change will affect China's military is in the rapid ageing of society that will more than triple the number of elderly, while leading to a fall in the tax-paying workforce. Other consequences include sharply-rising welfare costs, an increasing number of parents (fathers and mothers) with only a single child to support them, many children living long distances from their parents and a growth amongst single children of selfishness and defective in filial piety. All this is happening while economic growth is in long-term decline.

---

8   https://chinadigitaltimes.net/2021/01/weibo-users-denounce-plan-to-stop-feminization-with-more-gym-class/

9   Two years earlier Xinhua warned that public obsession with 'little fresh meats', if left unchecked, could result in the destruction of Chinese society. http://www.xinhuanet.com/politics/2018-09/06/c_1123391309.htm (in Chinese).

This raises the issue of how to divide the revenues. Allocation of funds to the military, both stated and unstated, has experienced buoyant growth in the decades since the 1980s. The world, and in particular regional neighbours, have been deeply apprehensive about the growing projection of military power. And yet President Xi has referred to welfare as being his top priority. It seems as if we are now moving into a new period in which not every interest group can have what it desires. This became more public in spring 2019 with the major political meetings in Beijing. With the explosion of the cost of the elderly, military expenditure growth will begin to be curtailed.

If China is obliged to spend (much) less on its military in future, we should ask what it will mean. Xi is the first recent Chinese leader to call for a major change in the country's place in the world. In 2017, he unequivocally stated that China is in a 'new era' and should 'take centre stage in the world'. Will Beijing have to drop its interest in global power projection and opt for a regional role? Or will it have to settle for a solely defensive posture? Or, given that there is no country which is looking to invade China, will the financial effect be so strong that its military posture becomes nominal? Will it continue to strengthen its military relationship with Russia, possibly hoping to save costs as a result?

I would suspect that, given the propaganda offered as history in the school system, the country will be unwilling to cut too much further. We really do not know what public pressure may oblige in the coming decades. My guess would be that the policy will eventually move to somewhere between the regional and the defensive options. What can affect this expectation? Clearly one possibility is a rearming of Japan, a 'forward policy' by India or an unlikely resurgence of Russia. Another is that technology may lead to a sharp reduction in the cost of sophisticated weaponry, which would make it less controversial to purchase.

The world has increased its trade with China substantially in recent years. It is a consensus view that countries which trade together do not fight each other. History, however, suggests otherwise. The First World War is a good example. From 1900 to 1913, British trade with Germany rose by 105 per cent, Russian trade by 121 per cent and French trade by 137 per cent, but by

1914 all those countries were at war with Germany.[10] We should not see trade relations as a promise of peace.

One of the possible negative aspects of the peaceful scenario outlined here is that some elements in the country may react with horror. The thought that China will look less like the future world superpower may lead nationalists to decide that it may be better to launch aggressive military action earlier rather than never. A specific short-term example could be an attempt to incorporate democratic Taiwan by military force. So, perhaps it is too soon to say whether a sharp cut in military spending will have peaceful consequences or not.

We can say that normative low birthrates, specifically single-child families and greater longevity will, from several respects, exert adverse pressure on military funding and performance. Or more simplistically, we can say that fewer babies will eventually mean less military power. For many Chinese this is an unwelcome outlook but perhaps a relief globally.

---

10 Peter Liberman, International Security, Vol 21: issue 1 (Summer 1996) p.166

8

THE INTERNATIONAL CONTEXT

While there are echoes of some of China's challenges in other countries, there are also contrary trends at work. In addition, there are also many examples of policy action taken overseas to address the challenges. We will be able to see a close nexus between demographic change and economic developments, especially in the US and Japan.

1.   A Decreasing Workforce

A reduction in a country's workforce is usually a precursor to a falling overall population. Increasing longevity temporarily masks certain evils. There are at least 25 countries where the working-age population will be seriously smaller in 2050 than in 2020. Eleven countries will have a sharp loss in their workforce. These include Bulgaria, Korea, Romania and Taiwan. Other countries that will experience a serious reduction include China, Germany, Japan, Poland and Thailand. The 25 major losers are heavily concentrated in East Asia and continental Europe. There are also contracting workforces in other countries, including Armenia, Cuba and Jamaica.

The Steepest Falling Working Age Populations amongst Countries Worldwide

Millions of 15-64-year-olds in 2020 and 2050 and the percentage fall

2020	2050	%	
2.1	1.4	-33%	Armenia
2.7	1.8	-33%	Bosnia
4.6	3.2	-30%	Bulgaria
771,000	501,000	-35%	Estonia
370,000	260,000	-30%	S Korea
1.2	0.7	-42%	Latvia
1.8	1.0	-44%	Lithuania
2.3	1.3	-43%	Moldova
402,000	275,000	-32%	Montenegro
14.5	10.1	-30%	Romania

| 17 | 11.6 | -32% | Taiwan |
| 840,400 | 570,900 | -31% | **Average** |

Source: USCB

Taiwan

Labour costs affect Taiwan's businesses in that they cannot respond well to China's increasing lack of competitiveness by withdrawing home, as Taiwan's workforce itself is shrinking faster than China's. Taiwanese companies need to become more innovative and less labour-intense. Alternatively, they must find less demographically challenged societies which also have a work ethic and a functional infrastructure accessible to the global supply chain. This is being encouraged by the government's New Southbound Policy which focuses on South and Southeast Asia.

United States

The Federal Reserve Bank in Washington published research in 2016 suggesting that since 1980 demography has had an important dampening influence on the US economy. The declining trends are particularly noticeable after the early 2000s. The low growth since the 2008-10 recession coincides very closely with demographic changes. It was largely predictable if one follows demographic data, resulting in a 1.25 per cent reduction to average annual GDP growth. This has been driven principally by a reduced supply of new labour.[1]

The Fed's research 'implies that demography - rather than fiscal or monetary policy, technology or other changes in productivity - are (*sic*) responsible for almost all of the decline in economic growth over the past 35 years.' The demographically driven model suggests a continuation of low US output growth. However, we should note that in the US it is only reduced new labour supply, not a reduced workforce. The OECD has also seen weak labour supply as a factor which will reduce economic growth in the US.[2]

---

1   Etienne Gagnon, Benjamin K Johannsen, and David Lopez-Salido, 'Understanding the New Normal: The Role of Demographics', *Finance and Economics Discussion Series 2016-080*, Board of Governors of the Federal Reserve System, http://dx.doi.org/10.17016/FEDS.2016.080. See also Kim, Jinill, 'The Effects of Demographic Change on GDP Growth in OECD Economies', *IFDP Notes*, Board of Governors of the Federal Reserve System, 28 September 2016: https://doi.org/10.17016/2573-2129.22.

2   https://www.oecd-ilibrary.org/sites/9b89401b-en/index.html?itemId=/content/publication/9b89401b-en

The US Federal Reserve seems now to have identified a new environment. In 2020 directors commented that evidence suggests that there is still more availability in the labour market, particularly in lower-income areas. There is even a growing interest in tapping the relatively large bank of previously imprisoned working-age Americans.[3] Outside the regularly unclear data of China, the US has the highest incarceration rate in the world, giving it on release a potential additional workforce of over two million. We should, of course, recognize that even if released, there are many ex-prisoners who would be grossly unsuitable. However, many people in America are imprisoned for relatively minor issues such as cannabis possession, use or sale. There are also about four million Americans on probation and almost a million on parole.

It could be that there remains a clear link between labour supply and GDP growth, but the supply has been expanded in the US through changes of circumstance.

Japan

In early 2019, Japan's health, labour and welfare ministry produced its first ever long-range forecast for the workforce. It projected a contraction between 2017 and 2040 of 20 per cent, from 65 million to 52 million.[4] This is steeper than the predicted 13 per cent fall in total population and is a steeper fall than is projected by the UN and the USCB for the Chinese workforce (14 per cent) during the same period. However, neither of these bodies seems yet to have fully engaged with China's looming challenges.[5]

Japan is already experiencing many of the effects of a falling workforce. In July 2016, a 43-year record high was established of 1.53 job openings to every one applicant. Many restaurants have ended their practice of being open 24 hours a day. Torikizoku, a grilled chicken chain, announced price rises in 2016 for the first time since the market crash of 1989. Shortage of staff is an especially important factor.

Farming is another affected area. People are leaving the countryside and as a result services are also collapsing. There are

---

3   https://www.ft.com/content/d2652066-32af-11ea-9703-eea0cae3f0de
4   https://www.japantimes.co.jp/news/2019/01/15/business/japanese-workforce-projected-20-smaller-2040/#.XiEzN_4zaUk
5   https://www.ft.com/content/1199ff3c-189d-11e9-9e64-d150b3105d21

fewer farmers, who by 2018 had an average age of 67. Tractor drivers may be even older, and the average plot is now over 75 acres. Driverless tractors came on sale during 2018 - to the relief of elderly farmers, who are involved in 81 per cent of machine-related accidents involving farmers.[6] While initially expected to work alongside a manned tractor, if successful, unmanned vehicles should eventually be able to work un-minded and even at night.[7]

The workforce contraction in Japan is regarded as a national crisis and the government is considering several measures in order to mitigate the effects, including a 70-year retirement age and a determined drive to increase the proportion of women in the workforce. Female labour participation in Japan is now at 51 per cent, the highest since 1992. Prime-age Japanese women have increased their participation to a level higher than that in the US. However, there is still much more to be done. For example, in most of Scandinavia female workforce participation is 60 per cent.

For a contracting workforce, another solution is a judicious increase in immigration. It is being liberalized, but the topic is highly sensitive as Japanese citizens are diversity-averse. Between 2012 until the end of 2019, the number of foreign residents in Japan rose 40 per cent to reach 2.8 million.

What is less discussed is the limited role of entrepreneurs and the weak relative productivity of SMEs. In Japan, the image of entrepreneurs is not very positive and unsurprisingly there are proportionately fewer than elsewhere. SMEs are over 50 per cent less productive than large companies. These factors need to be in the debate.

The IMF has warned that without serious reform, demographic trends will reduce Japan's GDP by a quarter by about 2060. Goldman Sachs proposes two key solutions:

a. Encouraging female graduates by ensuring greater gender equality in critical areas such as scientific research;

b. Pushing female work hours up so that they are the same ratio to male hours as the OECD average.

---

6   https://www.thehindu.com/news/international/in-japan-driverless-tractors-are-on-the-move/article27172252.ece

7   https://www.japantimes.co.jp/news/2019/05/26/national/services-touted-key-future-japans-farming-sector/#.XQcXVxYzaUk

The latter may conflict with the current campaign to limit overtime work to be family friendly. However, the calculation is that the first measure could raise GDP by 10 per cent and the second, if achieved, by a further 15 per cent.[8]

Changing Japanese corporate practices to encourage more women will not be easy; in 2013 it was stated that 'Japan's punishing corporate world makes it almost impossible for women to combine a career and family, while children are unaffordable unless both parents work.'[9] Around 70 per cent of women who become pregnant leave their employment.

A widespread expectation is that the overall economy will nonetheless - inevitably - contract and therefore the policy focus should be on building per capita income and increasing productivity to compensate for population decline. One issue is whether rising per capita income alone will suffice. Can an estimated Japan government debt of 245 per cent of GDP be supported by a shrinking population without serious inflation? A related question is whether a smaller number of workers can support a rising number of elderly.

Europe

European countries and others with a similar political culture will find it increasingly frictional to maintain even current levels of social security expenditure when the balance between workers and retirees tips substantially against tax contributors and towards welfare beneficiaries. Pained US calls for NATO members to raise their contribution to their own defence are likely eventually to go unheeded. This is not because they do not wish to respond but because they will come to realize that they cannot. With fewer young voters, there are unlikely to be the votes in democracies to reduce welfare. Public budgets may eventually resemble a massive alchemical machine to convert youthful income into elderly expenditure. This could even lead to political instability. It is likely to add further stimulus to emigration from parts of Europe. Given its welfare policies and geographical location, Europe will of course continue to have immigration as well but there may be issues of quality in the exchange.

---

8   https://www.ft.com/content/e425060c-61c4-11e9-b285-3acd5d43599e
9   https://www.theguardian.com/world/2013/oct/20/young-people-japan-stopped-having-sex

Europe's working age population began falling in 2010. By 2020 there were 10 million fewer potential workers. By 2035, there will be 50 million fewer.[10]

Falling Working Age Population amongst the Remaining EU Member Countries

Millions of 15-64-year-olds in 2020 and 2050 and the percentage fall

Working Pop. 2020	2050	Percentage Fall	Country
5.9	5.3	-10%	Austria
7.5	7.6	1%	Belgium
4.6	3.2	-30%	Bulgaria
2.7	2	-26%	Croatia
0.904	0.856	-5%	Cyprus
6.9	5.8	-16%	Czechia
3.7	3.8	3%	Denmark
0.771	0.501	-35%	Estonia
3.4	3.2	-6%	Finland
42	41	-2%	France
51	40	-22%	Germany
7	5.5	-21%	Greece
6.3	4.8	-24%	Hungary
3.4	3.8	12%	Ireland
40	34	-15%	Italy
1.2	0.7	-42%	Latvia
1.8	1	-44%	Lithuania
0.427	0.541	27%	Lux'mbourg
0.294	0.277	-6%	Malta
11.1	10.7	-4%	Neth'lands
25	18	-28%	Poland
6.7	5.2	-22%	Portugal
14.5	10.1	-30%	Romania
3.7	2.7	-27%	Slovakia
1.34	1.05	-22%	Slovenia
33	29	-12%	Spain
6.3	7.4	17%	Sweden
291.4	248.1	-15%	Total

Source: USCB

---

10   https://www.ft.com/content/49e1e106-0231-11ea-b7bc-f3fa4e77dd47

In the European Union over 80 per cent of countries will see their available workforces decline by anything up to 44 per cent. The grouping will see an overall reduction of 15 per cent. This compares with China experiencing a 20 per cent fall (with controversy over the data, as usual) and on the other hand the US, the UK, Canada, Australia and New Zealand expecting workforce increases – although that could change if wages rise in countries with labour shortages.

Summary

If workforce contraction continues as currently projected, Europe and East Asia are under severe threat of seeing their workforces shrink. The US and other English-speaking countries are in a different and happier position. Technology and innovation should be the saviour to compensate for shrinking workforces. However, it is probably too early to judge that any country has solved the challenge.

2.   *An Ageing Workforce*

The issue of ageing societies is becoming a global challenge. Poverty alleviation, better social services and improved medical care all combine to enhance longevity. First, life expectancy has been continually extended. Not only is life expectancy at birth projected to rise 18 per cent from 71 in 2015 to 83 in 2100, but the people of ten countries are expected to have an average life expectancy at birth of over 93 years by the end of this century. This means it will be quite normal then for many Australians, Italians etc. to live for over a century. However, underneath this is a contrary undercurrent. Longevity enhancement has slowed recently in many countries.

There are several results from this combination of increasing longevity and falling birthrate. One is that the median age of the world's population is estimated to rise by the end of this century to 41.7. However, 34 countries will have a median age in the 50s. These will include Brazil, Cuba, Mexico and Thailand. Second, young people will become scarcer. Currently under-15-year-olds are over a quarter of the world but by 2100 they are expected to fall to one-sixth. There will be 43 countries where there are more over-80s than under-15s.

In a study published in *The Lancet* in 2017, research across 35 industrialized countries on several continents indicates that life expectancy will continue to rise in all.[11] The leader for both sexes is South Korea. There is a 90 per cent chance that South Korean women born in 2030 will live for more than 87 years and there is a 95 per cent chance that South Korean men will live more than 80 years. This conflicts - to an extent - with data from the World Bank since 2010 showing substantial slowdowns in longevity enhancement and even some reversals. The authors stated that 'while a marker of progress, ageing populations also pose huge challenges to health care systems and social services and may require pushing back the age at which people stop working.'

Demographers have noted that 'the US, Western Europe and Japan have all reached the "tipping point" when the numbers of people in work compared with old and young dependants has peaked and started to fall'.[12] The number of over 60-year-olds in the world is expected by the UN to triple by 2100 to 3.2 billion. Of the 2015-2050 increase, 66 per cent will be in Asia. In 2010, AT Kearney, the management consultancy, noted that 'for the rest of this century, the world's fastest-growing age group -and therefore its fastest-growing consumer group - will be people over the age of 60. This is the most powerful mega trend of the future.'[13]

Among larger countries leading this trend have been China, Italy, Japan, Poland, Korea, Spain, Thailand and Turkey, all of which have been forecast to have around 40 per cent of their population over 60 by 2100. A major reason why falling birthrates have not yet - in many countries - led to falling populations is that the process has been delayed by increased longevity. We need to understand more about why longevity increases have slowed in so many countries since 2010.

The AT Kearney research notes that 'in 1950, some 200 million people were in the "over-60" group ... by 2050, the number will

---

11   https://www.thelancet.com/journals/lancet/article/PIIS0140-6736(16)32381-9/fulltext

12   https://www.ft.com/content/df61dc42-99fa-11e6-8f9b-70e3cabccfae

13   https://www.atkearney.com/documents/10192/682603/Understanding+the+Needs+and+Consequences+of+the+Aging+Consumer.pdf/6c25ffa3-0999-4b5c-8ff1-afdca0744fdc

have reached 2 billion'.[14] The combination of ageing with lower birthrates means that business is likely to transition from marketing based on a cult of youth to focusing on a cult of age. Overall, the world population is increasingly stabilizing 'and so future growth will depend on demand driven by technology and innovation rather than by raw population numbers'.

Although Stanley Fischer, then deputy chairman of the Federal Reserve in Washington, said in 2016 that 'an increase in the average age of the population is likely pushing up household saving in the US economy', there is nonetheless a widely held view that in an ageing society interest rates rise as the elderly need to draw down their savings to live. Alternatively, the elderly may choose to work longer as they are healthier. This could merely delay the raising of interest rates and the weakening of the economy. It is a contested topic. We must realize that we live in an unusual period where major governments have a vested interest in interest rate direction and silently need rates to stay low. Regardless, there needs to be more flexibility in many labour markets to accommodate the needs of the elderly if they are going to stay at or return to work.

Dependency ratios - the number of those working to those retired or at school - have been falling around the world. The calculation is often based on comparing those of working age with those of retirement or school age. However, this overlooks the long-term tendency for those of working age not to work. Both globally and in the US specifically the 'labour participation' rate had until recently been falling and, in both cases, stands now at about 62 per cent. In other words, worldwide, 40 per cent of people work and support the other 60 per cent. Using this approach turns the dependency ratio in the US dramatically from 1.9 to 0.7. Tax revenues are being increasingly stretched by providing income and healthcare for growing numbers of older - and not so old - people who are no longer contributing to the state.

The consensus response is to delay retirement age and thus reduce pension payments and increase employer pension receipts. However, not all citizens welcome delayed retirement and older people can be a very effective political force.

---

14   https://www.atkearney.com/documents/10192/682603/
      Understanding+the+Needs+and+Consequences+of+the+Aging+Consumer.
      pdf/6c25ffa3-0999-4b5c-8ff1-afdca0744fdc

Hong Kong

Hong Kong is more aged than China. In 2016, 16 per cent of its population was over 65. By 2036, this figure will be 30 per cent. In 2035 the UN projects China's over-65s will make up 21 per cent of the population. While Hong Kong's position looks worse, it is much more affluent than China. 'Resting and sitting' is apparently the preferred occupation of over 60 per cent of Hong Kong retired people. Lam Ching-choi, 57, who runs the Elderly Commission, has said that 'asking a person to suddenly stop working and contributing to society can lead to health hazards'.[15] Lam has also noted that 'retirement can kill. Retirement lets you feel lonely and alienated. You'd be depressed or even commit suicide.' There is the sense of some clear thinking in Hong Kong.

Britain

The number of people requiring elderly care in Britain is expected to double from 2015 to 2040 but the population will do no such thing. The total population could increase by 9 per cent and the over 65s by 43 per cent. This means more expenditure per working resident. On the other hand, we should note that the extension in years of reasonable health has resulted in raising the state retirement age, in stages, to 70.

Europe

In Europe, fortunately, older people are increasingly re-joining the workforce and elderly purchasing is rising in significance. Spending by the over-50s is forecast to rise by more than 70 per cent between 2015 and 2025. It will create 40 per cent of all new jobs during the period.[16]

However, European policymakers are deeply concerned about how increased ageing will affect both growth and public finance. The IMF has forecast that GDP per capita in developed countries will fall. For the EU region, the falls will be 'substantial'. France, Spain, Italy and Germany will see unwelcome cuts in per capita income. Even the EU Commission estimates that 'spending on

---

15   https://www.scmp.com/news/hong-kong/society/article/2167355/forced-retirement-age-discrimination-head-hong-kongs-elderly

16   https://www.ft.com/content/49e1e106-0231-11ea-b7bc-f3fa4e77dd47

healthcare for older people and pensions, which already accounts for 25 per cent of GDP in the EU, will rise 2.3 percentage points by 2040'. It is not surprising that they struggle to fund their membership of NATO.[17]

China and South Korea are both ageing countries with mean average ages over 40. However, Europe's - as an entire continent - stands at 43. This makes Europe by far the oldest continent by mean age of citizens.[18]

India

Yi Fuxian, a US-based demographer at Wisconsin Madison University, has made some parallels between China and India which were debated in Beijing's *Global Times*. Adjusting for overstatement, he estimated in 2017 that China's population was actually only 1.286 billion. A result of this is that India would already have surpassed China to become the world's largest country. He then notes that 'India has many more young people than China. Its economy in the future will be more dynamic and the pension burden will be much lighter.'[19]

Several of those interviewed by *Global Times* proposed that the total population number is no guide to economic prospects. In a sense this is true but - were all other things equal - a more populous country might be expected to have a larger economy, which can support more research and development. This is then immediately affected by intangibles such as work ethic, tangibles such as robotics, machine tools etc. and variables such as value added in industries. Education is a difficult issue and is usually assessed quantitatively - what percentage goes to university - whereas qualitative factors such as quality of education and its suitability to the economy are rarely fully assessed.

Points which emerged from the piece by *Global Times* were that India appears to have some strong advantages underlying its growth prospects. An official of the Confederation of Indian Industry made the point that youth will have a positive impact on India's relative savings, investment, market size and workforce. He also mentioned rising productivity and youthfulness as important factors here. The

---

17   Ibid.
18   Ibid.
19   http://www.globaltimes.cn/content/1050069.shtml

IMF has been forecasting India's GDP lead over China to grow markedly.[20] We should bear in mind, however, that both economies suffer from severely criticized performance measurement systems.[21]

One Indian professor interviewed stated that India will have over 30 years of demographic dividend until 2050 and as a result could overtake China and become the world's major economy. Another academic noted that the 'large number of young people, vast domestic market and low labour costs are the most significant contributors to the increase of foreign direct investment in India'.[22] There is some exaggeration here in that there is a vast number of people but not yet a vast market. However foreign investment is likely to increasingly flow into India for these reasons.

The pledge by Foxconn, the world's largest contract manufacturer, to employ 1 million people in India and the arrival of several major Chinese property developers are cited as examples of imminent change. India could become the premier manufacturing country and 'may take away millions of jobs from China'.

The growth rate of Indians studying overseas seems to have overtaken that of Chinese. Indians obtain almost six times as many H-1B temporary worker visas in the US as do Chinese. Most of these go to workers in IT. The number of Indian CEOs in global technology companies keeps growing. There are signs that India is more successful than China in the global employment market, and in IT in particular.

A number of points were not made in this debate. The contrast in the relative youth of India compared with the ageing of China focuses on one of the relative prospects. The very fact of India becoming the most populous country in the world will mean that many companies, belatedly, will decide they need an India strategy in the same way that most large companies already have some kind of China strategy. Inevitably this will lead to greater engagement in terms both of foreign direct investment into India and trade between India and the world. India is likely to outgrow China per annum much of the time during the coming decades but whether it will overtake the Chinese economy is less clear.

---

20   https://www.imf.org/en/Publications/WEO/Issues/2019/01/11/weo-update-january-2019

21   https://www.ft.com/content/25b0b690-360c-11ea-ac3c-f68c10993b04

22   http://www.globaltimes.cn/content/1050069.shtml

Russia

Not so long ago, Russia promised pension increases to the elderly, who tend to vote for Putin. However, by 2016 Prime Minister Medvedev was admitting that there would be no further increase in pensions to compensate partially for inflation. Instead, there would simply be a one-off payment equivalent to $77. 'We don't possess enough resources to carry out [an] extra pension adjustment,' he said.[23] Moscow has even had to divert pension savings at the state pension fund from individual accounts towards paying pensions owing to shortages of money. According to Evsey Gurvich, a Russian pension specialist writing in 2013, 'today there are 100 workers for every 87 pensioners ... by 2020, that figure will be 100 workers for 100 pensioners'.[24] This suggests dependency ratios which are increasingly out of control and unsustainable.

Russia has not only had one of the earliest retirement ages - 60 for men and 55 for women - but beyond that, early retirement rules create an effective retirement age of 54-58 for men and 52-54 for women. The state pension fund pays out more than it receives. The Russian pension system is in desperate need of reform. And it has been reformed regularly. Yet the crisis continues to worsen. And this is in a society where as recently as 2000-2005, male life expectancy was 59 years.[25]

In 2018, Putin's government had to announce a five-year delay for pension eligibility. This made the limit 65 for men and 60 for women. However, the average Russian man currently lives to 66, or less in the Arctic Circle where expectancy can be 56.[26] In other words, the age for men to receive their pension was the same or higher than their life expectancy. Clearly a major problem for Putin's own voters, he tackled the question head-on at his 2018 annual press conference: 'this is an unpleasant and, clearly, not a fun thing to do, but it has to be done nonetheless. To reiterate, if I

23   https://www.wsj.com/articles/russia-cant-help-pensioners-much-with-inflation-medvedev-says-1471982232
24   https://www.coursehero.com/file/p2ahosd9/11-Migration-from-Poland-and-aging-population-effects-volume-of-labor-force/
25   https://www.towerswatson.com/en/Insights/Newsletters/Global/global-news-briefs/2015/03/russia-social-security-pension-system-revamped-beginning-in-2015
26   https://www.arctictoday.com/russians-arctic-circle-putins-pension-reform-feels-like-trap/

was not convinced that it would have to be done some time down the road, I would have never allowed it to happen.'[27] The good news is that the WHO pointed out in 2019 that the traditional extreme alcohol consumption rate is tumbling and so there is hope for extension of life expectancy. This may, of course, not be welcomed by the Russian treasury.[28] As things stand, the average Russian state pension is around $220 per month.

Japan

With an average age of 46.5 in 2015, Japan is currently the world's most aged major society, with a medium-term outlook of further ageing approached only by Spain, Portugal and Korea. The cost for Japan is a rising dependency ratio (number of retired to those of working age), increasing - when not capped - social security costs and growing senile delinquency, such as increasing shoplifting stemming from inability to survive on low fixed pensions. In 2012, nappies for the elderly outsold those for babies for the first time.

In rural areas of Japan where depopulation is happening most quickly, the country's National Institute of Population and Social Security Research says 'it will become necessary for local governments to concentrate essential facilities such as medical institutions and government organizations in certain areas and *take administrative steps* to relocate elderly people who need such services'.[29] By 2035, it is estimated that a third of Japan's population will be over 65, compared with 21 per cent for China. However, China will catch up quite fast.

As in Britain there are calls in Japan to raise the retirement age to 70. The country is not generous in its pensions. Indeed, it has sought to hold them down to the point that their value is minimal. The welfare burden is exerting huge pressure and there is already very substantial public debt. As early as 2010 a fifth of the population was over 65. At the same time, over 25 per cent of arrested shoplifters were over 65. The numbers had nearly tripled since 1999 mainly because social security payments were too low

---

27   http://en.kremlin.ru/events/president/transcripts/press_conferences/59455
28   https://www.theguardian.com/world/2019/oct/01/russian-alcohol-consumption-down-40-since-2003-who
29   https://www.japantimes.co.jp/opinion/2013/04/17/editorials/japans-depopulation-time-bomb/#.XC3NmlUzaUk

for subsistence. Old people are lonely and prison provides company - as a result, this group is highly recidivist.

Former Prime Minister Shinzo Abe made clear in 2018 that he wanted to raise Japan's retirement age beyond 65 and allow people to defer their pension beyond 70. Such a major social security reform may make financial sense but is unlikely to be particularly popular.[30]

The OECD notes the economic challenge, saying that 'to achieve continued prosperity in an ageing economy, output per worker must rise faster than would be necessary in a different demographic context. In productivity terms, Japan will have to run faster simply to maintain its position vis-à-vis other economies.'[31]

Summary

Most of the real 'sunset' countries are members of the European Union. The rest are from the Caucasus, the Balkans or Russia, Cuba, Japan and Taiwan. Ageing is affecting most of the world, albeit at different speeds. The more developed countries may have worse numbers but are generally in a rather better financial position to address the issue. China ranks among the less developed countries in this respect.

Gender Disparity

It is normal for there to be a surplus of male babies worldwide, as we have noted. This is presumed by researchers to be a natural reaction to excess male infant mortality. However, that excess situation peaked at greater than 30 per cent in 1970 and has, largely unnoticed, abruptly declined. Nature has not responded. What is interesting is that two countries - China and India - virtually alone have brought the world excess male infant mortality down because they now have excess female infant mortality.[32]

Although global excess male mortality has fallen it is still the rule. It almost halved worldwide between 1995 and 2015. However, China by the early 2000s had fallen to 0.75:1 male to female infant

30   https://www.ft.com/content/702de9c8-b001-11e8-8d14-6f049d06439c
31   http://oecdinsights.org/2016/04/11/the-case-of-the-shrinking-country-
      japans-demographic-and-policy-challenges-in-5-charts/
32   https://www.un.org/en/development/desa/population/publications/pdf/
      mortality/SexDifferentialsChildhoodMortality.pdf

mortality. The suspicion is that this is not nature but prejudice against girls in their early nurture. The world average sex ratio at birth (SRB) for five-year periods has fluctuated from 106 to 108 boys to 100 girls between 1950 and 2015. It is currently about 107 boys to 100 girls. When we note that China is producing around 113 male babies to every 100 females and yet male mortality is 25 per cent less for boys, nature is clearly struggling to keep up with the actual birth conditions.

The World

China's present gender disparity - as measured by SRBs from the World Bank and USCB - although it has fallen, is very high at 113. The only competitor also at 112.5 is Azerbaijan, a country with fewer than 10 million people. Apart from three countries in the Caucasus - Azerbaijan, Armenia and Georgia - the only comparable countries are Vietnam and India with 110 and 111 respectively. After that we can note the Maldives, Taiwan and Pakistan; followed by Albania, Suriname, Papua New Guinea and Samoa, all with around 108.[33]

Some regions in certain countries are conspicuously skewed. Haryana and Punjab states in India were about 116 in 2016. The Red River delta region in Vietnam is approximately the same. Similarly, there are religious differences. Sikhs and Jains have high SRBs; Buddhists and Christians have low ratios.[34]

This is at some variance from Chinese research in 2005 from the People's University in Beijing which states that 'oriental SRBs tend to be higher than white SRBs which are higher than those of blacks … it may be suspected that SRB variation across the three main races is partly caused by variation in maternal gonadotropin levels…' It is unclear why this might be the case and appears to conflict with the global evidence. Notwithstanding, it is hard to find any common factors among these diverse countries. They are not the richest, nor the poorest. There seems no ethnic or religious similarity. They are distributed across the continents.

One outlier is Sweden where it was calculated in 2015 that the ratio of boys to girls at 16 and 17 had gone from 108 to become 123. This is the result of proportionately heavy migration, particularly from Afghanistan and Kurdistan. As immigrating minors have

---

33   https://data.worldbank.org/indicator/SP.POP.BRTH.MF
34   https://www.tandfonline.com/doi/abs/10.1080/17441730.2010.512761

the ability, if accepted themselves, to bring in their families, this would at the same time increase immigration further but potentially redress the gender imbalance.

Azerbaijan, Armenia and Georgia were all subjugated by the Soviet Union which imposed its own value system. Academics suggest that what we are seeing now in the Caucasus is a strong increase in the proportion of male babies fuelled by a reversion to traditional family values facilitated by liberal access to ultrasound equipment and therefore abortion. However, with a combined population of less than 20 million, trends in the three Caucasus states are irrelevant.

India and China

Both India and China have a historic preference for sons due to cultural and economic reasons. But they have taken it to many extremes. There is known to be strong son preference in large numbers of families. The UN hints that the fact that infant mortality has actually reversed to a female excess is suspicious. The world experiences male excess. China and India have female excess. They have high SRBs at birth. Nature is not taking its course.

When couples in India and China decide to limit the number of children they will have, they are often willing to break the law in using ultrasound to identify the sex of a foetus and, if the unborn child is female, they will frequently resort to abortion. UNICEF has estimated that gender analysis of unborn children in India, though illegal, is a business worth $244 million a year. In 2011 *The Lancet* reported that over 12 million Indian girls were aborted over the previous 30 years. As in China, many Asian countries have made it illegal for a doctor to reveal the sex of a foetus to expecting parents.

On this subject, we should note that in India and China there is considerable regional disparity. As noted, some larger provinces had SRBs of 1.16 in India in 2016 and the same in China. In India they are not necessarily the poorest provinces, indeed sometimes the reverse. Delhi has had one of the higher SRBs. In China, remote and rural does tend to characterize the higher rated provinces but with Han Chinese rather than minority populations.[35]

---

35   https://iussp.confex.com/iussp/ipc2017/mediafile/Presentation/
     Paper4760/IUSSP.pdf

If there were no human intervention, high SRB ratio countries would have more normal ratios. Some prefer to present the issue as one of missing women rather than surplus men. Simulations in a report in 2012 from the UNFPA have created an estimate of 117 million 'missing women', absent from the global population in countries where there are high SRBs.[36] Of these, 57 per cent would be in China and 30 per cent in India. This, of course, is in no way reflective of the respective population sizes. There were an estimated 39 million missing girls not born worldwide after 1990, of which 60 per cent would have been Chinese and 35 per cent Indian.

The large-scale absence of girls from certain societies has the understandable result of creating huge gender disparity. For men born after 2000, they will enter a very different world. The UNFPA estimates that 'the number of prospective grooms will exceed that of unmarried women by 60 per cent by 2030 in China and by 2050 in India'. The principal alleviation envisaged is that men will considerably delay the timing of their marriages and yet there will still be tens of millions of unwilling permanent bachelors.

Summary

China and India both began extreme levels of SRBs in the 1980s and 1990s respectively and Vietnam only as recently as after 2005. Other countries may feel demand for their females as brides. The principal impact of gross gender disparity will be in and from China and India.

Falling Population

Unfortunately, there is a steady sinking of global fertility. All kinds of country are seeing their fertility fall. The only exceptions have been in recent years those which fell hugely a few decades ago. These latter have seen a degree of stabilization and even signs of a small increase in rates. It may be surprising but fertility is falling in India, in much of Africa, in many Muslim countries as well as in non-Muslim ones, in Catholic as well as non-Catholic ones. Development specialists will point out that the data in parts of North Africa are often flawed as governments wish to show falling

---

36 https://www.unfpa.org/sites/default/files/pub-pdf/Sex%20Imbalances%20
at%20Birth.%20PDF%20UNFPA%20APRO%20publication%202012.pdf

fertility in order to secure further grant aid. When greater longevity is combined with the steady fall in birth rate, we can see ageing: the balance of social composition shifting radically from the young and middle-aged towards the elderly.

One of the most substantial demographic changes in the last half century has been the near halving of fertility worldwide. According to the UN, the global Total Fertility Rate (TFR) in 1970-75 was 4.5 and in 2010-2015 was 2.47. UN research as early as 2000 stated that the principal causes are urbanization, higher marriage age, greater use of contraception and increased female education. It was made clear then that continuation of these factors 'will ensure continuing fertility declines'.[37]

Most countries appear to have experienced a rising marriage age but some have not. In most countries, the marriage age - or what is called the singulate mean age at marriage (SMAM) - has been increasing since the 1970s or 1980s. The UN and the World Bank databases are patchy but there is clearer data from a private service called Knoema. In all, there is enough evidence to link later marriage with lower fertility. What seems curious is that in this respect a rising marriage age seems more important than the actual age. For example, the marriage age in China has gone from around 21 to 25 and in Europe has frequently risen to the early 30s and they have both witnessed falling fertility.

Indeed, both China and Russia seem aberrational in having relatively low ages of first marriage and yet low fertility. The conclusion might be that marriage age alone is not the driver of their low fertility. There are probable several other factors driving it down.

A Comparison of First Marriage Ages and Fertility by Random Countries 2005-11

	Female 1st Marriage Age		TFR 2005-10
Mali	17.8	2006	6.46
Bangladesh	18.6	2011	2.38
India	20.2	2006	2.73
DR Congo	20.8	2007	6.07

---

37 https://www.un.org/en/development/desa/population/events/pdf/ expert/4/population-fertilitylevels.pdf

Guatemala	21.6	2002	4.15
Pakistan	22.7	2007	3.65
China	24.7	2010	1.56/1.2?
Russia	24.4	2010	1.44
S Korea	28.8	2005	1.29
Brazil	29.7	2010	1.9
Japan	29.7	2010	1.32
France	31.6	2009	1.97
Germany	31.7	2011	1.36
Britain	31.8	2009	1.83

Sources: Knoema https://knoema.com/nleioce/age-at-first-marriage
   World Population Prospects 2010 Revision, UN

One UN survey of 26 countries showed that in all but two there was a clear correlation between female secondary or higher education and lower fertility. UN research has also concluded that 'urban fertility has consistently been found to be lower than rural fertility'.[38] Indeed, in 2000, 44 per cent of the world population lived in countries with at or below replacement fertility. Now, according to Global Burden of Disease (GBD) research, it is well over half, including the four most populous countries.[39]

Most Populous Countries are Non-replacing

Country	Population	TFR
China	1,428m	1.3
India	1,353m	2.1
US	327m	1.8
Indonesia	268m	2

Sources: Global Burden of Disease and UN
https://en.wikipedia.org/wiki/List_of_countries_by_population_(United_Nations)
https://www.thelancet.com/journals/lancet/article/PIIS0140-6736(18)32278-5/fulltext

---

38 'Completing the Fertility Transition', *Population Bulletin of the United Nations*, nos. 48/49, 2002, p. 160.
39 https://www.thelancet.com/pdfs/journals/lancet/PIIS0140-6736(18)32278-5.pdf

The adjustment from increasing to contracting population can be slow if fertility is just below replacement and longevity is increasing as well. However, even the relentlessly positive UN says that - increasingly - countries are now moving into the net of absolute falls. Geographical group after group is moving into the declining column. After the 2050s only Africa plus Iraq will be left with growth. The UN again in 2019 reduced its expectation for global population at 2100 but still shows growth. More regions are concerned by the implications of contraction. And yet, somehow the world has continued fretting about growing overpopulation.[40]

Another factor is deteriorating male semen. This seems to obtain in North America, Europe and Asia. World Health Organization data suggest a long-term marked deterioration. The standards by which the samples are measured by the WHO appear to have been gradually lowered. Reasons which have been suggested include chemicals, pollution, stress and diet.[41] The potential link between chemical pollution and male fertility receives little public discussion.

Of course, sometimes demographic change can creep up without much warning and bring substantial repercussions. An example of such change with rising population is the explosion of births in the Shi'a community in Lebanon in the 1970s. This is a country which does not hold censuses for political reasons. The situation developed that the average Christian family had six members, Sunni Muslim families had eight members but Shi'a families averaged nine members. This took the Shi'a from the third largest community in the 1930s to probably the largest. It enabled Hezbollah to emerge as one of the most potent forces in Levantine politics.[42]

One of the earliest observations of a society with very weak fertility was fifth-third century BC Sparta in Ancient Greece. Here the blame for a low birthrate has been ascribed to an obsession with luxurious living at the cost of the responsibilities of marriage and procreation.[43] This is perhaps not so different from the consumer

---

40 https://population.un.org/wpp/Publications/Files/WPP2019_DataBooklet. pdf

41 https://www.businesstimes.com.sg/life-culture/rise-in-male-infertility-in-singapore-mirrors-global-sperm-crisis

42 Augustus Richard Norton, Hezbollah: A Short History, Princeton University Press, 2018, pp. 12-13.

43 Peter Green, *Alexander the Great and the Hellenistic Age*, Weidenfeld & Nicolson, 2008, pp. 86-91.

culture of twenty-first-century Shanghai. It has been noted of rich young Spartans that 'the doubly propertied young couple would try not to rear too many children between whom their newly gained economic superiority would have to be divided. Consequently, landholdings were concentrated into fewer hands by a familiar narrowing of inheritance... It eventually contributed to a decline in the number of Spartan citizen-males.' It has been said the number of male Spartan citizens fell from 9,000 in 640 BC to 1,000 by 330 BC.[44]

The Greek historian Polybius takes this further and dissects the problem more widely: 'In our time all Greece was visited by a dearth of children and generally a decay of population, owing to which the cities were denuded of inhabitants, and a failure of productiveness resulted … this evil grew upon us rapidly, and without attracting attention, by our men becoming perverted to a passion for show and money and the pleasures of an idle life, and accordingly either not marrying at all, or, if they did marry, refusing to rear the children that were born, or at most one or two out of a great number… For when there are only one or two sons, it is evident that, if war or pestilence carries off one, the houses must be left heirless: and, like swarms of bees, little by little the cities become sparsely inhabited and weak.'[45]

More recently, using data from the GBD research survey, a striking fact is that now one third of all Muslim states - 17 - have a fertility rate at or below replacement. This includes countries as large as Iran, Turkey and Indonesia. Iraq is different. There the population is growing at 2.5 per cent a year. As a result, 40 per cent of the population is estimated to be 13 or below. One of the principal reasons is extensive child marriage. Almost 25 per cent of girls are married before they reach 18.[46] Both growing at 2.5 per cent annually, Iraq and Afghanistan have the fastest growing major populations in the world outside Africa. They are decidedly not following global trends. It is difficult to believe that there is not a connection between births and battlefields.

44 Robin Lane Fox, *The Classical World: An Epic History of Greece and Rome*, Penguin, 2006, p. 76.

45 http://www.perseus.tufts.edu/hopper/text?doc=Perseus%3Atext%3A1999. 01.0234%3Abook%3D37%3Achapter%3D9

46 https://www.ft.com/content/89bbcf7e-3380-11e9-bd3a-8b2a211d90d5

Nine countries - almost all in Eastern Europe - have regressed to population levels not seen for half a century. Probably the most extreme example is Bulgaria where the population has fallen so far that it is now lower than it was in 1950. It is reported to be the poorest country in the European Union. With the steady emigration of the young, it has lost almost a quarter of its population since 1980. The pension system, which in 2003 used 13 per cent of the central budget, recently absorbed 38 per cent and it may, by 2025, take 70 per cent. However, it is not simply emigration, low fertility and extended longevity which create a dystopian environment. In addition, 41 per cent of students are 'functionally illiterate' and one in eight of the population is claiming disability benefits. According to the UN, at least 30 countries and territories are now shrinking, including Greece, Hungary, Portugal and the Ukraine.[47]

A study by Tomáš Sobotka in Vienna has noted several examples of extremely low TFRs, lower than China nationwide today. In Vienna in 1934, TFR fell to 0.61, in East Germany after reunification it was 0.77, 0.9 in Hong Kong in the early 2000s and 0.6-0.9 in Shanghai recently. We have seen cases where low fertility rates have been reversed. Sobotka mentions that 'around 2000, half of Europe's population lived in countries with TFR<1.3; by 2008 no European country was below the threshold'.[48]

Academic research is usually loath to ascribe any part of such reversal to immigration. However, some demographers are more candid. Government statistical offices are also slowly showing greater frankness. Countries which reject immigration will have an uphill battle, although, as Sweden is finding, immigration can increase gender disparity.

Falling fertility is a global phenomenon, which should lead to a plateauing and ultimately a shrinking in the world population. Many others report rates falling but which have not reached that level. Naturally, we must be careful about statistics, even more about official ones and distinctly dubious about Chinese official statistics. There can be powerful political reasons to falsify data. As has been noted, contemporary West Africa is often identified as a

---

47 https://population.un.org/wpp/Publications/Files/WPP2019_DataBooklet. pdf
48 http://www.un.org/en/development/desa/population/events/pdf/ expert/24/Presentations/Sobotka_EGM_02Nov2015

good example of dissimulation in birth data. However, the global trend seems fairly clear. India, which may already be the most populous country in the world and, if not, certainly soon will be, has already according to some researchers seen its TFR fall below replacement rate.

It was not long ago that books were written about the out-of-control growth of global population. Soon the debate will shift to when stabilization in total population will occur, when we will see sustained reduction and how to cope with it.

Japan

Since 1973, Japan has not produced enough children to replace the existing population. The TFR per woman has been below the critical 2.1 level every year without exception. In fact, from 1951 to 2017, the TFR averaged 1.77, well below replacement rate. As a result, by 2017 the country had had seven decades of averaging sub-replacement performance which establishes a deeply grounded pattern difficult to break. Births in 2018 hit a new low of 921,000. This was not only the third consecutive year with fewer than 1 million births. It is also the lowest number since records began in 1899.

Masaaki Shirakawa, a past governor of the Bank of Japan, has said the country's fertility has waned because 'the cost of raising children grew, medical services improved and social security provided a safety net, leading people to want fewer offspring'.[49] This does not seem very credible, as Japan's social security for the elderly is far from generous. Perhaps it seemed more generous some decades ago when low fertility was becoming the norm.

There are three distinctly different expectations for the country's population. One is the UN Population Division forecast. Another is the Japanese government's aspiration and the third is the Japan National Institute of Population and Statistical (IPSS) research. The population peaked at 129 million around 2010. The government hopes to hold the line at 100 million - a fall of under 25 per cent. The IPSS is forecasting 106.4 million people by 2045 and the UN 112 million. Both of them estimate the population will have sunk below 100 million by the 2050s and 2070s respectively.

---

49 https://asia.nikkei.com/Opinion/Emerging-Asia-should-learn-from-Japan-s-demographic-experience

Using the IPSS forecast of 51 million by 2115, the country should have the population it last had in 1910. This will have economic implications.[50]

One response is to introduce more foreign workers. To use this approach, certain assumptions have to be made. A key projection is that while 500,000 a year of net immigration could stabilize the population at around 127 million. IPSS suggests a minimum 69,000 net migrants by 2035. Japan is one of several societies which are immigration averse. For example, as recently as in 2010, Japan's foreign-born population was just under 1.7% of the total, far below the levels found in OECD countries.[51]

Share of foreign residents in total population, 2010

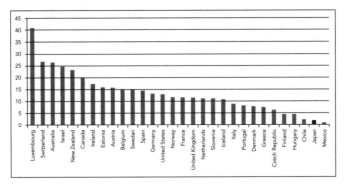

Source: OFCD Popilation Statistics

However, Japan has changed since then. Masaaki Shirakawa observes that 'not many people have noticed that Japan has already been receiving significant numbers of foreign workers in recent years, so that in terms of gross inflow of foreign-born residents in 2016, Japan matches the UK and surpasses France and Canada, for example.'[52] In the five years from 2008 to 2013, the average annual increase in foreign workers was 40,000 per year. In the five years from 2013 to 2018, the average increase was 156,000 a year.

50   https://www.ft.com/content/00df659e-1dcf-11e7-a454-ab04428977f9
51   http://oecdinsights.org/2016/04/11/the-case-of-the-shrinking-country-japans-demographic-and-policy-challenges-in-5-charts/
52   https://asia.nikkei.com/Opinion/Emerging-Asia-should-learn-from-Japan-s-demographic-experience

Number of Foreign Workers in Japan

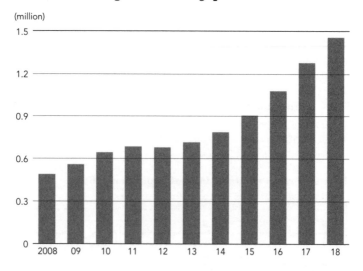

Complied by *Nippon.com* based on data from the Ministry of Health, Labor, and Welfare.

We should note that even the gloomy outlook from Japanese demographers incorporates some improved trends. The average TFR is now estimated at 1.43 rather than 1.35 owing to an increased tendency by 30-year-old women to have more children. This has the effect of delaying the decline a little but not preventing it. It is looking difficult to reach the government's target of rebuilding TFR to 1.8 by 2026.

One of the factors behind Japan's low TFR is perhaps peculiarly cultural. In 2011, '61% of unmarried men and 49% of women aged 18-34 were not in any kind of romantic relationship'. Their attitudes were more extreme. In 2013, 45 per cent of women aged 16-24 'were not interested in or despised sexual contact'. Over 25 per cent of men shared this sentiment.[53] It is estimated that women today have a 40 per cent chance of remaining childless.

The authorities have been placing a greater focus in recent years on pronatal and gender equality policies to let women work

---

53   https://www.theguardian.com/world/2013/oct/20/young-people-japan-stopped-having-sex

and at the same time encourage childbirth. There is a view that Japan's birthrate is fickle and can be revived. If the disincentives are societal constraints, they can be removed. Government believes that Japanese women would be willing to have more children - to the point of keeping the total population at over 100 million. This is the basis for the pronatalist strategy of creating an environment which encourages and nurtures child-rearing.

A major problem has been that it is difficult for a Japanese woman to consider childbirth before her late 20s and by the early 30s it is often thought to be too late. There are barriers to claiming maternity leave and taking time off for childcare. However, costs encourage a woman to have a career. The result is that women rarely have a child until their late 20s. The Tokyo authorities discourage starting a family after 35. Childbirth costs are progressively raised. This creates a short window in which to have a family. Traditionally a female employee in Japan who married found her career stopped, as in Korea. Employers assumed she will have a child and leave. Clearly conditions in this respect are improving.

Of course, these policies could be changed but will they be and when? Government policy has taken a pronatalist direction. Much work has been done. There are more female politicians to influence policy. Female participation in the workforce has risen and could increase further with the right stimuli. But is there reason to think that the birth decisions made by families in Japan will differ markedly from those in East Asia generally? This is a society which is deeply patriarchal. It is encouraging that Japan is now one of the countries which is discussing and introducing child-friendly policies. We do not yet know the full likely outcome.

The OECD stated in 2016 that 'what Japan is experiencing now is without precedent in recorded history: such a contraction of population in the absence of a major epidemic or prolonged war has never occurred anywhere, let alone in conjunction with the rapid population ageing that is now under way'.[54] In fact, except on a very small scale, disease or war have not depleted countries to the extent that we shall see in Japan. Once China starts its at least as steep population decline - and with a population ten times larger - then the world will really see the impact of population contraction.

---

54   OECD *Territorial Review Japan 2016*, p. 40.

Iran

Iran had a TFR of 6.5 in 1980-85. This was very high by world standards. Fear of population explosion caused a policy switch by government to birth dissuasion. This was not as coercive a policy as China's but - along with modern social drivers - it has contributed to a fall in the TFR to 1.8. This is a collapse in national fertility of 72 per cent in only 25 years. The significance of this transformation can be gauged by the fact that 2.1 is the recognized 'replacement rate'. In other words, to maintain existing population levels without growth or reduction requires two children plus an allowance for infant mortality. Iran is one of the 16 Muslim countries having fewer births than the replacement rate - and this has continued since the 1990s. Stuart Basten, a leading demographer, said that 'during the 1990s, Iran secured one of - if not *the* - fastest fertility declines of any country in history'.[55]

The official Iranian attitude to population growth has changed dramatically, in a volatile and bewildering manner. The 1980-88 Iran-Iraq war resulted in an estimated 1 million Iranian dead. For a country of then 50 million, it may have lost 4 per cent of its males. Nonetheless, Iran in the 1980s seems to have feared its population might later hit 140 million. It thus sought to dissuade birth. In 2018, the population was estimated at 82 million and Tehran has been calling for it to reach 'at least 150 million'.

We should note that Iran is not just hostile to the West but as the largest Shi'a nation it is the leader of a global religion outnumbered some 7:1 by Sunni Muslims. Gently declining population growth, such as we are currently seeing in the country, is not an acceptable strategy for Tehran. Several factors drive the population outlook. Young people are marrying later; they are frequently not marrying at all. The young are pursuing university studies instead of marrying after school. Housing is expensive. Marriage age has gone from early 20s to late 20s. This is a global problem and reduces fertility. Iran is 50 per cent more urbanized than the world average and this is steadily continuing. Yet, urbanization is the principal global enemy of fertility.

One of the other major factors adversely affecting birthrates is the steady rise in infertility. This is estimated to affect 10-12 per

---

55   http://www.openpop.org/?m=201404

cent of the world's couples but in Iran it is maybe 20 per cent. The principal factors affecting infertility in Iran are obesity, cigarette smoking, later marriage and higher education. We should also note that its Environmental Performance Index ranking is only about 80th out of 168, when ecological impact on fertility is so serious.[56]

Owing to high levels of infertility and a rising interest in growing the population there has been a surprisingly strong interest in infertility treatment. For some time, there have been subsidized state-owned clinics. Iran has become the IVF capital of the Middle East and even of the Muslim world, despite being a Shi'a country. In 2016, Tehran announced that the government would in future assist couples financially in paying for treatment. The deputy minister of health has said 'state insurance will cover 85 percent of the costs'.[57]

Iran has utilized *ijtihad*, a key feature of Shi'a Islam which allows for Koranic exegesis, or critical interpretation, of the scriptures. This contrasts sharply with the usually more literal interpretation by most Sunni Muslims of the Koran and the *hadiths*, the retained remarks of the companions of the Prophet Mohammed. Not every *marja*, or school, of Shi'a Islam has been willing to issue interpretations of theology permitting IVF treatment but certainly the school associated with the supreme leader Ayatollah Ali Khamenei has done so. The Sunni world has generally resisted fertility treatment.

One distinguishing characteristic of Khamenei's school is that it is of course influential in state policy and thus has national political, as well as purely theological, imperatives. The political elite would like to project greater power overseas, dampen feminism at home and address the weak birthrate. Encouraging motherhood over women's education, achieves all of these goals.

Faced with a demographic meltdown, Tehran has responded quite briskly. Family planning was scrapped. IVF is encouraged. Vasectomies and abortions are discouraged and have recently been banned. Cash is offered for babies. Such a swift, coherent, consistent and disciplined response is not forthcoming in other threatened societies. In China the UN tells us that from 1970 to 2015 the TFR collapsed from 6.3 to 1.55. This would be a slump

---

56   https://epi.envirocenter.yale.edu/epi-topline
57   https://www.businessinsider.com/afp-iran-govt-says-to-cover-infertility-treatment-costs-2016-8

of over 75 per cent in 45 years, slower than Iran but even deeper. However, according to the National Health and Family Planning Commission, by 2011 the TFR was only 1.04, a collapse of well over 83 per cent.

United States

Having four women graduates for every three males is reportedly having a negative impact on marriage rates. The problem is that female graduates are disinclined to marry non-graduate males. Furthermore, Susan D'Agostino at Johns Hopkins University states that $1.5 trillion of student loans is delaying marriage and childbearing.

India

India's current 'demographic dividend' has been welcomed as shifting from the young as dependents to the young in the workforce. However, fertility levels in India have been falling. They have plunged 56 per cent since 1970. While China's fertility has been below replacement rate for 25 years, Indian fertility is only recently - on some estimates - just below replacement rate. According to the Indian census authority, fertility in India after the age of 22 has been collapsing since 1971. For 22-year-olds it has not changed in 50 years. However, by 2010 it was down 40 per cent for 28-year-old women, down 56 per cent for 30-year-olds and down 79 per cent for 35-year-olds. We should not be surprised to see the estimates that India is now below replacement level, with a future impact on the demographic dividend.

When we speak of working-age population, the arithmetic for the economy looks very attractive. However, a structural problem in India is that there are many young people but very few formal jobs.

Russia

In Russia, the prospects for falling population have caused concern for over 20 years.[58] There had been some modestly good news on births, but the 2017 data showed that births fell by 11 per cent to a decade low. This is despite a series of pronatalist policies laid out for 2017 and beyond. Russia is one of the major countries expected to be particularly hit by weak future birth numbers. As with China and Japan, Russia will not welcome immigration as a solution.

---

58   https://www.rand.org/pubs/conf_proceedings/CF124/CF124.chap1.html

In 2019, deputy prime minister Tatyana Golikova made several points about the birthrate. She stated that there were fewer than 35 million women of child-bearing age in the country, they tend to marry too late to have more than one child and there are 750,000 abortions a year of which 80 per cent are quite unnecessary. This is one of the highest abortion rates in the world. While there are fertility problems, Golikova's remarks suggest that much of the problem is attitudinal.

In his annual speech in January 2020, President Putin said 'the birthrate is falling again… The aggregate birthrate … was only 1.5 in 2019… I want to say once again that we are alarmed by the negative demographic forecasts… We must not only get out of this demographic trap but ensure a sustainable natural population growth by 2025. The aggregate birthrate must be 1.7 in 2024.'[59] So the situation is alarming, and there is a prospect of being trapped in a downward childbirth spiral. The country must return to 2.1 births per woman, the replacement rate, and must get to 1.7 in the next four years. Many countries harbour the same hopes.

President Putin offers policy initiatives to achieve the desired results. These include expanding day nurseries, subsidizing low-income families to have children, raising the applicable age, providing capital sums, providing subsidized mortgage rates and offering free hot and healthy school meals. Putin has declaimed on this issue since 2000 without material effect. It is not clear that this package of measures and improvements will result in a material increase in national fertility.

Hungary

Hungary has been threatened by population collapse for many years. This is through both weak birthrates and persistent emigration flows. There are estimates of a 15 per cent fall by 2050.The government has taken several measures to staunch the trend. In 2019 the Orban government offered money for couples marrying. Loans were made available of an average two years' salary to couples if they are not homosexual and the wife was under 41. If the couple has a child within five years the interest will be cancelled. If they have four children, the loan will be cancelled. Prime Minister Orban said subsequently he

---

59   http://en.kremlin.ru/events/president/news/62582

would study whether this could be extended to families with three children. The government has declared IVF a strategic industry and nationalized clinics. Treatment will be offered free.[60]

Croatia

As with Hungary, emigration is a material challenge. Between 2013 and 2017, the country lost 5 per cent of its population to emigration. This is forecast to continue. The government notes that several pro-natal policies have been tried but they do not appear to be effective. The prime minister has described the challenge as 'existential'. The European Bank for Reconstruction and Development has made much of the injunction that better governance would markedly reduce emigration in such countries.

Albania

The population of Albania peaked in the early 1990s at 3.28 million and has then steadily declined. By 2020 it had fallen 12 per cent to 2.9 million. This is a predominantly Muslim country, one of only two in Europe, and yet the birthrate in 1958 was 6.5 and by 2018 had fallen to 1.37. This is a collapse of 80 per cent in 60 years to well below replacement. It is almost as precipitous as the collapse in the birthrate in China during the same period.[61]

Albania appears to have the highest level of emigration in the whole of Europe over 40 years - from 1980-2020.[62] By 2018, one-third of Albanians had emigrated. Incredibly, this is more than the current workforce.[63] These data are controversial and contested, inter alia, on the basis that those who go abroad do sometimes return. However, domestic interest in emigration has grown recently. From 2007 to 2018, it has risen to involve over 52 per cent of the population. A sharp difference is that 'now the skilled, the educated with a job and good economic standing want to migrate'.[64] Albania is one of several European countries at risk of political and cultural collapse.

---

60   https://www.ft.com/content/72f71db2-32ed-11ea-9703-eea0cae3f0de
61   https://balkaninsight.com/2019/11/14/the-clock-ticks-for-albanias-demographic-dividend/
62   https://www.ft.com/content/49e1e106-0231-11ea-b7bc-f3fa4e77dd47
63   https://www.migrationpolicy.org/article/embracing-emigration-migration-development-nexus-albana
64   https://www.reuters.com/article/us-albania-migration-trends/albania-migration-trends-change-52-percent-mull-leaving-idUSKCN1MT2HF

Italy

Italy is an interesting case for the sheer size of its national debt and pension liabilities as a proportion of its economy. With debt at 140 per cent of GDP in 2019, it is one of the most indebted major countries in the world. In the decade from 2009 to 2019, it never achieved 2 per cent growth. This makes it difficult to pay down debt. The country's birthrate went below replacement in 1976 and for over 30 years from 1986 to 2019, it stagnated between 1.2 and 1.4.[65] Births in 2019 were the lowest since Italy became a country in 1861. Births also were less than half the number of deaths. Of those Italians alive, one-quarter are over retirement age. Emigration in 2019 mostly involved young people and was the highest number in almost 40 years.

This guarantees that Italy will have a declining population for a long period. In such a situation of massive debt, negligible growth and falling population, it seems condemned to a vicious debt trap where repayment is unlikely and even debt servicing is totally dependent on foreign governments continuing to manipulate interest rates at distorted low levels. The relationship between high debt and low birth in Italy and Japan has been remarked on by several observers.

Paternity leave in Italy at five days is extremely low by European standards. Judging by the birthrates in the more generous autonomous region of Bolzano South Tirol, it may be that some pronatalist policies could help. It is not easy for Italy to fund a steep increase in welfare payments such as paternity leave. However, it is frequently said that childbearing is weak owing to the precarious economic and debt situation.[66]

Official data explain that the 2019 TFR was only as high as 1.32 owing to the contribution of overseas-born women, who average 1.9 children. Based on Italians alone, the TFR would only have been 1.2.[67] This aspect introduces a political element to the already difficult situation. It also suggests that native Italian birthrates have not recovered at all since their collapse to 1.22 in 1998. Matteo Salvini, leader of Italy's largest political party, has said, 'Are we as a country facing extinction? Unfortunately, yes.'

---

65   https://www.macrotrends.net/countries/ITA/italy/fertility-rate
66   https://www.thelocal.it/20191030/how-ageing-italy-plans-to-bump-up-its-birth-rate-in-2020
67   https://www.ft.com/content/a9d1fe0c-2306-11ea-92da-f0c92e957a96

Europe

The UN forecasts that Europe's total population will start contracting from 2021. Analysts suggest that in Southern Europe, few jobs, poor wages, lack of pronatal policy and inflexible labour markets are causing later childbirths or fewer.[68]

It appears in recent years that Britain and several European countries stand out as having rising fertility rates. This is, of course, after the falls between 1970 and 1980. European fertility rates had largely collapsed by around 2000. They fell by over 40 per cent but then recovered by anywhere up to 8 per cent. However, the native population does not seem to have driven the revival. According to German and British statistical offices, it appears that - as with Italy - foreign-born women with greater fertility were probably crucial in the improvement. We cannot necessarily rely on this factor as a support to European fertility levels. Research in Norway demonstrates declining fertility rates amongst immigrants, falling below replacement by 2017.[69]

The entire population in 10 of the 27 European Union states fell during 2018. The problem is tripartite. There is a very low birthrate, a noticeable increase in longevity and certain countries - especially in the Balkans and the Baltic - are experiencing net emigration which does not all go to other European countries. They are shrinking sharply and the emigrants are not even all staying within Europe.

Israel

We might think that Israel is the exception to the falling fertility rates. In 1975-80 the TFR was 3.47. By 2015, the Central Bureau of Statistics recorded TFR at 3.13. This looks like no real change. However, when we look within the numbers, it is more complex. Most assume that the Arab population enjoys a substantially higher TFR than the Jewish population. Yet in 2015 Jewish and Arab women had each an average 3.13 children. Fifteen years earlier in 2000, Arab women had 4.3 children and Jewish women had 2.6. What has been happening is that the Jewish community has had a rising TFR and the Arab one a falling rate. Although not all Arabs are Muslim, the Arab birthrate reflects the falling rate in much of the Muslim world.

---

68 https://www.ft.com/content/49e1e106-0231-11ea-b7bc-f3fa4e77dd47
69 https://link.springer.com/article/10.1007/s10680-019-09541-0

The ultra-orthodox Haredim community has an extremely high birthrate, higher even than that of the Arab community. However, even their birthrates are coming down. They simply remain higher than the Muslim community or the rest of the Jewish community. The non-Haredim Jewish birth rate keeps rising but has not reached anywhere near the Haredim birthrate, which is falling. In fact, the non-Haredim birthrate has now reached 2.6, which was the average rate for all Jewish women in 2000. The Haredim are expected by many eventually to become the principal Jewish community. However, there is continuing defection to a more secular or less closeted life which erodes the effect of the high birthrates.

The important point here is that there is no national trend in the birthrate in Israel. There are three very different trends and the national result is merely a residual.

The Sahel

Another area with high fertility rates encompasses the African countries south of the Sahara. There are several different definitions of those countries wholly or partly in the Sahel, ranging from five to eleven. For the purposes here the hard core five are used - Burkina Faso, Chad, Mali, Mauritania and Niger. The UN records their modest reduction in fertility levels over recent decades.

Sahel Fertility History and Forecast

The table shows the 'actual' TFR for 1970-75 and 1980-85, the UN forecast for 2010-15 and then the actual for 2010-15.

	1970-1975	1980-1985	2010-2015(est)	2010-15 H
Burkina Faso	6.70	7.06	5.75	5.65
Chad	6.60	6.75	5.74	6.31
Mali	6.93	7.07	6.12	6.35
Mauritania	6.75	6.28	4.36	4.88
Niger	7.52	7.76	6.92	7.35

Sources:
World Population Prospects 2010 Revision
https://www.un.org/en/development/desa/population/publications/pdf/trends/WPP2010/WPP2010_Volume-I_Comprehensive-Tables.pdf
World Population Prospects 2019 Data Booklet
https://population.un.org/wpp/Publications/Files/WPP2019_DataBooklet.pdf
UN Population Data Query
https://population.un.org/wpp/DataQuery/

What is striking is not only how high the birthrates are and how stubbornly they stay up, but also how the UN forecasts are generally for a much more rapid reversion to a mean than is happening. Yet the UN projects a collapse in the coming decades. For example, it records Niger as having enjoyed a fall in TFR over the last 40 years of 2.3 per cent but claims that over the next 35 years it will fall by over 40 per cent. The region has had an overall reported fall of 12.3 per cent over the last 40 years and is forecast to have a fall of over 40 per cent in the coming 35 years.

Niger is a good example of resistance to lower birthrates. It has the world's highest TFR: 7.4. There are strong cultural reasons for this. Men are polygamous; spouses compete to bear children to please their husbands. Only a low 12 per cent of women use contraceptives. Men traditionally tended to obstruct women seeking birth control. There are fears about side-effects of contraception. Only around one-quarter of women show any wish to space out their births. Reducing them is even less popular. There is little political desire to change this situation. Indeed, a study in 2011 by the Guttmacher Institute concludes, 'family planning is not a realistic option'.[70] Guttmacher noted that 'according to an analysis of family planning trends in 13 West African nations (including Niger) between 1991 and 2004, contraceptive prevalence in the region increased by only 0.6% per year over that period, strongly suggesting that those UN projections are unduly optimistic.' In fact, 'unduly optimistic' is a description which could be given to several UN projections.

Several other specialists in African development also doubt these figures and suggest that governments report falling birthrates because donor countries are disbursing money and want to see progress in population control. Some suggest that there may be no reduction at all in birthrates in the Sahel. There is also a theory suggesting a slow reduction in pregnancies but that families breed to outwit infant mortality. However, infant mortality is falling almost as fast as pregnancy. The result is only small or no decline in births.

Guttmacher reported that in Niger, 'the median age of marriage among women is 15.5 and the median age at first birth

---

70   https://www.guttmacher.org/journals/ipsrh/2011/06/niger-too-little-too-
     late

is 17.9'.[71] They further mention that there is 'a strong pronatalist culture in which the desired family size is higher than the actual family size. In 2006, married women and men reported wanting an average of 8.8 and 12.6 children'. Population growth has been running at roughly twice economic growth. In other words, the Sahel is a family planner's nightmare.

For a number of decades, annual grain output has fallen. Lack of fallow periods for agricultural land raise the likelihood of soil exhaustion. Weather patterns are changing. Reportedly 44 per cent of children suffer from chronic malnutrition and this is forecast to increase. Mortality decline halted in the 1990s owing to deteriorating health services. In 2000, there was one doctor for every 47,000 people. Exploding population and falling grain production sit ill together. In a country where most of the land is arid and desert-like, 90 per cent of the population lives in the third of the land which is at least somewhat fertile. Dosso and Maradi, with 6 per cent of the land, house a third of the population and see the greatest number of conflicts over land, many of which are very violent.

The combination of suspect data, desire to attract a husband's attention through outbreeding his other wives, a disdain for contraception, a positive desire for children and falling infant mortality appear to create an atmosphere conducive to maintaining high birthrates.

The good news is that Mali is introducing community health care workers on a national scale, having seen the programme work locally. The impact of going to the families to look for illness rather than waiting for people to come to a clinic allows illness to be identified earlier. The impact on reducing infant mortality has been impressive. Research suggests that lowering infant mortality leads to lower fertility. Although this does not appear so far to be the case in this region, it is possible we could be hopeful.[72] If there is no improvement, what we may see in the Sahel is a dystopia of deliberate overpopulation regulated by nature through emigration, starvation and war.

---

71   *Ibid.*
72   https://www.ft.com/content/63294e4a-3a88-11e9-b856-5404d3811663

Singapore

Singapore has one of the lowest fertility rates in the word at just over 1. In 2019 the government decided to subsidize 75 per cent of the cost of IVF treatment.[73] Academic response has been lukewarm on the basis that many believe the problem is one of attitude rather than any physical obstacle. The median age for female marriage has risen between 2010 and 2019 from 27.7 to 28.5. Overwork discourages childbearing and perfectionism delays until marriage, home, job and savings are all satisfactory.

Taiwan

In Taiwan, over the last decade the marriage age for women has risen from 28 to 31 and the age of first-time mothers from 28.5 to almost 31. Later marriage reduces childbirth markedly. The average fertility rate is even lower than Singapore at about 1.

South Korea

One of the most extreme examples of low fertility is South Korea. In the third quarter of 2018, the national TFR fell to 0.95. By third quarter 2019 it was 0.88, possibly the lowest in the world.[74] The total population is estimated to start shrinking in 2028. This is not a high-wage society but extensive overtime hours are typical. This combination makes childcare difficult to afford and parental assistance can also be hard to provide.

In January 2021 it was revealed that for the first time in its history South Korea had registered more deaths the previous year than births. Only 275,800 babies were born, down 10 per cent from 2019, while around 307,764 people died. The figures prompted the interior ministry to call for 'fundamental changes' to its policies. Already in December 2020, President Moon Jae-in launched several policies aimed at addressing the low birthrate, including cash incentives for families. Under the scheme, from 2022 every child born receives a cash bonus of 2 million won ($1,850; £1,350) to help cover prenatal expenses, on top of a monthly pay-out of 300,000 won handed out until the baby turns

---

73   https://www.scmp.com/week-asia/health-environment/article/3032557/singapores-ivf-fertility-drive-symbolic-ultimately
74   http://www.xinhuanet.com/english/2019-11/27/c_138586793.htm

one. The incentive will increase to 500,000 won every month from 2025.[75]

Female workforce participation has crept above 50 per cent - from a low 47 per cent in 1990 - but in this patriarchal society women's employment is not widely appreciated. Stereotypical views are that when female employees have children they become less useful to the company. Resignation is often encouraged. However, as in other regions, women want careers and do not want them to end with childbirth. The current situation has been described as a women's 'birth strike'. Furthermore, Korean births will not improve with the 2019 decision by the constitutional court to legalize abortion.

Summary

The halving of global fertility since the Second World War is an unprecedented shock. There are several egregious cases of collapsing population. Even in the Muslim world - as has been noted - a third of countries are at or below replacement rate. When the effects of increased longevity wear off, severe falls in population will become visible. There are already 20 small and medium-sized countries registering negative population growth. By the end of this century, we may see Russia lose one-third of its population, Japan one-half and China well over one-half.

Overall, a falling workforce is an experience here and now for many countries. Eleven will lose over 30 per cent of their workforce by 2050 according to the UN. Countries as small as Montenegro and as large as China have begun the contraction. Gender disparity is really only a problem in China and India and a few much smaller countries. Overall, there is a fairly normal global ratio. However, China and India are both very large and important countries. Ageing is rising rapidly but birthrates have been falling in many countries. The problem is not longevity but low birth.

The global population increase is slowing sharply. It has been estimated that after twice doubling in the twentieth century, the world population will not double at all in this century but the number of those over 65 will double in just 25 years. We might not

---

75   https://www.bbc.co.uk/news/world-asia-55526450

even see a 50 per cent rise in population this century. Encouragingly, agricultural technology will probably well outpace population growth.

The turning point has started for falling overall populations. At least 27 countries are already seeing annual falls, even if these are mostly small apart from Japan. During the Black Death in the fourteenth century probably a third but possibly up to half of the population died in Europe. Plagues also caused this level of mortality in the fourteenth, fifteenth and sixteenth centuries in such various European states and cities as England, Norway, Naples and Venice. The Native American population lost countless lives in the colonization of North America. Otherwise there may not be any international examples with which to compare our century's demographic implosion. In the foreseeable future a halving of the population of several countries -small and big - is increasingly likely.

9

HAS PRONATALISM WORKED?

If births are falling to undesirably low levels, it would be sensible to examine pronatalist policy for what has and has not been tried, and effectiveness. Pronatalist policy is usually seen in very specific terms. It is quite right to examine such policymaking. However, policy to support births can be construed much more widely and this chapter seeks to take both a conventional and wider approach.

The state can attempt pronatalist policies, but where they have been tried these have generally had a low impact, such as in Singapore. There is some sign that greater maternal welfare provision has had an effect in Scandinavia. Indeed, politically difficult as it often is, there is some evidence that Sweden has taken action to favour the young over the old. However, as political correctness often discourages ethnic determination, it can be difficult to differentiate between the impact on birthrates of changing social trends among the indigenous people and fluctuations in immigration.

In China, pronatalist policy needs to succeed antinatalist policy but the minds of officials are still so imbued with yesterday's thinking that it may be too difficult to go into reverse and call for all-out mass childbearing too quickly. Too many officials have waxed fat on the 'fines culture' of the one-child policy. In China today there are still hundreds of thousands of people whose main job is to enforce and implement family planning regulations.

One of the problems with pronatalist policymaking is that is difficult to determine the causes of outcomes. As one recent paper remarked, 'the key problem in estimating the effect of pronatalist policy on fertility is that other factors can drive them both, giving the illusion of causation. Economists would say that the policy change is *endogenous*.'[1]

---

1   https://journals.plos.org/plosone/article/authors?id=10.1371/journal.
pone.0192007

We can identify two kinds of pronatalist policy: coercive (in varying degrees) and voluntary.

Coercive Policy

China has a government which rarely shrinks from taking tough measures against opposition. If there is concern about the political impact of the expression of opinion, officials are willing to jail those responsible. Is there room for coercion to increase procreation? From 1979, as noted above, there was an entire 'family planning' industry employing half a million people which did not shrink from forcible sterilization, abortion and compulsory abduction and transfer into institutions of children born without permission. Of course, it is harder to make people do something than prevent them committing an act. The state would probably find it easier to stop citizens expressing an opinion or having a child than making them express a pro-government opinion or have a child.

Second, it was only very recently that procreating beyond a specified limit was against party regulations and liable to lead to inhumane punishments. To move from coercion against to coercion in favour in a handful of years risks making the party look indecisive and flawed. However, as this is a proudly coercive society, authoritarian policy can be an advantage in stressing collectivism. After all, *People's Daily* has said, 'The birth of a baby is not only a matter of the family itself but also a state affair.'[2]

Abortion

First, we need to consider the vexed issue of abortion. Statistics, as ever, are problematical. In 2015 the National Health and Family Planning Commission – since 2018, the National Health Commission - said that there were 13 million abortions a year in China. Qi Rongyi, chief physician of the gynaecology and obstetrics department at a Tianjin hospital, stated that 'The number of abortions performed is believed to be higher. This is because the statistics were collected from registered medical institutions and do not include abortions carried out at unregistered clinics.'[3] Statistics are also likely to exclude the large number of families

---

2   https://www.theguardian.com/world/2019/mar/02/china-population-control-two-child-policy

3   http://www.chinadaily.com.cn/china/2015-01/27/content_19412949.htm

responding to an unwelcome ultrasound reading, whose data are unlikely to be collected. According to the *World Population Review*, in 2021 the abortion rate in China was 24.2 per 1,000 women. When multiplied by the population of 1.444 billion, this gives a total of almost 35 million abortions per year, more than three times the number of live births.[4]

In 2016 the NHFPC said that 62 per cent of these abortions were performed on women aged between 20 and 29, most of whom were single. Nearly 20 per cent had had more than one abortion. If the real figure is not 13 but more than 30 million, that implies that 21 million 20-29-year-olds were having abortions. In 2015, we estimate the number of women between 20 and 29 at 98.3 million. This implies that one-eighth of all women in this age group have had an abortion and 2.5 per cent of all those in the age group each year may be on their second abortion.

Shan Dan, an obstetrician at the Beijing Obstetrics and Gynaecology Hospital, said in 2015 that 'abortions increase the risk of ectopic pregnancies and also the potential for bacterial infection. Abortions also cause sterility in 2 to 5 per cent of women who have them.'[5] That suggests maybe 3.5 per cent of those undergoing an abortion are becoming sterile, or 430,000 a year. Heavy use of unregistered and unlicensed clinics can only increase the risk of complications. One of the reasons advanced for rising infertility is unprofessional 'backstreet' abortions. Maybe an estimated 5 per cent rate of sterility following abortion is more realistic.

Given the drastic national situation, there are grounds for a blanket ban on abortion with appropriate exceptions. Already a number of provinces have stopped abortions after 14 weeks. The number of abortions in the country is currently so large that it seems to represent a lifestyle choice for sexually active women. China probably cannot afford this option. Unlike other forms of legislation, as abortions rely heavily on unlicensed clinics, there must be thorough enforcement of the law. The benefits of legislation are to reduce a public health risk from unlicensed abortion clinics and to increase the prospect of births.

---

4   https://worldpopulationreview.com/country-rankings/abortion-rates-by-country

5   http://www.chinadaily.com.cn/china/2015-01/27/content_19412949.htm

Social Credit

One coercive measure in China which has attracted considerable attention recently is the creation of a 'Social Credit' system. This Orwellian scheme collects data from various sources and generates an overall social credit score. Internet chat services will be obliged to keep records of conversations and 'score' their customers. Prison records and court fines will be sources. The composite score will then rate people and determine whether they can buy tickets to fly or take high speed trains, whether their children get into schools, they get a mortgage or can travel overseas. It can be used by potential employers, bank credit officers or even potential spouses. Endorsements by the government or by economic players help one's score. If someone you know posts a 'negative' comment on social media, your score is reduced. Higher scores even enhance profile positioning on a major dating website. Low scores reduce access to restaurants and internet speed, nightclubs, holiday areas and golf courses for parents, private schools and higher education for the children. Of course, there is no discussion about who guards the guards.

One of the technology companies involved in the project said the system is designed so that 'untrustworthy people can't rent a car, can't borrow money or even can't find a job'.[6] One official document explained that the system would 'allow the trustworthy to roam everywhere under heaven while making it hard for the discredited to take a single step'. By spring of 2019, 13 million Chinese - about 1 per cent of the population - had been classified as untrustworthy. Their lives will now be very different.

The vice governor of China's central bank has urged aspiring bridegrooms to show their central bank credit scores to prospective mothers-in-law to give them reassurance. Others have said that possession of high social scores will encourage mutual confidence in young people looking to marry. From a demographic perspective, it is debatable what effect these will have on the marriage rate, and thus the chance of more children. On the one hand, the possession of two high scores may encourage young people to marry but, on the other hand, the generation of a lower score could prevent

---

6   https://www.wired.co.uk/article/chinese-government-social-credit-score-privacy-invasion

marriages which might otherwise have happened. The net impact on marriage promotion looks marginal. However, the system could be extended to serve national policy. A society introducing social credit scores could consider a further measure whereby those born - say after 1990 - would have higher scores if they have two or more children. Having no children could lead to a negative score.

There can be other elements of coercion but not necessarily for the public. If the top priorities for party cadres are now social stability (absence of riots) and births, they will find ways of strongly encouraging births which may for some appear coercive. Since 2017, the Communist Youth League has been in the dating business. It has stated that it 'will help young people develop a "correct attitude" towards love and marriage'.[7] It even organizes events for members to meet and marry. These include mass blind-dating sessions. It is quite imaginable that young members may conclude that a 'good file' with their supervisors would include a marriage and some children. Without a good file, the best job opportunities may not be open.

This system of coercion can go a lot further. Could we see, for example, new regulations introduced that rule that from a given date all party and government posts up to level 'X' will only be available to natural parents of two or more children? Then, after maybe another ten years, all posts above level X will only be available to similarly qualified people. That means officials will be forced to set an example to the country. Of course, this would be hard on couples who were unable to have children.

Non-coercive Policy

James Crabtree, professor at the Lee Kwan Yew School of Public Policy in Singapore, has observed that 'at base, increasing birthrates means lowering the cost of having children - in particular for women'.[8] It is likely that pronatalist policy will be developed largely through non-coercive means. Yet a glance around the world suggests that non-coercive measures often fail. Voluntary measures can take a variety of forms. Local officials in China have shown some originality in their policies. Shanxi province experimented in 2018 by launching a programme to reimburse part of a couple's marriage

---

7   http://www.globaltimes.cn/content/1081451.shtml
8   https://www.ft.com/content/1e683ca0-77f8-11e9-be7d-6d846537acab

expenses. Hangzhou in Eastern China has been experimenting with extra days' leave at Chinese New Year for female employees in their 30s for the specific purpose of 'dating'. Not surprisingly the proposal has been met with enthusiasm. Xianning city in Hubei has offered to cut kindergarten costs and give subsidies of almost $5,000 to families having problems conceiving a child. It will also prioritize for low-cost housing those families with a second child.[9] Some people noted that stamps issued to commemorate the Chinese New Year of the Pig in 2018 showed two adult pigs with three baby piglets, suggesting official endorsement for larger families.[10] The stamps, though, were met with derision on social media site Weibo with many saying they could not afford more children and the state should not encourage them to live like pigs.

Remaining Controls on Births

As we have noted, Beijing has allowed all families to have two children. However, this has not had the desired effect of raising the birthrate very much. One overdue reform is to scrap all controls on families having the number of children they choose. Shaanxi province (not to be confused with Shanxi) proposed this in 2018.[11] Although there are millions of couples who want no children, there must be some families with two children who would be willing to have three.

Childcare Support

In 2018 Beijing announced a series of allowances including Y12,000 per child for education costs. While welcomed by parents, it seems a small sum compared with the huge expenditure on private tutoring. In 2019 Beijing for the first time allowed a deduction of children's education expenses against tax. This is one of the barriers to child-bearing most frequently mentioned so we must see how it affects couples and whether it is extended.

In the US there is said to be a 'childcare crisis' over costs. The Economic Policy Institute in Washington DC states that in 33 out of 50 states infant care costs exceed in-state college tuition and for two-child families childcare can vary between half and three times their rent. It is very difficult to meet childcare costs on US minimum

---

9   http://www.ecns.cn/news/society/2018-08-17/detail-ifyxccrz0966902.shtml
10   https://www.bbc.co.uk/news/world-asia-china-45124502
11   http://www.ecns.cn/news/society/2018-08-17/detail-ifyxccrz0966902.shtml

wages and yet if childcare is not sought, one of two parents is out of the economy and for single parents it is difficult to work at all. At the high end, a Washington DC minimum wage worker would need over 80 per cent of his or her wages to afford childcare for a four-year-old. In 20 of the 50 states these costs would absorb over half of an average worker's wages.[12]

A two-job, two-child, English family spends about 40 per cent of its disposable income on childcare. This is the highest proportion in the OECD. The average is 12 per cent.[13] So childcare is a problem in many major countries. Childcare costs are also proportionately a big cost in China. There are issues where half of all Chinese urban workers are in informal, low-pay employment and childcare is, relatively, quite expensive. The absence of affordable childcare there is one of the factors deterring Chinese working couples from having children.

We should note, though, that research from the US' National Institutes of Health suggests that children who spent 30 or more hours in childcare each week showed more problem behaviour in childcare and in kindergarten (but not at home) and had more episodes of minor illness than children who spent fewer hours in childcare each week.[14] It also indicates that the family environment is - by two or three times - the more important determinant of a child's development. However, childcare can spur both births and economic activity and thus creates a double benefit to society.

Only 7 per cent of US companies offer childcare centres but there is evidence that they reduce staff turnover and increase productivity, 'as children are the No.1 reason for absenteeism and tardiness'.[15] This is an area where China could consider offering incentives to employers and it is a way to employ retirees in a field directly beneficial to productivity. It is perhaps ironic that in the 1990s, SOEs closed their Mao-era creches to slim their structure and get ready for 'marketization' and even IPOs, but may now need to reinstate them to generate greater productivity.

---

12 https://www.epi.org/files/uploads/EPI-Its-time-for-an-ambitious-national-investment-in-Americas-children.pdf

13 https://www.ft.com/content/c3bd628a-6f2e-11e8-92d3-6c13e5c92914

14 https://www.nih.gov/news-events/news-releases/family-characteristics-have-more-influence-child-development-does-experience-child-care

15 https://www.studymode.com/essays/Tardiness-And-Absenteeism-As-Main-Reason-1492546.html

Parental Leave

In the West it is argued that parental leave is a major issue and reluctant employers tend to reduce it where possible and conceal their obligations from potential employees who are reluctant to inquire in case their applications are consequently disregarded. Activists argue that such retrograde behaviour reduces labour force participation by steering female applicants into the informal sector, where they receive lower pay and less security, or keeping them from active engagement. This has been described as 'the motherhood penalty'.[16] China has highly traditional employment attitudes and it is likely that similar deterrents apply there as in the West.

It is also reported that breastfeeding tends to tail off when a working mother returns to her job. However, breastfeeding plays a vital role in preparing a child for life. It strengthens the immune system, including creating microbial resistance in the gut. It reduces the risk of obesity which in maturity can be life-shortening and it reduces the chance of infant mortality. By curtailing the opportunity for breastfeeding, a woman may be discouraged from having a second child or maybe a child at all. The WHO has called for 'properly paid maternity leave'.[17]

Gender Equality

In early 2019, nine Chinese government ministries issued a set of rules to govern employers' relationship with females. Women at job interviews should no longer be asked questions about marital status or plans for children. There should be no policies that discouraged pregnancy. Childcare provision for working mothers would be improved. The intention appears to have been to encourage greater female participation in the workforce and childbearing at the same time. One of the structural problems in China is that rules are often ignored and this is particularly true if the penalties are exceptionally light. However, it is important to try to create the right environment. Lu Xiaoquan, a Beijing lawyer, has said, 'it's impossible that women would be willing to raise more children if their basic rights at work were not guaranteed'.[18]

---

16   https://www.ft.com/content/3dc1a0e0-35fa-11e9-9be1-7dc6e2dfa65e
17   https://www.ucd.ie/newsandopinion/news/2019/may/01/
      breastfeedingcutschildhoodobesityrisknewwhostudyfinds/
18   https://www.scmp.com/news/china/society/article/2187353/chinese-
      working-women-wooed-new-sex-discrimination-policies

Bride Price

The practice of young men - or their families - paying a 'bride price' in small towns and rural areas has frequently attracted official attention. Several local authorities have tried to limit the ever-rising amounts. In some areas the bride price exceeded $100,000 and continues to rise. In Henan province, when it reached over $20,000 in 2019, the local government tried to set limits at less than half that figure. The National Bureau of Statistics survey in 2017 estimated that there were 1.5 unmarried men for every unmarried girl over 15. The extraordinary gender gap is pushing up the bride price across the country, making marriage more difficult. Seeking to regulate the bride price when there is such a rising gender disparity is understandable but official efforts have borne no fruit.

Internal Immigrants

The central authorities in Beijing should give more thought to the 250 million internal rural migrants who have no clear status in the cities where they work. Even if the wife accompanies her husband, or vice versa, the knowledge that access to medical care and education in the cities is problematic is a disincentive to having children. It has been estimated that there are over 60 benefits which are disproportionately available between urban and rural residents. The laws which brand every person in China as urban or rural create a divide which has been likened by some observers to the much-criticized apartheid system in South Africa before the mid-1990s. Reform of the household registration, or *hukou* system, could instil more stability and thus confidence for couples in the cities. This could improve the birthrate. Policy work is being done in this area but it is woefully slow and thus not currently producing results.

Unintended Consequences

There has been considerable discussion of raising the retirement age from 60 for most men and 55 for most women. The purpose would be to relieve pressure on the pension funds and increase the labour force, given the contraction under way. This would assist in both those areas but has not yet been implemented. A negative consequence is that it could deprive working mothers of grandparental childcare and thus influence the mothers either to give up work or give up childbearing. Beijing may have to decide which result is more desirable: strengthening the falling workforce or encouraging women to bear children.

Infant Mortality

Given the poor survival rates for infants in Western China, more effort could be made to bring infant mortality closer to the levels of Eastern China. There needs to be not only a reduction of infant mortality as a whole in Western China but a specific reduction nationwide in the excess female infant mortality which scarcely exists outside China and India. Most important, given the looming shortage of young women, is to redress the unnatural excess female infant mortality in China. Male excess infant mortality was the rule in the 1970s. By the 1980s there was parity with females and by 2000-20 there was a 33 per cent female excess in infant mortality.[19]

The WHO strongly advocates breastfeeding to protect infants against early disease. Raising sales taxes on infant formula, banning the sales staff from maternity hospitals and making their incentive arrangements illegal could be combined with thoroughgoing maternal education programmes starting during gestation.

Social Media

In 2019 some publicity attached to the discovery of an open database which contained the age, education, address, telephone number and identity number of 1.8 million women with an average age of 32, together with their 'BreedReady status'. Although the shortage of women is accompanied by an increasing reluctance to marry, it is unlikely that such an approach will produce desirable results.[20]

Pollution

The impact of pollution - whether soil, air or water - on fertility and infant health is evident. Unfortunately, China is one of the most polluted countries in the world. In recent years Beijing has declared its determination to change its environmental status. However,

---

19 https://www.un.org/en/development/desa/population/publications/pdf/
    mortality/SexDifferentialsChildhoodMortality.pdf
20 https://www.theguardian.com/world/2019/mar/11/china-database-lists-
    breedready-status-of-18-million-women

the practical reality is that pollution persists at excessive levels. A more assiduous government focus on reducing national pollution and cleaning up the country would materially assist in permitting pregnancy and fostering infant health.

Foreign Models

It is worthwhile to survey pronatal policies around the world and the results. They differ in their emphasis but tend to be similar.

The Franco-Scandinavian Model

There is European research suggesting two important conclusions. One is that more childcare and support equates to more women in the workforce and higher TFR, which sounds logical. Scandinavia and France are at the higher end; Japan and Southern Europe at the lower end. The second seems somewhat counterintuitive: societies with high levels of open relationships, such as cohabitation without marriage, appear to have higher fertility. Again, France and Scandinavia provide the evidence. The suggestion is that traditional marriage where the husband works and the wife stays at home lends itself to gender inequality and women find the environment unconducive to childbearing. As French demographer Laurent Toulemon told *The Guardian*, 'If family traditions cannot be adjusted to suit the new political reality of gender equality, it results in a *de facto* refusal to bear children.'[21]

The argument is that in France and Scandinavia the state has taken a major role in allocating significant budget finance to childcare. More activities, wider availability and longer hours in childcare correlate closely with higher fertility. If child-rearing is made easier and allows a woman to work, births will follow. It is ironic that this is a reversal of the situation of even 30 years ago. Another French demographer, Olivier Thévenon, also told *The Guardian*, 'Up to the end of the 1980s the countries with a high fertility were, on the contrary, the ones where women didn't usually go out to work.'[22]

Reconstituted, or blended, families, unmarried couples and single parents are examples of more open relationships and are more

---

21   https://www.theguardian.com/world/2015/mar/21/france-population-europe-fertility-rate
22   *Ibid.*

common in Scandinavia and France than in Southern Europe or Japan. Over 50 per cent of births in France, Sweden and Norway are outside marriage. *Post hoc ergo propter hoc.* The academic argument has been made that such social units are freer and thus less patriarchal and create more gender equality, which encourages childbearing.

High spending on childcare raises some concerns. Reportedly it can reach 3-4 per cent of GDP in France and Scandinavia. There are likely to be debates over the relative merits of defence spending and the need for smaller budgets. The second point may raise even more heated debate as to the desirability of less marriage in society.

There is some criticism of the amount spent on pronatal policy towards children who may not be born rather than on the aged who are definitely here. The totals are high and weigh heavily on France's budget deficit.

TFRs for Selected European Countries 1975-2015

TFR	1975-80	1990-95	2005-10	2010-15
Denmark	1.68	1.75	1.85	1.73
Finland	1.66	1.82	1.84	1.77
France	1.87	1.71	1.98	1.98
Norway	1.81	1.89	1.92	1.82
Sweden	1.66	2.01	1.89	1.90
Britain	1.73	1.78	1.87	1.88
Germany	1.51	1.30	1.36	1.43
Greece	2.42	1.42	1.46	1.34
Italy	1.89	1.27	1.42	1.43
Spain	2.55	1.28	1.39	1.33

It is interesting to see that the other major countries in Europe, such as Germany, have TFRs that are about 25 per cent lower than those of France and Scandinavia. Academic research corroborates that in France unmarried cohabiting couples display the same fertility rates as married couples. However, research also shows that in the US cohabitation tends to lead to lower fertility than marriage, possibly because it often happens later in life. Thus we might - cautiously - assume that cohabitation can produce lower fertility results than marriage.[23]

---

23   https://www.ncbi.nlm.nih.gov/pmc/articles/PMC3576563/

We cannot be sure that what makes the whole difference is childcare, working women and open relationships. There is another factor at work: immigration. French immigrant women are almost 80 per cent more likely to be mothers than long-term French residents. This may translate into raising the national TFR by something over 5 per cent. Later, however, the birthrate tends to converge with the national average, particularly with higher education.[24]

Immigration and Fertility: Britain, Sweden, Italy and Germany

Researchers seem highly reluctant to discuss the extent to which immigration may affect national fertility rates. Until 2016 Sweden, with a mere 2 per cent of the EU population, regularly took a disproportionately high proportion of the asylum seekers accepted into the bloc.

Proportion of Incoming Asylum Seekers to the EU Taken by Sweden each Year

%	2012	2013	2014	2015	2016
	11.7	11.7	12.3	11.7	2.2

Estimates in 2016 suggest that there were then 123 boys to 100 girls in the 16-17-year age group in Sweden. This improbable fact emerges because asylum seekers are included and there is an extremely high number of under 18-year-old Afghan boys. It is possible that immigration may be as relevant to the fertility rates of France and Scandinavia as childcare and gender equality.

In Italy, demographer Marcantonio Caltabiano writes about the period since the mid-1980s and observes a modest improvement in fertility but in northern, not southern, Italy. He writes: 'In the northern regions of Italy, period fertility has returned to the levels observed in the early 1980s, in part due to an increasing number of babies born to immigrants, whose fertility tends to be higher than that of native Italians. Overall, however, there has also been a slight increase in native fertility, coupled with the diffusion of new forms of family arrangements

---

24   https://www.ined.fr/en/everything_about_population/demographic-facts-sheets/faq/france-fertility-level-no-immigrants/

among the younger cohorts. Today in the northern regions, about 30% of births occur outside of wedlock, while about 20% of births have at least one immigrant parent.'[25]

So Caltabiano ascribes the small fertility improvement to immigrants, cohabitation and lastly native fertility levels rising slightly. His observation does not necessarily mean that cohabitation produces more births than marriage. He probably means that it adds to the choices of living arrangements which can sustain child-rearing. If people are not going to choose marriage, then the option of cohabitation increases overall births.

In Germany, TFR bottomed at 1.24 in 1994, shortly after reunification, and had risen close to 1.45 by 2017, to 1.57 by 2018 before dropping back to 1.54 in 2019. This is partly the result of heavy social expenditure but also of a liberal immigration policy. For example, from 2014 to 2015, the fertility rate of immigrant women in Germany rose from 1.86 to 1.95. In 2016 all births in Germany rose by 3 per cent but births to non-German women rose 25 per cent. Births to non-German women became 23 per cent of all births in the country. A government report noted the rise in births to older German women encouraged by better family benefits and also the impact of rising births to non-German women, many from countries with traditionally high birthrates. There was no conclusion on which was most important.[26]

In the UK, there are many similar trends. TFRs have risen since the low of 2005 to around 1.8 in 2020 - albeit on a declining curve.[27] The Office of National Statistics says there is no single explanation for the increase, but notes that foreign-born women tend to have higher fertility than UK-born women. In 2018, the ONS said that the percentage of live births in England and Wales to mothers born outside the UK rose every year from 11.6 per cent in 1990 to 28.4 per cent in 2017 and 'in recent years, the percentage of births to women born outside the UK has been higher than the percentage of the female population of childbearing age born outside the UK'.[28] The data seem clear.

25   https://www.demographic-research.org/volumes/vol21/23/21-23.pdf
26   https://www.politico.eu/article/germany-migration-helps-bump-birth-rate-to-highest-in-decades/
27   https://www.worldometers.info/demographics/uk-demographics/#tfr
28   https://www.ons.gov.uk/peoplepopulationandcommunity/birthsdeathsand marriages/livebirths/bulletins/birthsummarytablesenglandandwales/2017

Foreign-born women in Britain definitely do have higher fertility rates and this is a material factor in the TFR which, although falling, is still higher than the regional average. A second point made by the ONS is that 48.1 per cent of babies born in 2017 were to unmarried mothers although two-thirds of them were living with the father. So in Britain we may note in particular the contribution of foreign-born mothers and the high proportion of unmarried parents.

There is widespread cynicism in the demographic community about the effectiveness of pronatalist policy. Yet it seems likely that the success in high TFRs in France and Scandinavia may be partly due to childcare policy, partly the extra dimension of cohabitation and also the contribution of high immigration. Although TFRs in Western European countries are generally higher than East Asia, Audrey Donnithorne has suggested that 'large immigrant communities mask the host populations. These societies are not stable but in rapid near-future demographic decline.'[29]

Poland

The Polish government is instinctively pronatalist and in October 2020 the country's top court banned all abortions, including in cases where there are foetal defects.[30] These are the strictest rules in Europe. Plan 500+ gives $1,520 per year for each child after the first. Although it is relatively more generous than the US Child Tax Credit of $2,000, it has not had sufficient effect. In the year to July 2018, births were 400,000 but needed to be 600,000 to reach replacement rate. The first half of 2019 was almost 5 per cent below 2018. Even the births of children by Polish mothers overseas do little to fill this gap.[31]

Finland

The homecare allowance for families to hire help for childcare was widely praised when introduced. It gave public money to allow families to make private choices. However, TFR has fallen since 2010 by 20 per cent to 1.49 in 2017, and 1.41 in 2018, the lowest in the

---

29   https://www.ft.com/content/00ccc058-7311-11e9-bbfb-5c68069fbd15
30   https://www.bbc.co.uk/news/world-europe-54642108
31   https://stat.gov.pl/en/topics/other-studies/informations-on-socio-economic-situation/statistical-bulletin-no-82019,4,104.html

country's history.[32] Research published in 2019 gives clear reasons for the low birth levels in the country: 'Women are postponing childbearing to a later age, mainly because of enrolling in tertiary education, focusing on employment, having housing and economic uncertainty, engaging in premarital cohabitation and delaying marriage at later ages. In addition, men play an important role in delaying parenthood because of having inadequate knowledge about reproductive lifespan and postponing forming partnerships and parenting with women. These complex trends, which affect the decision of having a child, may differ across socioeconomic groups.'[33] This is all very cogent but was probably true five years ago or ten years ago. It does not really explain why popular pro-natal policy cannot improve the weak birthrate.

United States

Influenced by pronatalist thinking, the US started the Child Tax Credit in 2018. It is a step in the right direction but not with very high sums. Families can claim a tax credit of up to $2,000 for every child under 17. The TFR for the US in 2021 was 1.781, a 0.11 per cent increase from 2020. It was 1.779 in 2020, 1.778 in 2019 and 1.776 in 2018.

Russia

National TFR in Russia had been falling since 1950, but in recent years has begun to rise. Having reached a low of around 1.16 in 1999, the TFR has risen steadily over the past 20 years to around 1.8. In 2021 it stood at 1.823. Pronatal policy dates back to at least 2007, with continually mounting incentives. These involved a mixture of lump sums, childcare allowances, kindergarten rebates, maternity leave allowances, tax deduction, rural land allocation and, more recently, extra midwife centres in rural areas and extra nursery places.

Russia is a leading example of a population on the edge between flat-lining and falling. The government has pursued pronatal policies with a focus on cash payments and interest rate subsidies on mortgages. The continuing weak birthrate does not suggest that this is very effective, despite the nation's reduction in vodka consumption.

---

32   https://www.tandfonline.com/doi/pdf/10.1080/00324728.2020.1750677
33   https://www.ncbi.nlm.nih.gov/pmc/articles/PMC6340426/

Japan

Japan also has one of the world's lowest fertility rates. Its TFR sank below replacement in 1974, never recovered and bottomed at 1.26 in 2005. It recovered to 1.43 in 2013 and has oscillated around that level until now. Shinzo Abe, former prime minister of Japan, has claimed that 'Abenomics' is 'womenomics'. Japan has not been known for its enlightenment in terms of gender equality. Recent developments have included limits on overtime working, mandatory disclosure of gender diversity, equal pay for equal work and lavish parental leave. There is a drive for many more places at childcare centres to reduce or eliminate the waiting lists. This has also been driven by employers' difficulties in getting staff. However, that may have been a second factor in Abe's mind; Japan is short of labour as well as babies.

The national birth rate in 2018 fell to a new low. On the other hand, female participation in the workforce grew by an important two percentage points, while it kept falling in the US and China. This amply illustrates the frustration of policymaking. Some of the objectives may be reached through policy measures while others are not. It is possible that there is a longer lead time to changing birthing behaviour.[34] In 2019, Abe made infant school - from 3 to 5 - completely free and day care free for those up to 2 from poorer families.[35]

Republic of Korea

In the decade from 2006-2016 Korea spent $68 billion on encouraging its citizens to have children. Gone are the 1960s and 1970s when the government subsidized sterilization to keep the population in check. By 2016 it had a TFR of 1.19 and a TFR below 1 for the whole of 2018. This could be the lowest rate among countries in the developed world. There is a 70 per cent graduation rate, high average marriage age and a falling rate of marriage. All is linked and uniformly negative for childbearing.

34   https://data.worldbank.org/indicator/sl.tlf.cact.fe.zs
35   https://www.japantimes.co.jp/news/2019/05/10/national/japan-enacts-legislation-making-preschool-education-free-effort-boost-low-fertility-rate/#. XOJO-FIzaUk

Hungary

The generous pronatalist policies introduced by the conservative government of Victor Orban in Hungary after its election victory in 2010 are of particular interest. The population situation was dire. TFR was low even by European standards, longevity weak and making little progress and emigration a constant threat. In 2011 the new constitution gave a special position to the institution of marriage. This measure and the associated policies are more expansive and aggressive than those of other countries. Hungarian women with four or more children have a lifetime exemption from income tax. Young couples can have interest-free loans worth $36,000. These will be written off when they have three children. There is government support for buying seven-seat vans. Extra nursery places will be created. Government housing subsidies will be expanded. The Institute for Family Studies in the US analysed these benefits just up to mid-2018 and concluded: 'Given that the average salary in Hungary is only around $11,000 to $15,000 per year, an equivalently-impactful subsidy for Americans, based on our higher incomes, would need to amount to somewhere between $40,000 and $250,000.'[36] The Orban government has taken Hungary's severe population challenge much more seriously than many other countries.[37]

As a result, Hungary has enjoyed a marked increase in fertility rates since 2011, from just above 1.2 to almost 1.5. This is particularly the case for the critical 20-29-year-olds, but up to now there has not been so much success on the multiple child front, although it is too early to judge some of the more recent policies. Analysis suggests that the combination of government incentives and constitutional recognition may have encouraged marriage with the secondary effect of the birth rate rising. It is noteworthy that Hungary stresses the opposite of the 'Franco-Scandinavian model'; it affirms the value of marriage over cohabitation. Gender equality is not a priority.[38]

If we take account of the impact of immigration in Singapore

---

36   https://ifstudies.org/blog/is-hungary-experiencing-a-policy-induced-baby-boom

37   https://www.bbc.com/news/world-europe-47192612

38   https://ifstudies.org/blog/is-hungary-experiencing-a-policy-induced-baby-boom

and decide that it is a significant feature in France, Britain and Scandinavia, then Hungary may be the most successful country in its pronatal policies.

Financial Considerations

Many pronatal policies are an effective cost on the employer or a constraint on him/her. However, several would constitute a financial cost to the public budget. The world's impression of China is of a country becoming ever stronger and capable of projecting itself powerfully in a number of directions internally and externally. The reality is different. This was exemplified in 2019 when Xi Jinping offered a further $60 billion to African countries when a senior education official had earlier said that the country would not extend its present nine years of compulsory education to 15 as it could not afford it. In 1993 Beijing set a target of spending 4 per cent of GDP on education. It failed every year. Only in 2012 was the goal achieved and by international standards it is in any case a low ambition. Military veterans have been atrociously treated and yet - for political reasons - one might imagine that they would be a cosseted sector. Budgetary constraint is an important issue in Beijing and it will be increasingly apparent in funding the impending ageing society. This suggests that pronatal policies which require large-scale spending will be hotly debated by policymakers as well as the childless public.

One possibly reassuring fact is that at times when taxes have recently been cut it does seem to have led to more tax revenue being raised. This appears to bear out the US Laffer Curve thesis that lower tax rates raise revenue. But it is probably too early to draw any such conclusion in China. Nonetheless, Liaoning province, particularly poorly positioned, has decided to offer incentives on education, housing and tax to couples who have a second child.

Political Barriers

Creating a pronatalist climate that works will not be easy. As with many issues it requires political will. From social media, for example, it is clear that too much policy rebalancing towards financing child-rearing raises anger from other sectors of the public.[39] For example,

---

39   https://www.ft.com/content/f34bb0b0-2f8b-11e9-8744-e7016697f225

in 2018, two Nanjing professors proposed a 'birth fund' into which everyone below 40 would contribute and draw out at retirement, but which parents with two children could draw on early. This was met with abusive responses from people who felt it was biased against couples without children and just another form of tax.

Summary

Professor Wang Feng of University of California, Irvine, has expressed some considerable scepticism as to whether Beijing can - or even wishes to - enact policy solutions to arrest and reverse the decline in births. It would require 'fundamental social restructuring … this is not something that the Chinese government is capable of doing, let alone has any resolution to do.'[40] That does not mean it cannot be done; merely that it is not easy.

---

40   https://www.ft.com/content/f34bb0b0-2f8b-11e9-8744-e7016697f225

10

POTENTIAL POLICY SOLUTIONS

In this book we have examined the four principal demographic challenges facing China: labour shortage, ageing, gender disparity and falling population. As we have seen, the outlook for China appears bleak. The working-age population is set to continue falling, suggesting a less competitive economy and less growth. The country is ageing rapidly, implying increasing fiscal pressure and less innovative spirit. Gender disparity is excessive and may cause social instability. It should diminish but it cannot be swiftly eradicated. Falling birthrates do not reverse quickly. All forecasts show falling population long into the future. Demographic changes develop slowly but the trends can then be colossal and durable. China's future in this century will be shaped largely by its current population structure. As CASS said in 2019, 'the long-term population decline, especially when it is accompanied by a continuously ageing population, is bound to cause very unfavourable social and economic consequences.'[1]

James Carville, former adviser to President Bill Clinton, once said he wanted to be reincarnated as the bond market because he could then intimidate anyone. He could have said that he would like to be reborn as demography, which will be governing most decisions in most countries for at least the rest of this century. It is therefore crucial to take an original look at potential policy responses. They may not be solutions but could be powerful mitigation. In parallel it is essential to plan for adverse developments which cannot be avoided.

Responding to Ageing

We have already noted that one standard response to ageing is to encourage greater participation by older people in the workforce. For example, working life could be lengthened by delaying

---

1   https://www.express.co.uk/news/world/1067686/china-news-economy-trade-population-decline

pensionable age in the absence of illness. Even when it is feasible, however, the immediate effect of elderly people continuing in employment reduces the provision of in-family childcare. The related impact could be to endanger China's fragile fertility through making childbearing less practical and palatable for working mothers. This is one of the critical conundrums in the demographic crisis.

We have seen the observation of the World Bank that China is a middle developing power which 'even with sustained productivity growth, however, ... will not reach the income levels of ... (richer and older) East Asian and Pacific economies or OECD and middle-income countries ... at similar points in the demographic transition', and even if it does , it will be an 'aged society at much lower levels of income than the (more developed ones)'.[2] So, we are seemingly faced with a large but not highly affluent society which will confront a growing aged population with a collapsing workforce and income and sales tax base.

We have noted the rising criminal behaviour of the elderly in Japan. In Korea, elderly criminality is growing rapidly and also disproportionately as a share of the population. There may be cultural differences between elderly Japanese, Koreans and Chinese but there are also similarities. Increasingly children of the Chinese elderly are spending less time with their parents. This is a major change. There are also underdeveloped social security and pensions arrangements. We should probably expect a similar trend to emerge in China.

An ageing society in the West would normally be expected to have a substantially higher budgetary cost. In Asia, elderly care has often been provided by the family. However, China has managed to break with its Asian heritage. In the large-scale absence of siblings, combined with internal migration and greater longevity, the burden on working children is becoming less bearable.

Rapid ageing and the retreat of the family from social provision will also place a very heavy burden on public finance and is likely to drive up government debt. Although not a first rank developed world power, China has already accumulated,

---

2   http://www-wds.worldbank.org/external/default/WDSContentServer/
     WDSP/IB/2015/12/17/090224b083cb86bc/1_0/Rendered/PDF/
     Live0long0and00ast0Asia0and0Pacific.pdf

in recent years, very high levels of debt. A future pension fund deficit, estimated at $14 trillion, could undermine the financial capacity of the state.[3] Unless some highly innovative funding mechanism is created, this suggests that either the economy must grow at an unimagined rate, debt must exceed rational levels, fiscal imposition will weigh more heavily on the productive economy, possibly encouraging further emigration, or certain budgetary areas must be curbed or stopped.

Bank of America Merrill Lynch has estimated that in North America just one year of added average longevity 'could more than double the amount of aggregate pension underfunding'. Moreover, 'worldwide, annuity and pension-related longevity risk exposure is already a "worrying" $15tn-$25tn - about three months' worth of global gross domestic product'.[4] Despite alarmist commentary, China has no more debt as a share of GDP than the US and less than Japan. The problem is that those are both modern, developed and rich economies. History suggests that the debt-bearing capability of developing countries is a substantially smaller share of their GDP than is the case for more mature economies.

Younger citizens may chafe at a wholesale reversal of budget priorities in favour of the old. This could lead to anger and even to civil instability. In future the Chinese state may feel the expectations of the young are becoming so inimical to social stability that the voice of the many old should be given some electoral prominence to drown out the young. It may be ironic that as the state leaders become younger, they increasingly identify with the elderly. The price may include accepting comprehensive social provision. Similarly, the damaging impact of seniority in a rapidly ageing society could block promotion prospects for, for example, younger scientists and thus dampen innovation and encourage emigration.

The widespread absence of siblings helps to explain the decreasing enthusiasm by youngsters for supporting their elderly relatives. Let us then assume half of the over-65s may need state care by 2040. This is a marked increase on today's estimated 2 per cent. We are using a working estimate of 400 million over-65s by 2040. If we assume low-standard care provision at the level

---

3   http://knowledge.ckgsb.edu.cn/2016/10/17/demographics/silver-age-
     chinas-aging-population/
4   https://www.ft.com/content/0066d01c-1e74-11e6-b286-cddde55ca122

of Y1,400 (say $200) per month as obtains currently in many municipal facilities, the annual cost per capita would be around $2,500. For 200 million people, this is an annual budgetary cost of $500 billion. Let us note that this does not include medical or health costs, merely living costs.

To put it in context, for China this is the equivalent cost of building 70 aircraft carriers every year. China currently has two carriers. It ignores the high maintenance costs; carriers spend six months a year in dock. However, in 2013 President Xi said that improving welfare was the 'No.1 priority'. This suggests another critical conundrum in choosing between ballooning welfare costs for the aged and military projects.

Future welfare provision will inevitably affect budgeting. If China cannot invest in every desired area, it will need to make uncomfortable choices. Inevitably this will raise structural questions. Can China maintain global military power projection and the growing internal security provision? In 2019 several large-scale military capital investment projects came under question owing to the slower economy. It seems clear that not all political constituencies can be well served.

The financial solutions will probably need to be a combination of encouraging much more foreign and domestic private-sector elderly care provision and pension provision, reluctantly accepting the disadvantages which stem from delaying the pension age and moderating military expansion. Hard-headed analysis would conclude that China has no real external threats.

It seems clear that ageing will be very costly. Increasing criminality by the elderly and accompanying recidivism is likely. Keeping the aged at work through delaying retirement age to reduce pension outflows could severely reduce in-family childcare and thus risk accelerating the fall in birthrate. Pensions will either be funded by some imaginative private-sector or foreign solutions or will present a defining budget challenge. Either global military projection will be continued or welfare can be reformed and expanded. The two are unlikely to be sustainable together. Ageing may cause China to become a large, angry and threatening version of Japan. This ambiguous outcome may lead to the condition described in the common expression: 'they veered between apathetic torpor and hysterical fanaticism'.

Addressing Gender Disparity

The initiatives begin by considering the effects and then looking at the causes. Inevitably, some measures may have a short-term impact, but others may only take effect in the long term.

A Search for Brides

Many Chinese single males currently have to look outside China for wives to complement the diminished national stock. In fact, many academics discard the term surplus males in favour of 'missing girls'. To address this fully, there might be two approaches: seeking women from the neighbouring region or, more imaginatively, seeking women wherever there seems to be a substantial surplus of women.

Marrying women from within the East Asian region would not be a novel approach but each community in Asia tends to have its own specific features which assist or hinder this process. To a significant extent the South Koreans looked overseas to address their own recent gender disparity. This was short but sharp, running from just before 1985 and ending by 2007. It thus affected 18-year-old girls in the region from 2002 and is still continuing. As an example, 'In 2010, half of all middle age men in South Korea were single.'[5] By 2006, 13.6 per cent of all Korean marriages involved a foreign partner. One of the drivers was the substantial gender imbalance which peaked with the 1990 sex ratio at birth of 116.5 (116.5 boys born to 100 girls). The number of Koreans marrying foreigners has subsequently subsided from 31,000 in 2005 to 18,000 in 2013, but remains high. This experience in Korea has not been universally successful. Inability to share language and having different cultures both play their part. At one stage, 40 per cent of Korean mixed-race marriages ended within five years. Owing to unhappy marriages, Seoul banned marriages by men whose income is below a certain level. Furthermore, levels of abuse within marriages became so high that the Korean government banned marriage to foreigners by any Korean men with a history of violent behaviour.

Highly educated and career-oriented East Asian women are frequently uncomfortable with the patriarchal aspects of Asian marriage and often eschew marriage altogether. Research from

---

5   https://www.hbs.edu/faculty/Publication%20Files/12-082.pdf

Harvard Business School suggests that 'a college-educated woman in developed East Asia is 50 to 200 percent more likely to remain single than a less-educated counterpart'.[6] For example, in 1981 fewer than 10 per cent of Korean women went to college; by 2006 it was 60 per cent. Thus there is a pool of often high-achieving single Asian men who look for overseas brides from more traditional cultures. These men are characteristically from Taiwan, Singapore, Japan and South Korea.

We should note that in 2006 over half of mixed-race Korean families earned under the minimum wage of $8,000. Since 2014, Korean bridegrooms seeking a foreign spouse are legally required to have annual income above $14,000. This means that all four of Japan, Singapore, Taiwan and South Korea will have large numbers of relatively high-income single males seeking brides from traditional and, more importantly, poorer countries. This will present a challenge for single males in China. We can see that the eight Chinese provinces with the most severe gender disparity in 2010 were generally poorer than the national average. Indeed, four of them rank among the seven poorest provinces and autonomous cities (out of 31) in the whole country.

Given the social and economic structure of East Asia, it is relatively easy to see the countries where Chinese singles might find a bride. Those singles are likely to be rural, less educated and over 20 per cent poorer than the national average. This does not suggest that they possess foreign language skills. There are likely to be cultural clashes between Muslim women from Pakistan and Bangladesh and pork-eating, baijiu-drinking Chinese farmers. Malaysians, South Koreans and possibly Thais are likely to be too affluent. Indians and Nepalis are often Hindu and ethnically distinct; there is probably no great logic to such unions. Mongolians seem to be better disposed towards the Russians than the Chinese.

Seeking a Wife in Southeast Asia

The Philippines might seem a possibility as there is now a larger proportion of the population in poverty than there is in China. However, it is generally English-speaking and Christian. There has also been the Sino-Philippine dispute over the South China

---

6   https://www.hbs.edu/faculty/Publication%20Files/12-082.pdf

Sea and, perhaps, unease towards China among many Philippine citizens. Any initiative would need to comply with the 2003 and 2012 laws on trafficking in which Manila includes any matching for a profit of Philippine and foreign nationals for marriage.

The more promising possibilities are Vietnam, Burma, Cambodia and Laos. They have per capita GDP s of $1,000-2,000 and have rather more familiarity with Chinese culture. Proximity does not, of course, always generate amity; there are tensions towards China in Vietnam, Laos and Burma.

If we think of Burma, we might imagine that it would be the 69 per cent of women who are rural and outside an institution who might be the target for single Chinese males. As we lack very clear cross category data, we might apply this percentage to other groupings. In 2014 there were 6.54 million Burmese women in total who were single, widowed or divorced. Applying, somewhat experimentally, the 69 per cent factor to rural women outside an institution, we would come to a target group of 4.5 million available rural women. For the future, perhaps we should include 3.76 million rural girls between 0 and 15. This would make 8.3 million. It is improbable that most would cross the border and marry Chinese farmers who do not speak their language, know their culture or who are unlikely to appreciate Buddhism. Most of these are young single girls who are likely to be planning to marry a compatriot. Perhaps - thinking liberally - we could assume that one-quarter of these women might be tempted to marry a poor, uneducated and unattractive Chinese peasant over the coming years. This suggests that there might be 2.1 million Burmese brides for, maybe, 45 million Chinese men. If we are lucky, 4.5 per cent of the problem solved.

Cambodia in 2015 was estimated to have 7.2 million women and girls below the age of 54. In the unlikely event that in the coming years one-quarter of them married Chinese farmers, it would only amount to 1.8 million. Laos with a total population of 7 million will not play an important role here either.

The Prospects in Vietnam and Taiwan

Vietnam has a large population, estimated in 2021 at 98 million. There is a very small surplus of women, but the TFR has been running just below replacement for several years. Therefore the future surplus may shrink. Moreover, the country has its own infant gender disparity almost as extreme as that of China. In 2014 it had risen to 112.4:100. If anything, it is believed to be rising whereas China's disparity may be falling.

It was noted earlier that Taiwan has a sex ratio at birth of 108. However, in 2002 the average age for first marriage in Taiwan was 31 for men and 26.8 for women. By 2012 it was 32 for men and 29.5 for women. The important point is that it rose by three times as much for women as men. By 2016 it was 30 for women. More pertinently, for Taiwanese women it was 30.8 in 2012, as opposed to 29.5 for all women married in the country. This shows two facts. In Taiwan women's age of marriage is rising faster than that of men and Taiwanese women are marrying later than other nationalities living in the country. This indicates a diminishing enthusiasm for marriage amongst Taiwanese girls.

The falling interest in marriage combined with the high gender imbalance towards men creates a profound difficulty for Taiwanese men seeking wives. As a result, there has been a major drive among Taiwanese men to marry girls from Vietnam. Broadly half of all foreign brides in Taiwan are from Vietnam. Almost 90 per cent come from rural districts where income levels are below average. In these poorer provinces, the vast majority of international marriages are with Taiwanese. The most evident characteristic of these marriages is the average age of men at 35 and women at 22 - a gap of 13 years. The brides have low education and their Taiwanese husbands are similar. The Taiwanese grooms pay an average $10,000 for a bride. In 34 per cent of the cases, the marriage decision for the girl is made entirely by parents. After the meeting and agreement to marry, the average time until the wedding is 3.5 days. The reasons for the girl marrying are almost entirely economic and generally speaking their families move from near poverty to relative comfort after the marriage.

Poorly educated Taiwanese men are missing out on marriage at home as it becomes less appealing to women and those women considering it will seek to marry upward not down. However, these men are considered a good economic catch in Vietnam amongst poor and poorly educated rural women. If millions of Chinese farmers started trying to marry Vietnamese girls in a large-scale, organized way, it is likely the Hanoi government would take measures to halt the activity to prevent disturbance to Vietnam's own demography. But, more importantly. they are unlikely to be seen as attractive husbands compared with the Taiwanese.

Casting the Net Wide

The limited number of surplus women in East Asia might lead potential Chinese husbands to consider women from further afield - in fact, from anywhere. There are certain countries which currently have surpluses of women in the age group 25-54 and even some within the ages of 15-24. This is despite the global surplus of males up to the mid-50s when a female surplus became predominant. These countries could in future attract the attention of Chinese men, or more likely, those whose business it is to assist them in achieving their goals. This group may in future include the government in Beijing, in the interests of public order.

There are about 45 countries which have a surplus of women over men of marriageable age. As may be expected there are several complexities. The surpluses range from 50,000 to possibly 3 million. Fewer than 20 countries have surpluses below the age of 25. The range from 25 to 54 is doubtless in many cases weighted heavily to the higher ages. The surpluses may often be deceptive as some are in countries where polygamy is practised.

The Central Asian republics which border China are ethnically distinct and predominantly Muslim. Kazakhstan and Uzbekistan have about a quarter of a million surplus women. Tajikistan and Kyrgyzstan are home to returned migrant workers from Russia who can no longer find work with the rouble collapse in recent years and may not be able to enter into marriage. Although recovered from the 2016 nadir, the rouble is still at around half the level of 2008-14. Remittance income has been the largest contributor to both economies. The weak Russian economy has made it difficult for the men to find gainful work abroad. This has led to unemployment and lower marriage prospects for them at home. The women might be attracted to China and Beijing may propose that marriage facilitation be made a stipulation for loans under the Belt and Road Initiative. However, it is unlikely that a significant number of women would be found or unions forged, not least because of Chinese antipathy towards Muslims and the treatment of Uyghurs in Xinjiang.

If there are around 50 million Chinese bachelors, then the solution needs to involve millions of brides. There are only three countries with millions of surplus women of marriageable age. After that, solutions will involve painful stitching together of piecemeal prospects from different countries for relatively small numbers.

Bangladesh appears to have the largest surplus of marriage-age women. It is a society where one-third of women are married before 15 and three-quarters by 18. Thus there may be interest among surplus women in considering marriage to a foreigner rather than being unmarried for life. This is a Muslim society where polygamy is permitted but seems very little practised in reality. Being Muslim and racially distinct may make marriage to Chinese spouses less practical as an option. The typical Bangladeshi girl is already married by around 20 to a man around 26. The surplus of men from 40 and above is probably academic as they have lived through a period with a surplus of women and presumably not married. Over 10 per cent of women are widowed or otherwise separated by their late 40s. The number of women over 20 who never marry or are widowed or divorced is around 3 million.

The other two countries with large surplus female populations of marriageable age are Mexico and Russia. Mexico's surplus of around 2.5 million is evenly distributed from 20 to 55. Russia's surplus is about 2 million and runs from the ages of 30 to 55 but is concentrated almost 50 per cent in the age group 50-54, perhaps linked to the historic prevalence of alcohol-related illness amongst Russian men. If the age range of 50-54 is thought of little interest to potential Chinese bridegrooms, the Russian surplus halves to 1 million. Although Mexico is a member of the high-GDP OECD, there are substantial numbers of poorer Mexicans. However, the country is over 90 per cent Christian. Apart from the potential for identifying unmarried rural women, it is difficult to see many cultural bridges between Spanish-speaking Christian women in Mexico and Chinese bachelors.

There is little point in spending time on small countries such as Cambodia and Laos, where there may be deemed to be some cultural affinity, when the populations are so limited. The realistic options - where scale is available - do not in general show obvious links: Burma, Bangladesh, Mexico and Russia. If China's agricultural labourers are to be encouraged to marry Mexican, Russian and Bangladeshi spinsters then some acculturation will be needed. China's rulers may need to sponsor a programme which private-sector agents will execute. They will need to think how geographically dispersed and ill-educated rural Chinese men can be prepared for communicating with women from such different cultures.

Addressing the Causes of Disparity

We looked earlier at how countries have dealt with the effects of gender disparity. Korea also addressed the causes. The country was previously egregious in the degree of its son preference, but in 30 years the country went from a sex ratio at birth of 106 up to 116 and then back to 105. The Korean government increased social security for the elderly and women's education, changed children's inheritance and wives' status through creating choice in children's family names and land ownership rights. It is unlikely to be unconnected that such changes coincided with a sharp reversal, indeed elimination, of the highly skewed gender disparity of Korea in 1990 within 17 years. Conditions are different in every country, but Korea is a shining example that governments can tackle the causes of major social problems and succeed.

If Chinese parents want sons because they will guarantee security in old age, social security can be introduced. Inheritance law can be reformed to treat girls equally. Women can be made more effective marriage partners through greater education. This would, of course, require lessening the geographical disparity in educational spending. Most societies would not relish the heavy hand of the state re-engineering their preferred family life and inheritance arrangements in order to achieve an important social goal. Most societies do not at present have the problem which Korea faced at the end of the 1980s.

One longer-range solution to China's disparity is to encourage parents who want two children to accept that one is a girl. Second, if they insist on only one child, policy measures can be taken to make daughters more welcome in today's homes. It is slowly becoming clear in urban society that a daughter is better equipped to look after parents and in-laws than a son. There is no longer a premium on farm work but on solicitude. Bride price is making sons more costly. This reality needs to be understood by young marrieds. State-directed propaganda is one of China's specialities; it would be very helpful in this instance.

Gender disparity is likely to work itself out in the coming years. As China becomes less rural, as mechanization on the farms rises and as plot sizes increase, the preference to bear sons to work the land is likely to diminish. Furthermore, there are already signs many families have more confidence in their future care from a daughter than from a son.

Dealing with a Falling Workforce

This question really means: if we are facing a falling workforce which can prejudice the country's economic future, what are the solutions? The measures that might be considered include new strategies for creating a workforce and alternatives to having the previous-sized workforce. We must address the causes and the effects of the issue. Interestingly, Wang Pei'an, deputy head of the National Health and Family Planning Commission, made a telling comment at a meeting with journalists in 2016: 'China's workforce is adequate … It's the quality of workers, not the quantity that's the problem'.[7] While noting that labour reduction is affecting the economy, his point is certainly in line with much research done at the higher end of the labour market on the 'skills gap' and graduate unemployment and under-employment in China. It would also corroborate research on the malfunctioning of vocational training.

There are three classic contributors to economic growth: labour, capital and productivity. We are seeing labour diminish. In fact, since 2011 almost the sole contributor to growth has been capital, and that has been with ever lower returns. In policymaking terms, we can either seek pronatalist measures to later turn the trend of falling native births, increase female participation, delay pensionable age, encourage immigration, find other ways to rebuild the workforce. or accept that the population will shrink. If, however, we are going to accept the fact of sub-replacement Chinese births and thus a falling population, we will need to examine solutions which can mitigate or balance this effect through other means.

---

7   https://blogs.wsj.com/chinarealtime/2016/01/22/chinas-working-age-population-sees-biggest-ever-decline/

Can the Workforce Be Boosted?

It is often proposed that Beijing should relax the rules for urban residence (*hukou*) to lure more labour from rural areas. Twenty years ago it would have been good strategy to relax the residence requirements for rural migrants working in the cities. However, there is now much less surplus or underemployed, rural labour contemplating life in the major cities. There is probably minimal unused surplus left in the villages suitable for urban work beyond that to be provided by future births. Indeed, there is considerable evidence of the diminishing attraction of city life for rural residents.

More promising is that if land ownership reforms were contemplated, mechanization resulting from the increased scale of rural farms could release some more labour, but it is unlikely to be substantial. A classic remedy for a decreasing workforce is to increase female participation. Unfortunately, China already has the largest female participation rates of any major economy; this is despite having lost 10 percentage points from 74 per cent in the early 1980s to 61 per cent over 30 years later in 2018. (This level of 61 per cent in China compares with 57 in Britain and 56 in America, 55 in Russia and 55 in Germany.) Contemporary China may have many blemishes, but it is no longer the totalitarian system of Mao. It is probably difficult for a now only semi-totalitarian China to increase female workforce participation by much. However, there are areas to consider.

Research indicates that relieving maternity problems and the use of infant formula has accounted for 'approximately 50 percent of the increase in married women's workforce participation between 1930 and 1960 in the US'.[8] According to the World Health Organization, China, to its detriment with a fifth of the world's population, uses a third of the infant formula so - even if this method were acceptable - there is little immediate boost there.

In the US, the Economic Policy Institute has been vocal about a 'childcare crisis' in which many poorer Americans cannot afford childcare. In a 2016 paper they concluded that 'the benefits of boosting women's workforce participation through the provision of more and better childcare access and affordability are potentially enormous. Women are, of course, half of the potential workforce,

8   https://ourworldindata.org/female-labor-force-participation-key-facts

and each 1 percent boost in the overall workforce increases total national income by 1 percent, or roughly $180 billion.[9] The numbers may be smaller and there are differences in the social structure but there is probably a lesson here for China.

There are estimated to be up to 25-50 million Chinese, both men and women, without appropriate papers because they were born outside the official system. They did not have their birth registered during the 'one-child policy' regime. As a result, their work options are limited. Government could facilitate their entry into the normal workforce. Indeed, Xi Jinping has referred to initiating such action. Any liberalization of their situation would free up for more efficient deployment a large number of young below the age of the mid-30s.

Another possibility is to accept increasing longevity and regularly raise retirement ages in order to staunch workforce evaporation. However, we should note the rapid replacement of traditional illnesses with the illnesses of prosperity. These include obesity, diabetes, cardiovascular illness and mental illnesses. As we have seen, 40 per cent of over-65s in 2013 were described as 'diagnosably depressed'. Such maladies may affect the deployability of the elderly. Indeed, many of these illnesses arise from modern work routines and particularly from a more sedentary lifestyle.

Research shows that Western workers are often more productive as they get older as they have the education to learn and improve. However, almost half of older Chinese workers have often not completed primary level education.[10] This may explain the success of German and other Western countries in postponing retirement and gaining extra productive workers. The results of retirement postponement in China may be more mixed.[11]

Any increased retention of the old in the workforce, in a semi-traditional society such as China, as noted earlier, will reduce the less obvious role they often play in providing childcare for two working parents. Such a reduction may have perverse consequences in the willingness of mothers to work and on the desire of parents to have

---

9   https://www.epi.org/files/uploads/EPI-Its-time-for-an-ambitious-national-investment-in-Americas-children.pdf

10   http://www.economist.com/news/briefing/21601248-generation-old-people-about-change-global-economy-they-will-not-all-do-so

11   https://www.ft.com/content/fd1078c8-03c7-11e9-99df-6183d3002ee1

a second child. Yet if longer working years and later pensionable age are possible solutions to two of our four problems - ageing and a shrinking workforce - it might just become necessary to do it. There is the potential negative consequence of longer working years by the elderly in slowing the promotion prospects of the young thus both inhibiting but also less obviously preventing the rise of novel and iconoclastic thought. Retirement postponement works in advanced societies. For example, in Japan, where one in three citizens will be 65 or older by 2025 and where there is expected to be a shortfall of 6.44 million workers by 2030, and where one in three Japanese will be 65 or older by 2025, the retirement age for men has been raised to 70. This is less helpful in China as older workers are, as we mentioned above, often insufficiently educated to offer the skills needed.

We need here to address a medical debate in China. If the elderly are to work longer, they need to be healthy. Many professionals believe that future medical gains will be predominantly for the benefit of the elderly. Research suggests that increasing life expectancy will be driven by improvements in the health of the elderly rather than children.[12] Further contributions were made by 'constant reductions in mortality from cerebrovascular disease, chronic lower respiratory disease, and gastrointestinal cancers'. As risk factors such as hypertension and obesity continue to rise, longevity has probably improved through international medical advances and greater access to treatment. Many cancers remain uncurbed. Clearly the slow pace of recent drug introduction may be a factor here in being at least as positive for the future. As a corollary, it is felt that there are few further gains to be had from reducing infant mortality. However, the gross disparity, mentioned earlier, between the situation in West and East China and between female and male mortality disproves this theory.

As noted earlier, a 2013 study blamed air pollution for cutting longevity in North China by 5.5 years. One of the authors remarked that this was rather like cutting the workforce by an eighth. If air pollution can be reduced, it can have the effect of decreasing the decline in the available workforce.[13] There has already been a

---

12   https://bmcpublichealth.biomedcentral.com/articles/10.1186/s12889-018-5112-7

13   https://www.pnas.org/content/pnas/110/32/12936.full.pdf

substantial cut in Beijing's air pollution with the obvious political imperative. It has even been suggested that it may fall out of the top 200 most polluted cities in the world. This can then presumably be achieved elsewhere. However, the fact remains that 23 out of the 50 most polluted cities in the world in 2018, according to the WHO, are in China.[14]

If efforts are made and any breakthroughs are found in infant mortality, China could in future be in the happy position of seeing marked improvements in the health prospects of the old and the young. With the old already alive and the future young not yet conceived, this situation suggests that the ageing percentage of society will continue rising. However, better health might enable the aged to continue working and paying tax rather than drawing on the fragile pension system. Overall, there could be two positive contributors to mitigating population fall.

Shanghai does enjoy seven years of greater life expectancy than the national average, but it is not that much advanced in its shift to non-communicable diseases. At the same time, it is experiencing ageing more rapidly than the national average. It is a useful lesson that this is where medical improvements can have the greatest impact. This will come as little surprise given the appallingly low birthrates in the city. Nonetheless, it is a useful check for policymakers that they need to weight their health spending towards the old.

In a society where perhaps 30 per cent of the young go to university or colleges, there is an unacceptably high level of graduate unemployment or underemployment, which at times approaches 30 per cent but could in fact be higher. The authorities plan to raise tertiary education participation to 50 per cent. This seems a pointless approach until the quality and effectiveness of university education is improved. Some measures are being taken but by no means enough. In the meantime, it might be better for the morale of the young and the health of the economy to reduce tertiary participation. The state could cut the number of Chinese youths at 18 going to university by, say, 20 per cent and get the young into the economy, after perhaps an improved course of vocational training.

It can be argued that opportunities for every young person leaving education are blocked by every elderly person who

---

14   https://en.wikipedia.org/wiki/List_of_most-polluted_cities_by_particulate_
matter_concentration

continues working. But if China were to become a genuine market economy, employment should not be a zero-sum game. Additional available people keep wages low and allow entrepreneurs to experiment with new enterprises and services which may not previously have existed. The negative factor is that if through ageing and birth reduction the average age keeps rising, it is likely to make the workforce less flexible and innovative. So, although in some contexts experience trumps age, the need for vitality and innovation is paramount.

If there is a need to bring in workers from outside China's borders, the most obvious place is to look at those citizens who have left. It is believed that half the estimated 3.5 million students who went abroad to study have not returned but have acquired residence overseas. As they went during the period of China's rapid growth, they presumably did not stay away for superior economic opportunity. There may be other aspects of life overseas which might be preferable for them. China's government needs to reflect on this situation.

The next place to look at is the Chinese diaspora, which was estimated in 2018 at over 60 million. Families often emigrated over the centuries owing to harsh governments and limited economic opportunity. Most are living in countries where Chinese are a minority and sometimes a not so well-treated minority. Why do more of them not move to China where the country is run by Chinese? Are they not convinced about either the government or the opportunity?

Out of politeness to the Communist Party, international sources tend to exclude 23 million Taiwanese from the overseas diaspora. However, Chinese seem to have been intermittently emigrating there from the seventeenth century to the point that the original culture has now been largely overwhelmed by Han Chinese. This, though, is a society where three times as many want formal independence as want unification with China, where just 4 per cent identify as 'Chinese' and 57 per cent do as 'Taiwanese'.[15] Although Taiwan's industry has invested heavily in China for cheap labour or markets, this seems to be decreasing and Taiwan does not seem to be an abundant source of future mainland citizens.

---

15   http://focustaiwan.tw/news/aipl/201907110012.aspx

A classic approach to a demographically-driven workforce reduction is to encourage multi-ethnic immigration, usually only on a temporary basis. Generally, but notably in 2015, the World Bank encouraged East Asian countries to 'embrace immigration' and offered the examples of Australia and Singapore with populations of 20 and 40 per cent respectively comprising immigrants.

Much like several other demographically threatened countries such as Russia or Japan, China is not culturally inclined to this route. The idea of resident foreign experts has been accepted - by China that is, not necessarily by the experts. These would be at the top end of the talent chain. At the other end, the situation is not so clear. One inducement for certain categories of foreign expert allows them to bring foreign domestic staff. There are quite a few overseas manual workers in China but often with dubious or no documentation. They have been reported as coming from Vietnam, Burma, Laos and Cambodia. In 2014, over 5,000 illegal labourers were reported caught in Guangdong province. While a principal magnet, it is not the only target area for such workers. It has been estimated by one source that there are 30,000 in the city of Dongguan alone. Ironically, some have even been employed building the fence along the Vietnamese border to reduce illegal immigration into China.

Given the culture of collusion and bribery between factories and officials, the existence of mass fake identity card production and the highly varied accents, dialects and languages of China's citizens, it would perhaps not be too far wrong to suggest that China may have over 100,000 illegal overseas workers. The demand for workers considerably exceeds such a number, however, and yet there seems no debate yet on mass legal immigration of labour.

There are also considerable numbers of African migrants living in China. The city of Guangzhou in the highly industrialized province of Guangdong was host to several hundred thousand at one point, many of whom arrived as traders, but then overstayed their visas. Recent estimates suggest around 15,000 in the city, many of whom faced discrimination and insults from Chinese during the Covid-19 pandemic.[16] Many complain they are not made to feel welcome.

---

16   https://www.theguardian.com/commentisfree/2020/apr/25/coronavirus-exposed-china-history-racism-africans-guangzhou

How Can China Encourage Productivity Growth?

If attempts to replace the falling workforce prove impractical, other measures will be needed. The most promising might appear to be to raise productivity in the widest sense. Unfortunately, research indicates that although productivity is very low and had been improving rapidly, from 2007 it has been falling.[17] While attempting to raise everything, China must rely less on inputs of labour and capital and focus more on areas such as improving total factor productivity (TFP), technological improvement, improving capital allocation and economic reforms. While accepting that these categories overlap, they are indicative of policy areas.

In the past TFP improvement arose from more efficient resource allocation through labour moving from rural to urban work. However, much of this has been done and so the opportunity has diminished. Furthermore, the early, easy gains to be achieved from exploiting the different levels of technology between China and overseas are reduced by the gradual narrowing of that gap in many areas. Some of the impact could be addressed through technology. Yet we must appreciate that technology needs to be easily usable by an older generation of less-educated Chinese workers. Smart technology is needed for unsmart users.

Both more efficient use of capital and greater innovation are possible. Some opportunities now are more available through mobilizing capital and labour and managing their allocation on a strictly sectoral basis to choose more productive sectors. However, reforms are needed to scrap the barriers to entry in a host of 'strategic sectors'. Researchers at CASS have concluded that efficient allocation of capital and labour - if allowed - across the whole economy could increase national TFP by 30-50 per cent. According to CASS, preserving the barriers to entry in industries dominated by state enterprises creates a 'great loss of allocative efficiency'. As they acknowledge, 'A competitive environment is vital for enhancing the potential growth rate in China over the next decade or so.'[18]

---

17 https://www.conference-board.org/retrievefile.cfm?filename=KBI-FY15---China-Slowdown---Final-Draftv2.pdf&type=subsite
18 https://papers.ssrn.com/sol3/papers.cfm?abstract_id=2236513

In 2018, AXA, the asset management firm, suggested TFP growth will come in future from three initiatives. Human capital must be upgraded through improving education. Urbanization must continue and the last elements of rural underemployment should be squeezed out of the villages through migration to towns and cities. Financial and economic reforms should be driven through even if politically unpalatable. Recent IMF research suggests that these reforms would add 0.5 per cent to annual TFP growth. If China can also succeed in carrying out its industry-upgrading policies, detailed in '*Made in China 2025*', then a whole percentage point of TFP growth can be added to the economy. If China can really get TFP moving it would offset negative labour and capital trends to create a 'soft landing'.

It is unfortunately the case that productivity growth has been disappointing globally over the last decade, with the exception of a recent pick-up in the US. We seem way past the peak in generating high productivity growth. In China in particular, productivity was exceptionally low and improved rapidly but this has stalled in recent years. However, there are distinct conditions in China which create specific opportunities.

The BBC believes that by 2030, 60 per cent of all graduates in STEM subjects (science, technology, engineering and maths) will be from China or India. The contrasting situation would be 8 per cent in Europe and 4 per cent in the US. This sounds encouraging for China but seems to be taking a rosy view of China's population outlook and probably underlying the remark is an optimistic view of academic quality in China.[19] Also, it probably overlooks the fact that recently the second most popular subject at Chinese universities has been literature.[20]

Innovation has proved an elusive and somewhat intangible commodity in China, which has for many years set targets and held ambitions. In the Global Innovation Index (GII), China has slowly struggled up the league table to reach the top 25 countries in the world in 2016 and no. 14 in 2019 and 2020.[21] Its ranking in no way reflects the size of its economy, its effort or its budgets. This

---

19   https://www.bbc.co.uk/news/business-35776555
20   https://theconversation.com/inside-the-worlds-largest-higher-education-boom-74789
21   https://www.globalinnovationindex.org/Home

is despite the quantified measures - as opposed to the qualitative - such as number of patent applications and scientific papers, which plays more to China's strengths.[22] One of the factors weighing down the ranking in innovation is the very low score for rule of law.

Official encouragement has focused understandably on hard targets. Research and development intensity, number of patents applied for and published scientific papers have been favourites. One of the negative by-products of these demands is that teaching has been downgraded. Unfortunately, the quantity of R&D spending as a percentage of GDP would be a useful yardstick if every country calculated in the same way and if the expenditure was closely related to research. Unfortunately. neither of these is the case. Patents applied for seem clearly less useful than patents granted. Even for the latter, there is the issue of innovation patents and the more incremental utility patents. The latter are rather popular in China. There is a pervasive sense of mediocrity about the patent store accumulated in China in recent years. Moreover, there is a very active culture of applying for patents not to manufacture but purely to harass foreign industrial companies when they bring manufacturing to China. There is also a concern about scientific papers and plagiarism. One report summarized this as 'systematic fraud and mass retraction of research papers from the Chinese academic system, and allegations of attempts to game the peer-review system on an industrial scale'.[23]

Scientific papers have been pushed high on the state agenda in recent years and the world is now flooded with Chinese-originated research. Unfortunately, this medium is riddled with plagiarism and deliberate misattribution. The British medical journal, *The Lancet*, said in 2015 that 'research integrity has not kept pace, and research misconduct, such as fabrication, falsification, plagiarism, and unattributed ghost-writing threaten to overshadow China's achievements'.[24] The long-term implications are ominous because 'current huge investments in biomedical research will not translate into new discoveries or more reliable medical evidence without a

---

22   https://www.wipo.int/export/sites/www/pressroom/en/documents/
     pr_2019_834_annex1.pdf
23   http://www.scmp.com/comment/insight-opinion/article/1758662/china-
     must-restructure-its-academic-incentives-curb-research
24   https://www.thelancet.com/journals/lancet/article/PIIS0140-
     6736(15)60700-0/fulltext

sea change in China's research culture and regulatory systems'. The situation not only exists in medical research. It is pervasive throughout the sciences.

This can, of course, be confronted if there is a will. It is possible to discourage such practices through appropriate punishments and rewards. There are signs of changing attitudes by the authorities, but it is difficult to transform a lax culture into one of strict measures. Second, we should remember that in China laws are one thing but enforcing them is quite different. While individual scientists criticize the academic environment, those in charge seem largely silent.

The subject of indigenous innovation is more interesting to a nationalist government than it is to a businessman. Business does not mind where a robot comes from as long as it is price competitive. If the savings are sufficient a German-made robot may suit the requirement. Perhaps one made in Japan would have lower transport cost. It is possible that overseas robot makers could lower their cost - and protect their intellectual property rights - while in future manufacturing in China. The issue of China's indigenous innovation should not be allowed to cloud the priority of effective automation.

The drive to develop home-made innovation, make patent applications and require academics to publish research papers is focusing too much on the quantitative rather than the qualitative, encouraging plagiarism and the short term in general. For example, Chu Zhaohui, a senior researcher at the National Institute of Education Sciences, has said, 'at present the number of papers published still plays too large a part in promotion and career achievement'.[25] James Lewis makes the point that 'the rate of progress is conditioned by Chinese domestic politics, since more restrictive policies create an outflow of money and talent'.[26] Jeffrey Ding makes another challenging point: 'As earlier analysis on megaprojects demonstrated, China's industrial policy approach to scientific innovation has been criticized for diverting resources from bottom-up, investigator-driven [sic] projects to large national projects run by mediocre laboratories, on the basis of personal connections.'[27]

---

25 http://www.chinadaily.com.cn/global/2019-10/18/content_37516693.htm
26 https://nsiteam.com/social/wp-content/uploads/2019/03/AI-China-Russia-Global-WP_FINAL2_fromMariah8mar2019_ndw11mar2019.pdf
27 https://www.fhi.ox.ac.uk/wp-content/uploads/Deciphering_Chinas_AI-Dream.pdf

As discussed earlier, specialists in innovation believe that what is required to create fertile soil is a populous society in a free-market economy, population concentration and a youthful society. China has a populous country but not a free-market economy, nor its corollary, strong property rights. There is population concentration, but society has ceased to be youthful and is on the way to become 'super-ageing'. This is not promising but some action could be taken to improve matters.

It has been observed that China's innovations are largely applications, thus dependent on foreigners, particularly for semiconductor chips. Its ambitions will depend on investment in basic research. However, China has won back the number one position in supercomputers and has announced a plan to have an exascale computer by 2020-22.[28] As China's workforce diminishes, wages and associated social charges continue to rise and intermittent improvements are made to factory working conditions, the balance will tip further towards robots. Of course, the skills of the robots may increase faster than their price, and thus become more cost-effective. As robots become more common, competition may drive down their prices. What is noticeable is the low number of installed robots in China in comparison to the workforce compared with the US, Japan, Germany and of course Korea, the global leader.

Robots Installed by Country 2017

(per 10,000 workers)

Korea	710
Germany	322
Japan	308
China	97

Source: https://ifr.org/downloads/press2018/IFR_World_Robotics_Outlook_2019_-_Chicago.pdf

However, when we look at recent purchases, the situation is very different:

---

28   Exascale means capable of performing a quintillion (or a billion billion) calculations in a second.

Robots Bought by Country 2018

	('000)
China	133
Japan	52
USA	38
Korea	38

Even more relevant is to look at the annual purchases in the light of the total population:

	A	B	A/B
Country	**Thousands Bought**	**Population (m)**	
Korea	38	50m	0.76
Japan	52	123m	0.42
USA	38	327m	0.12
China	133	1,428m	0.09

All major countries are buying each year. Owing to the large size of the current population, at the current rate it may take many years before China reaches parity.

Yet the productivity enhancement which most comes to mind is artificial intelligence (AI). PWC research suggests that AI could add $15.7 trillion to the world's GDP by 2030. Accenture, a US consultancy, has published research forecasting that China's GDP could be 27 per cent bigger by 2035 and its growth rate much higher if AI is harnessed effectively. It acknowledges that 'the economy has slowed significantly' and that 'productivity has dwindled' but believes that threefold benefit can be generated from AI 'via intelligent automation, which creates growth through a set of features unlike those of traditional automation solutions; labor and capital augmentation, which results from enhancing the skills and abilities of existing workforces and physical capital; and innovation diffusion, which trickles down throughout the economy in the form of increased total factor productivity.'[29]

Beijing has made a major commitment to artificial intelligence. Rafael Reif, president of MIT, says it is reportedly spending $1 billion each year on research into artificial intelligence. And yet the state of AI is still regarded by the experts as rudimentary and it does not always produce salutary results. There have been unsatisfactory

---

29 https://www.accenture.com/_acnmedia/pdf-55/accenture-how-artificial-intelligence-can-drive-chinas-growth.pdf#zoom=50

outcomes from applying machine learning in medical research. The systems are often required to produce predictions. Dr Genevera Allen of Baylor College of Medicine observed that 'they never come back with "I don't know" or "I didn't discover anything" because they aren't made to.' There have accordingly been results but often the results are not reproducible, for example in some recent cancer research projects.[30]

Research from McKinsey indicates that 51 per cent of jobs in China could be eliminated as a result of AI. This is higher than any other country.[31] It suggests that a falling population could be neatly compensated for by machinery. However, it overlooks the fact that today's jobs include many which will not need to be done anyway and others - possibility not yet invented - will need to be done. Nor does it reflect the future job requirements of the rising service sector and in particular the tech sector.

Research from Jeffrey Ding at Oxford benchmarks China's progress in AI versus the US. He concludes that China is behind in three of the four key areas and ahead in data alone. He rates China's achievement at 17 versus the US at 33.[32]

Data use is an interesting subject. The consensus is that it is a vital component and China has a huge lead in it. James Lewis at CSIS makes the controversial statement that

> China does not have a data advantage. This is a fundamental misunderstanding that is surprisingly common in the West. Yes, Alibaba and other Chinese companies have access to the data of hundreds of millions of Chinese users, but they are limited to China... In contrast, Facebook, Google and others service a global market and have access to twice as much data as Chinese companies. Facebook has 3.4 billion users, more than twice the population of China. Different kinds of AI require different kinds and quantities of data, so that comparing user data numbers is simplistic... Where China may have an advantage is in the scope of privacy regulations. These could hamper the access of Western companies to their larger data pool.[33]

---

30 https://www.ft.com/content/e7bc0fd2-3149-11e9-8744-e7016697f225
31 https://www.mckinsey.com/~/media/McKinsey/Featured%20Insights/China/Artificial%20intelligence%20Implications%20for%20China/MGI-Artificial-intelligence-implications-for-China.ashx
32 https://www.fhi.ox.ac.uk/deciphering-chinas-ai-dream/
33 https://nsiteam.com/social/wp-content/uploads/2019/03/AI-China-Russia-Global-WP_FINAL2_fromMariah8mar2019_ndw11mar2019.pdf

Ding also stated that 'a lack of experienced AI researchers, innovation in algorithms and hardware disadvantages are key factors expected to hold China back'.[34]

We should note that early high forecasts of redundancy in OECD countries owing to machine learning, or AI, were tempered after 2013 into much lower numbers by 2018. They are now modified to predict that a high proportion of the workforce will have change how they work, which should make them much more productive. This is not good news for countries facing collapsing workforces.[35]

National education quality will play a big part in determining the fate of individual workforces. China's education system presently offers more immediate redundancy than the economy actually requires. The higher potential redundancy in China's workforce compared to the OECD countries (14 per cent) seems to indicate a lower quality or lower ability to transition into other areas.

Can Returns on Capital be Improved?

If China cannot increase the size of its workforce, there will be higher labour costs and, maybe, a shortage of skilled workers. That requires more return on capital and more productivity to compensate. It was mentioned earlier that returns on capital have been steadily falling. This is partly because wages are rising owing to short supply; something we have not seen since at least the Black Plague in the fourteenth century.

There are other reasons for poor returns on capital. One of the principal problems is the institutional bias towards concentrating capital provision on the state-owned enterprises which have consistently underperformed against foreign and privately owned enterprises, as measured by return on assets. This is specifically true of the period 2001-12. Furthermore, it seems clear that the smaller the company the better the returns - although that conclusion may only be correct because SOEs tend to be larger.

---

34   https://www.scmp.com/tech/article/2166177/made-china-2025-china-has-competitive-ai-game-plan-success-will-need
35   https://www.oecd-ilibrary.org/docserver/2e2f4eea-en.pdf?expires=157103 5144&id=id&accname=guest&checksum=BAE872AC29728CA20E8346EB 5C1134A2

As we have seen earlier, the private sector in China represents 50 per cent of all tax revenue, 60 per cent of GDP, 70 per cent of technological innovation, 80 per cent of all jobs and 90 per cent of new jobs. The 70 per cent of innovation is very important.[36] Even so, Chinese financial markets currently discriminate against the private sector which provides both jobs and growth. The banks disproportionately supply credit to the state enterprises rather than private firms, they charge far higher interest rates and the regulatory authorities have prioritized state enterprise access to stock market listing over private companies. Liu Yonghao, a prominent private businessman, has said that the 'banking sector isn't fit for the age we live in... Our banks and financial institutions serve the state-owned sector and the government.'[37] If on the other hand, capital could get to the entrepreneurs who need it to grow, we could see a more productive economy as well as a larger one.

While these facts may seem evident, there are entrenched barriers in the Chinese system to increasing support for private and smaller companies. One is the fear among state-owned bank staff of losing money on loans to private companies as opposed to government companies. Another is the reasonably rational concern that the accounting at private firms can be poor and misleading, often for good reason.

When trying to put a percentage to bank lending to the private sector we immediately come upon serious problems. One is the unclear definition of 'private'. There are some major companies whose ownership is contested amongst analysts. For the clearly private firms, there are those built up by entrepreneurs and those acquired by relatives and friends of officials which gain many benefits from the state banking system. The ratio of lending to the private sector, however, is anywhere between 2 and 30 per cent. When compared with its role in the economy - maybe 60 per cent - this is derisory. Some 70 million of the 90 million smallest firms have no bank loans at all. The main sources of funding are shadow banking and retained earnings. This looks to be changing

---

36 https://www.bloomberg.com/news/articles/2018-11-19/why-xi-leads-a-chorus-backing-china-s-private-sector-quicktake

37 http://www.ft.com/cms/s/0/833c5208-3eba-11e6-8716-a4a71e8140b0.html#axzz4GNMb2mNl

with the rise of 'fintech' lenders such as Ant Group, an affiliate of Alibaba and the largest fintech company in the world – although in November 2020 it ran into serious regulatory trouble and was prevented from launching an IPO that would have valued the company at $37 billion.[38]

Even the widely used expression small and medium enterprises, SMEs, is a politically correct term which is ambiguous. It can mean what it says - enterprises measured by size regardless of nature of ownership - or it can be a coded expression for the private sector. After all, most SOEs now are larger companies, as smaller state companies have been largely disposed of.

One point to stress here is that it is not more capital that is required. China has - if anything - had too much capital investment. What is needed is better allocation of capital. The way to achieve this is by putting access to capital in the hands of those who will take personal responsibility - in other words private owners. The efficiency of investment has halved over the last 20 years. If there is more access to capital by entrepreneurs, we can assume that, in an overall sense, they will usually not borrow more than they need for productive deployment and will be more focused on creating economic returns on capital. There may also be fewer bad loans in the banking system.

It is not only bank credit which is important here. It is access to the stock market. Limited access for private-sector companies has helped to maximize the casino aspects of the market where unsuccessful SOEs crowd the market and share prices are driven more by rumours of SOE restructurings and liquidity bursts than by scrutiny of earnings prospects. If well-managed and growing private firms can gain access to the stock market without being asked to pay bribes, then the national economy will benefit, as will tax revenues. Until the banking system and stock markets become rules-based and market-driven we should not expect major improvements in return on capital. Policymakers should, of course, be aware that high growth often comes at a high price in inequality and indebtedness. This suggests that high growth, if it can be restored, may have political enemies.

---

38   https://www.cnbc.com/2019/01/29/chinese-fintech-companies-find-new-opportunities-in-business-loans.html

Addressing Falling Births

This is, of course, almost the same issue as the falling workforce. But the timetable is different, the scale is bigger and there are social, political and military implications. One problem is that the state believes too much in its own propaganda that policy was responsible for reducing births and by a correction to that policy direction it can grow births again. In reality, as we have shown, social drivers are the principal factors cramping births. We should look at some of the presumed factors.

It is not the rising divorce level, which is still lower than in the US. Neither is it women participating in the workforce, which has always been a major feature in China. Births peaked in the 1960s and then fell; female workforce participation also fell between the 1960s and 2020. However, later marriage is important. In Shanghai and Guangzhou it is now after the age of 30 for men and after 28 for women - and rising. This is later than in the US. We should see Shanghai and Guangzhou as harbingers of China's future. Late marriage irrefutably reduces fertility. The drivers of later marriage are diverse. They include starting a business, saving for an apartment, starting a career and female college education. We are unlikely to see earlier marriage or less divorce. Narcissism was the fruit of the one-child policy. Furthermore, the state urges higher consumer spending. This seems closely linked with low interest in childbearing.

Why are Chinese people not doing Beijing's bidding and procreating for their country? There are many separate reasons. A growing number of young women say that they do not like the young men who are available. Single male Chinese children may have been comprehensively spoilt, beyond what might be normal elsewhere. Some research suggests these young men are less trusting, less trustworthy, more pessimistic and less competitive, each of which may make them less attractive marriage partners.

Habitual use of contraceptives, disdain for illegitimacy and insouciance regarding abortion limit childbearing. Korea has experienced the highest rate of abortions in the world and has low fertility. There are signs in China, through surveys, that the one-child family is becoming widely accepted as the desired size unit. Normative pressures, in other words the attitudes of society, play an important part. If intensive parenting and other aspects of parenthood are regarded as normal and if childlessness is widely accepted, it will encourage reduced fertility.

For now at least there are still restrictions in place on birth choices for families, as we have noted. Substantial fines are still in force for breaching the rules. This is to the benefit of the extensive family planning apparatus. However, for the needs of the country all restrictions should be scrapped and free choice reintroduced. The first and – theoretically - most practical measure is to scrap all the many remaining restrictions on births. Not least of these is the general limitation to two children which impedes the small number of families who desire more than two children. Of course, this is not sufficient, but it is a clear starting point. Several demographers recommend this course including both Zuo Xuejin at the Shanghai Academy of Social Sciences and Yi Fuxian at the University of Wisconsin-Madison. It now looks if this is quite likely to happen in the near future.

The demography of north-east China bears some passing similarity to that of the Russian Far East across the border. Not only are ageing and low fertility taking their toll but so also is the dismal economic outlook for a region dominated by historically stranded state enterprises. By 2016, the particularly weak province of Heilongjiang had announced that families would be allowed a third child. This policy could be unrolled nationally. Better yet, of course, is that there should be no restrictions on family choice about childbearing. This is a *sine qua non* of any package of birth encouragement.

The UN Population Fund has said that a solution might be for single men in China and India to delay their marriage in order to allow the supply of women to accommodate the surplus of men. It seems a fact, however, that if a woman marries a man significantly older she reduces her own prospects of fertility. The most effective proven antidote to demographic decline is commensurate-scaled immigration. Yet the three largest countries most directly threatened by falling population - Japan, Russia and China - all strongly resist ethnically diverse immigration. It is hard to imagine China accepting even 100 million non-Han immigrants, or 7 per cent of the population. Whether our principal concern is 50 million angry bachelors by 2035, 250 million missing workers by 2050 or 800 million missing Chinese by 2100, we shall not find the solution from studying the atlas. However, some female migrant workers could possibly be channelled to domestic marriages.

Any improvements in sex ratio at birth in the next two decades will not remove the pain that will be witnessed over the next 30 years from the accumulated skewed birth ratios.

Environmentally driven infertility and infertility induced by unprofessional abortions are a multigenerational price paid for the undisciplined dash for growth and the one-child policy. They will eventually be soluble. Cleaning the soil, the water and the air of China will not be cheap. Estimates are in the trillions of dollars. But history suggests that it is achievable. It requires political will which has been noticeably absent in recent decades. The legacy of scarred bodies and minds bequeathed by the one-child policy will work itself out through the passage of time, even if it will leave a continuingly distorted society.

The rate of reported involuntary infertility seems to have been rising rapidly but is perhaps presently no greater than in other major countries. It looks like 10-20 per cent. However, as usual in China, the data are ambiguous. Of course, if it relates to individuals rather than couples, it is unlikely that an infertile man will necessarily have married an infertile woman. As a result, if only one-quarter of infertile men married infertile women, then well over 20 per cent of couples might be infertile. We should look out for any continuation or future deterioration in pollution leading to above world average infertility. Fortunately, at least Beijing is improving.

More intriguing would be to reassess the whole urbanization drive. Urbanization generally offers huge dividends to countries pursuing that path, and its indirect though clear contribution to reduction of fertility levels has assisted in managing global population growth far more than bodies such as the United Nations can imagine.

The point has been made that inclusive urbanization - where the whole community benefits from the urban dividend - has a pronounced downward impact on fertility. Where conversely there is an exclusiveness in urbanization and sections of society, such as the poor, are excluded from the benefits, there is less fertility reduction. An example can be seen in the large slums where three-quarters of Africa's urban population resides. While migrant families in China have been discouraged from sharing the temporary urban home, male migrant sex is unlikely to be geared towards procreation.

It is thought-provoking that China has managed to create urban landscapes suffused with inequality but because they have laudably avoided slum conditions, the cities lack the fertility benefits which are normally thought to attend inegalitarian urbanization. China has contracted its demographic prospects to such an extreme degree that in its case the balance of advantage from urbanization is quite different from other countries. Serious thought should be given not only to slowing urbanization but also to seeking an entirely new urban/rural planning vision of the future.

We have seen that while the birth control policy has been successively liberalized, it is not a free-for-all. Many families are still restricted to no more than two children. Fines and coercion are still abundant. Indeed, as recently as 2014 the UN Committee on Economic, Social and Cultural Rights urged China to 'take further action to prevent and criminalize effectively the use of coercive measures, such as forced abortions and forced sterilization, in the implementation of the birth control policy'. The continuation of certain restrictions on parental choice - number of children, fines - is a direct impediment to the national ability to raise the aggregate birthrate. In parallel, the good news is that in 2018 the Communist Party started to encourage members to have a second child and evangelize for this change among the public. The party needs to go much further and demand members have more children, with stiff penalties for failure.

Some Suggestions

It would be worth China experimenting with some maternal welfare measures along Scandinavian or Hungarian lines to see if they can generate results. Public investment in kindergartens and childcare has been shown to spur births. Encouragement of greater domestic partnership in the home and financial support for childcare and kindergartens would be positive steps. Another important step is to recognize the likelihood of a once-working mother returning to part-time employment. The usually lower rates paid for part-timers need to be considered. Greater parity would encourage women to view ceasing employment for childbirth and then gradually re-entering the employment market in stages as satisfactory, to the benefit of the economy and the national birth rate. This may require a combination of employer education and legislation.

The principal barriers to childbearing in China seem to revolve around cost and discrimination. Children are expensive, women are expected to lead the child-caring and women suffer discrimination in the workplace. School fees and family travel can absorb one-third of a middle-class family income. Money can be redirected and laws can be passed but also enforced. Unfortunately, local governments are not cash-rich, Beijing is likely to become tighter in its financing and China is not good at enforcing its laws.

Measures that would help would be longer maternity leave (the Chinese have one of the shortest in the world, at 14 weeks), extension of the Shanghai scheme to give young mothers longer holidays, tax breaks for childcare and kindergarten fees, greater encouragement for breastfeeding to minimize infant mortality and maybe even a discouraging high level of tax on infant formula. The Japanese government, for example, has committed to create 500,000 extra spaces at creches to enable mothers to work.

The whole field of greater benefits in cash, tax allowances on education, holidays for families and working mothers could be explored much more imaginatively. Tax credits and allowances for childcare, kindergarten fees and medical treatment offer a variety of options. Imposing on employers generous paternal leave arrangements is a possibility and also subsidizing employers to give maternity leave and to avoid any informal workplace discouragement. There could be some affirmative action policies such as cash bounties on female babies, given the distinct shortage of wives and the lingering suspicion of selective abortion.

Perhaps each country has its own distinctive issues. Chinese surveys continually cite cost concerns as a reason for opting against birth. The cost of education, which includes kindergarten and tutoring charges, and the cost of giving a son his own apartment in order to be a candidate for marriage, are frequently mentioned. These suggest that this is where the government should start. There is little point in having surveys if nobody listens to the results. Perhaps Beijing should prioritize kindergartens over battleships. Perhaps low-cost private housing estates should be built for occupation by families with two children.

It is often thought that rising female participation in the workforce correlates with falling births. But China seems an exception. Ironically it has a double negative of a substantial fall in female labour participation and a parallel reduction in births.

If women say they would like children, but it is too expensive, difficult or inconvenient, and if pronatal policy is having almost no effect, do we have to ask the question: do they mean it or are they too embarrassed to say that they do not really want children? It is possible that we have moved into a new era where many people make alternative choices - foreign holidays, motor cars, domestic animals - in preference to children. Is this a modern consumer culture?

Conclusion

This is a lengthy list of possible solutions. Although tried, many do not seem to have worked. Some are distinctly original. We need to consider those which look like they could be useful in the context of China. Beijing likes to refer to the distinct nature of China and pursuing policies with 'Chinese characteristics'. It will be undoubtedly necessary to adopt some policies that have never been tried before.

INDEX

abortion 10, 12, 43, 45, 75, 78-9, 81, 100, 105, 111-12, 119, 123, 158, 231, 245, 256-7, 303, 305-7
Africa 74, 108, 125-6, 129, 140, 207, 232, 235-7, 249-50, 263, 273, 292, 305
agriculture 3, 8-10, 163, 172, 190-1, 204, 212, 251, 254, 284
America, *see* USA
antibiotics 17, 21, 131
artificial intelligence 184, 194, 196, 298-9

bachelors 52-3, 57-8, 66-8, 70-3, 114, 232, 284, 304
Bangladesh 126, 208, 233, 280, 284
Beijing city 6, 16, 94-5, 97, 107, 129-30, 133, 136-7, 163, 199, 290
birth control
  regulations 1, 9-12, 43, 47, 75-6, 78, 175, 180
  relaxation of 81-5, 87, 90, 92, 94, 123, 306
breastfeeding 8, 16-17, 108, 262, 264, 307
bride price 44-5, 67, 72-3, 263, 285
Britain 18, 20, 22, 69, 102, 113, 191, 198-9, 224, 228, 234, 248, 266-7, 269, 273, 287 *see also* UK
Buddhists 45, 230, 281
Burma 73-4, 281, 284, 292

Cambodia 73-4, 281, 284, 292
cancer 17, 128, 289, 299
cardiovascular disease 16-17, 128, 288
CASS forecasts 28-9, 34, 53-4, 56, 59, 62-3, 70, 80, 115, 123, 151-2, 177, 275, 293

childbirth 41, 68, 75, 86-7, 94, 119, 241, 245, 306
childcare 101, 103-4, 111, 118, 140, 190, 260-3, 265-7, 269-71, 276, 278, 287-8, 306-7
Christians 230, 232, 235, 280, 284
cohabitation 111, 265-6, 268-70, 272
Communist Party 11, 62, 76, 78-9, 86, 91-2, 101, 114, 121, 134, 136-7, 170, 181, 291, 306
consumerism 26, 115-16, 125, 127, 134, 162, 170-1, 180, 192, 222, 235, 303, 308
contraception 9, 112, 149, 233, 250-1
Covid-19 22, 129, 162, 171, 181, 190-1, 292
crime 35-6, 51, 71-2, 102, 138, 174, 276, 278
Cultural Revolution 10, 134, 175

Deng Xiaoping 9, 80
dengue fever 129
depopulation 97-8, 228
depression 17, 31, 132, 210, 224, 288
diabetes 16-17, 22, 128-9, 288
diet 15-17, 108, 128, 212, 235
divorce 68, 72, 109-10, 112, 303
drugs 21, 71, 189, 289

earthquakes 6, 180-1, 209-10
emigration 93, 97-8, 119-21, 138, 237, 245-8, 251, 272, 277, 291
eugenics 7-8
extramarital activity 68, 112

family planning 10, 13, 75-6, 81, 86, 119, 145, 243, 250, 255-6, 304

fertility rate (TFR)
  in China 8, 12, 26, 76-9, 85-90,
    93, 98, 101, 111, 122-4, 142-3,
    147-8, 152, 155-61
    elsewhere 77, 88-90, 111, 142,
    183, 188, 233-4, 237-8, 240-4,
    247-50, 252, 265-72, 281
Five-Year Plans 46, 85, 132
formula milk 17, 108, 264, 287,
  307
France 97, 139, 220, 224, 234, 239,
  265-7, 269, 272-3

Gansu 1, 92
gender disparity 13-14, 37-74, 88,
  174, 229-30, 232, 253, 263, 275,
  279-80, 285-6
gender equality 110, 218, 240, 262,
  265-7, 271-2
Germany 18-20, 40-1, 88, 102,
  138-9, 144, 163, 169, 213-15,
  220, 224, 234, 237, 266-8, 287-
  8, 297
Global Burden of Disease 89, 142-
  3, 188, 234, 236
grandparents 42, 104, 190, 263
Great Leap Forward 10
Guangxi 92, 115
Guangzhou 130, 135, 292, 303

Han Chinese 5, 12, 38, 40, 45, 92,
  132, 231, 291
healthcare 28, 93, 177-8, 223, 225
Heilongjiang 95, 98, 118, 138, 304
homosexuality 114, 212, 245
Hong Kong 18, 35, 43, 78, 84, 99,
  123, 186, 199, 224, 237
hospitals 93, 128-9, 136, 256-7,
  264
housing 27, 43, 103-4, 109, 111,
  114, 125-6, 133, 136, 242, 260,
  270, 272-3, 307
Hubei 107, 115, 137, 260
hukou 95, 136, 263, 287
Hunan 115, 134
Hungary 18-19, 220, 237, 245-6,
  272-3

hypergamy 40, 65, 110

IIASA 64, 142-3, 150, 153-4, 156-
  7, 161
illiteracy 65, 70, 237
IMF 20, 218, 224, 226, 294
immigration 89, 97, 123, 188, 218,
  237, 239, 263, 267-8, 286, 292,
  304
India 11, 20, 34, 41, 45, 55, 67, 73,
  117, 126, 168, 200, 209, 213,
  225-6, 229-34, 238, 244, 253,
  264, 294, 304
Indonesia 41, 126, 234, 236
infant mortality 8, 18, 37, 40-1,
  63, 76, 79, 107-9, 124, 148, 158,
  229, 231, 264, 289-90, 307
infanticide 13-14, 37
infectious diseases 17, 21, 41
infertility 83, 100-1, 104-7, 118,
  123-4, 126, 242-3, 257, 305
infidelity 112
Iran 236, 242-4
Italy 220-2, 224, 247-8, 266-7
IVF 107, 243, 246, 252

Japan
  ageing 22-3, 34-6, 176-8, 186,
    222, 228-9, 278, 289
  birth rate 88, 122, 238, 241, 247,
    253-4, 271
  economy 163, 175-7, 182-3, 186,
    189, 191, 196, 215, 217-19,
    239-40, 277, 297-8
  lifestyle 115-17, 130, 138, 193,
    234, 266, 276, 280
  military 9, 14, 208, 213
  welfare 28, 33, 238, 265, 307
Jews 248-9

kindergartens 103, 113, 136, 260-
  1, 270, 306-7
Korea
  North Korea 73-4, 97
  South Korea 22, 44, 77, 97, 215,
    222, 225, 234, 252-3, 271,
    279-80, 285, 297-8, 303

Laos 73-4, 281, 284, 292
Li Keqiang 46, 127, 135, 138, 167
life expectancy 8, 15, 18, 20-3, 194, 221-2, 227-8, 289-90
lifestyle 16-17, 20-1, 100-1, 105, 108, 116, 118, 125, 128, 211, 257
longevity 8, 15-22, 25-6, 79, 129, 138, 177, 214-15, 221-2, 233, 235, 237, 253, 276, 288-9

Mao Zedong 2, 9-11, 80, 261, 287
maternity leave 241, 262, 270, 307
McKinsey reports 134, 187, 197, 200, 299
median age 23, 34, 176-7, 221, 250, 252
mental health 72, 127-8, 133, 164, 210, 212, 288
Mexico 129, 221, 284
military effect 30, 34, 72, 81, 179, 206-14, 273, 278, 303
miscarriages 16
Mongolia 6, 31, 74, 95, 280
Muslims 45, 89, 92, 125, 232, 235-6, 242-3, 246, 248-9, 253, 280, 283-4

National Bureau of Statistics 24-5, 51, 79, 85, 88, 91-3, 99, 115, 148, 155-6, 159, 163, 263
NHFPC 46, 55, 61-2, 84, 91, 93, 148, 151-3, 155, 159-60, 244, 256-7, 286

obesity 16-17, 22, 72, 128-9, 211, 243, 262, 288-9
One Child Policy 11-13, 75-6, 79-86, 98, 119, 123, 157, 255, 288, 303, 305

Pakistan 73, 126, 208, 230, 234, 280
pandemic 127, 131, 171, 174, 190, 292 *see also* Covid-19
patriarchy 109-10, 149, 241, 253, 266, 279

Pearl River 1, 163
Peking University 9, 79, 99-100, 142, 154, 170, 177, 185-6, 197
pensions 20, 26-30, 35-6, 133, 171, 178, 194, 223, 227-9, 237, 263, 277-8, 290
plagues 3, 6-7, 129, 254, 300
pollution 15-16, 100-1, 105, 109, 123, 125, 145, 235, 264-5, 289-90, 305
polygamy 40, 250, 283-4
pregnancy 43, 74, 158, 219, 250, 257, 262, 265
premarital relations 68, 270
primary schools 123, 165, 167, 199, 288
prison 35-6, 173, 217, 229, 258
pronatalism 123, 202, 240-1, 244, 246-8, 251, 255-74, 286, 308
prostitutes 73-4, 102, 157

Qin Dynasty 1-2
Qing Dynasty 3-8, 13-14, 18, 37

Republican period 7, 14
retirement 26-30, 35-6, 121, 171, 175, 190, 193, 223-4, 227-9, 247, 261, 263, 274, 278, 288-9
robots 115, 185, 194, 197, 202-3, 225, 296-8
Russia 122, 213, 227-8, 233-4, 244, 253, 270, 283-4, 287, 304

Scandinavia 218, 255, 265-7, 269, 272-3, 306
secondary infertility 104-5
secondary schools 166, 199, 202, 234
sedentary lifestyle 20, 100, 125, 128, 211-12, 288
sex ratio at birth (SRB) 14, 37-48, 51, 54-5, 57, 59-65, 67, 71, 230-2
sexual activity 111, 240, 257
sexual disease 157
sexual violence 72
Shaanxi 1, 91, 260

Shanghai 21, 33, 69, 95, 107, 113, 119, 130-1, 137, 199, 236-7, 290, 303, 307

Shanghai Academy of Social Sciences 27, 89, 154, 159, 304

Shanxi 107, 115, 259-60

siblings 32, 101, 103, 182, 276-7

Singapore 18, 77-8, 84, 105-6, 123, 169, 235, 252, 255, 259, 272, 280, 292

smoking 100, 128, 243

social services 27, 104, 135, 164, 221-2

SOEs 27, 96-7, 103, 137, 171, 261, 300, 302

Song Dynasty 3, 5-6

Soviet Union 96, 207, 210, 231

sperm quality 106-7, 235

sterility 257

sterilization 11-12, 75, 78, 81-2, 256, 271, 306

students 69-70, 166-7, 200-1, 237, 244, 291

suicide 17-18, 103, 164, 224

Taiping Rebellion 3, 7, 14

Taiwan 14, 44, 73, 77-8, 84, 123, 207-8, 214-16, 229-30, 252, 280-3, 291

Tang Dynasty 4-5

taxation 4-5, 30, 34, 86, 112, 170, 173, 183, 198, 212, 219, 260, 264, 270, 273-4, 290, 301-2, 307

technology 43-4, 168-9, 184-5, 190, 192-4, 196-7, 203, 213, 221, 223, 254, 258, 293-4, 301

tertiary education 79, 109-10, 119-20, 166, 198-9, 270, 290

TFP 293-4

Thailand 31, 73, 77-8, 88, 90, 215, 221-2

Tibet 5, 12, 38, 45, 81, 131-2, 207

trafficking 44, 72-4, 281

two-child policy 84, 99, 151, 256

ultrasound 43-4, 231, 257

unemployment 27, 40, 95, 98, 138, 167, 172, 191, 198, 204, 283, 286, 290

United Kingdom statistics 19, 139, 164, 221, 239, 268 *see also* Britain

United Nations 102, 117, 120, 153, 155, 208, 234, 305

reports by 23-5, 30, 34, 47, 50, 52-4, 89-90, 117-18, 120, 143-4, 146, 151-3, 160-1, 177, 179, 195, 217, 222, 224, 231, 233-5, 243, 248-50, 306

UNFPA 47, 51, 54, 60-1, 64-7, 117, 122, 232

UNPD 23-4, 48-9, 66, 77, 90, 150-2, 154-5, 238, 249, 304

UNPF 53, 58

UNPOP 142-3

United States of America

economy of 3, 21, 126, 130, 158-9, 163, 169, 171, 174, 176-7, 179, 181, 185-8, 190-3, 196-7, 199, 216-17, 223, 270, 277, 299

population of 12, 17-20, 23, 35, 40-1, 68-9, 74, 109, 176-8, 189, 191, 216-17, 221, 234-5, 244, 254, 261, 266, 270-1

reports by 16, 43, 73, 102, 179, 184-5, 187, 216, 260, 272-3, 277, 287, 298

USCB 24-6, 34, 48-64, 100, 115, 117-18, 142, 150-2, 156, 158-60, 216-17, 220, 230

unmarried

men 14, 52, 58-60, 65, 67, 69, 71, 114-16, 182, 240, 263, 265-6

women 59, 65, 69, 111, 114-16, 232, 240, 263, 265-6, 269, 284

urbanization 27, 79, 95, 100-1, 125-41, 145, 190, 202, 212, 233, 242, 294, 305-6

Uyghurs 12, 92, 283

vasectomy 11, 81, 243

Vietnam 44, 73-4, 90, 208-10, 230, 232, 281-3, 292

welfare support 28-30, 33, 36, 86, 103, 133, 179, 212-13, 217, 219, 228, 247, 255, 278, 306

well-being 102-3, 204

World Bank 15, 18-19, 22, 30-1, 38, 46, 62, 88, 90, 107-8, 120-1, 130, 135, 152, 154, 156, 164, 166, 194, 222, 230, 233, 276, 292

Xi Jinping 2, 34, 136-8, 168-9, 207, 210-11, 213, 273, 278, 288

Xinhua 56, 96, 136, 144-5, 151, 196, 212, 252

Xinjiang 5, 92, 132, 283

Yangtze River 1, 131

Yunnan 81, 115